IMAGES
of America

ELIZABETHTOWN

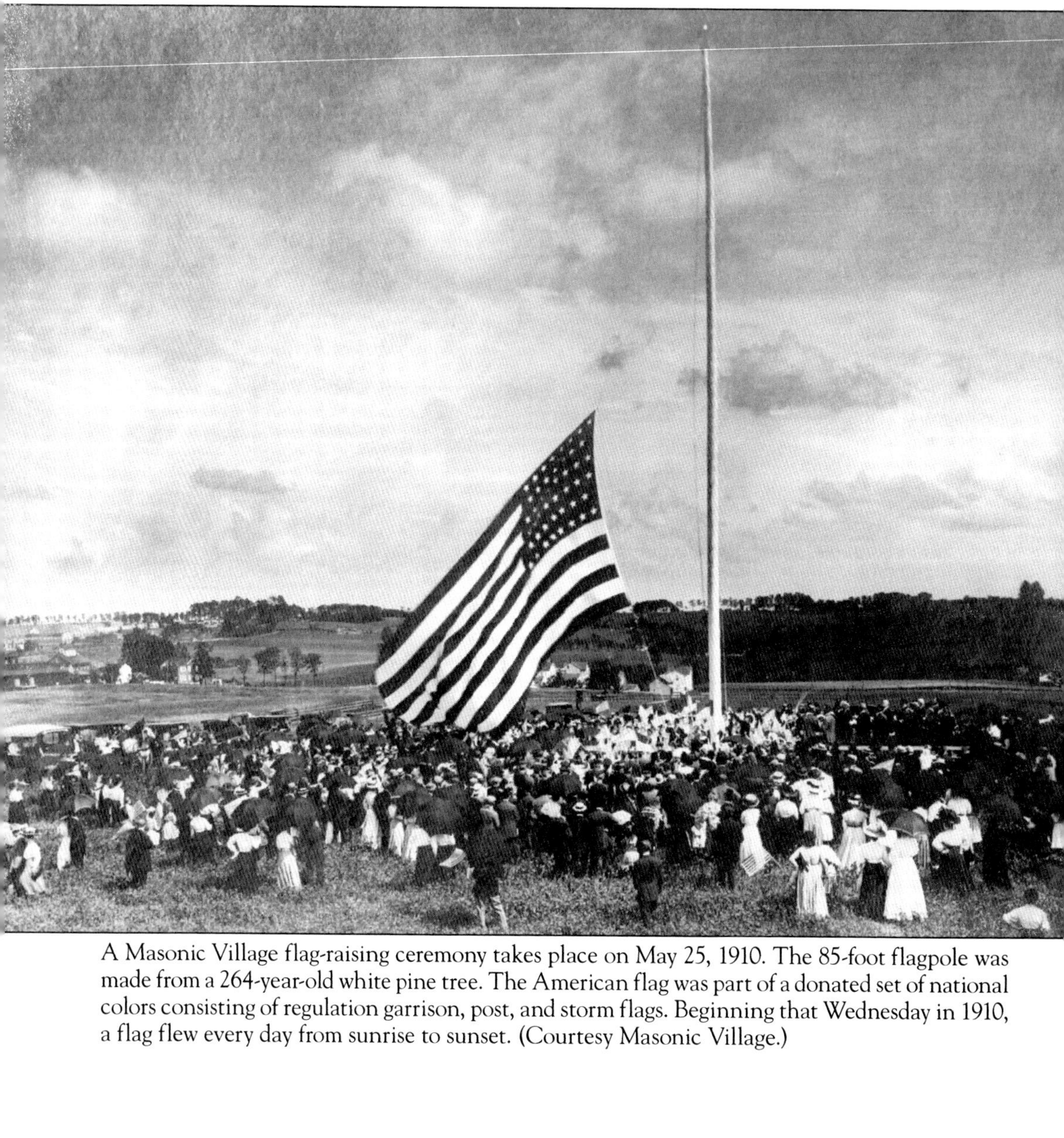

A Masonic Village flag-raising ceremony takes place on May 25, 1910. The 85-foot flagpole was made from a 264-year-old white pine tree. The American flag was part of a donated set of national colors consisting of regulation garrison, post, and storm flags. Beginning that Wednesday in 1910, a flag flew every day from sunrise to sunset. (Courtesy Masonic Village.)

On the Cover: A 1946 Victory Parade marches north on Market Street. A banner is being carried by officers of the Elizabethtown Lodge No. 128, Independent Order of Odd Fellows, established on September 29, 1845. The banner displays the triple link chain, representing friendship, love, and truth, with the higher-degree branches of Washington Encampment and Canton Lincoln and the women's division. Betsy Ross Rebekah Lodge No. 129 was established in May 1935. (Courtesy Winters Heritage House Museum.)

IMAGES
of America

ELIZABETHTOWN

Jean-Paul Benowitz

ARCADIA
PUBLISHING

ISBN 978-1-4671-2355-6

Published by Arcadia Publishing
Charleston, South Carolina

Printed in the United States of America

Library of Congress Control Number: 2014957241

For all general information, please contact Arcadia Publishing:
Telephone 843-853-2070
Fax 843-853-0044
E-mail sales@arcadiapublishing.com
For customer service and orders:
Toll-Free 1-888-313-2665

Visit us on the Internet at www.arcadiapublishing.com

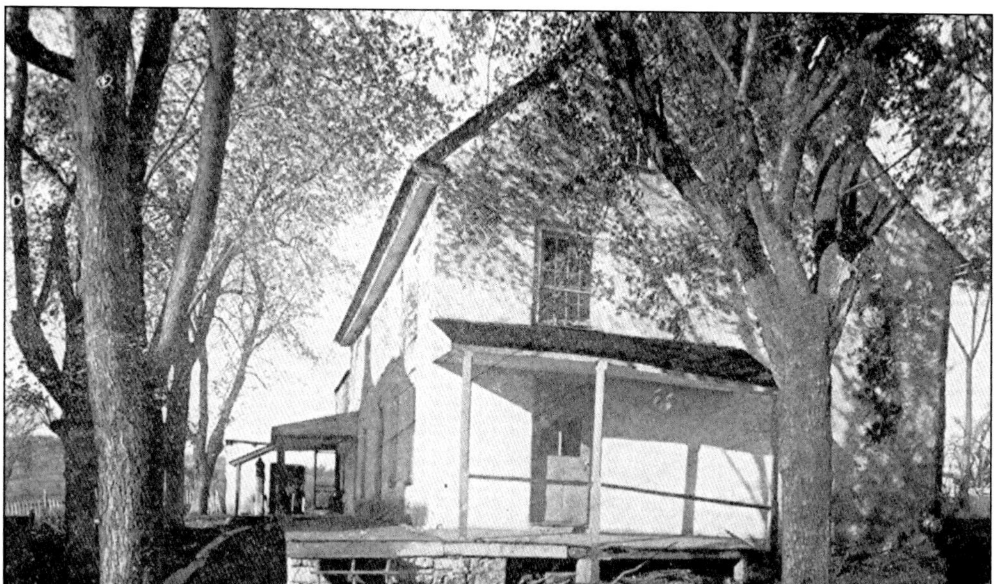

This postcard image depicts the Sign of the Bear Tavern, built in 1745 by Thomas Harris. Through his photography, George Falkenstein preserved and documented the history of Elizabethtown. He sold the photographs as postcards from his bookstore and lending library at 39 South Market Street. Presently highly collectable, the Falkenstein postcards make this kind of book possible. His historical legacy proves how a picture is worth a thousand words. (Courtesy Winters Heritage House Museum.)

Contents

Acknowledgments

This project has been a collaborative effort. Thanks go to Susan Asbury, Thomas Campbell, Phil Clark, Nancy Landis, and Jeff Myers of the Winters Heritage House Museum, Seibert Library and Research Center, Elizabethtown Preservationist Associates, Inc.; Kathleen Forney, Lloyd Reed, Patsy Reed, and Maryann Swartz of the Elizabethtown Historical Society; Marianne Heckles, Barry Rauhauser, and Martha Tyzenhouse of LancasterHistory.org; Peter DePuydt, Louise Hyder-Darlington, and Beth Young Miller of Elizabethtown College High Library, Brethren Heritage Room, Earl and Anita Hess Archives and Special Collections; Amy Benowitz and Barbara Shank of Elizabethtown College; Blake Banta and Richard Johnson of the Masonic Village; John Buch of Abraham C. Treichler Lodge No. 682; Missy Dedman-Hiner and Michael Dooley of the Pennsylvania Department of Corrections Training Academy at Elizabethtown; and the Reverend Steven Fauser, Stephanie Rankin, and Eileen Rider of St. Peter's Roman Catholic Church.

Unless otherwise noted, all photographs are courtesy of the Winters Heritage House Museum, Seibert Library and Research Center, Elizabethtown Preservationist Associates, Inc.

Introduction

The heart of Elizabethtown, Pennsylvania, is the Conoy Creek. Named Conejoholo (Anglicized as "Conoy") by the Piscataway Nation (referred to as Conoy Indians), the creek is a tributary of the Susquehanna River. The creek is created by the convergence of two waterways; the headwaters for the first begin at a spring on the farm of Kenneth Myer, and the second, Negly Run, starts at a spring on the former Leonard Negly farm.

Measuring 465 miles, the Susquehanna is the longest river on the East Coast, flowing from New York and Pennsylvania through Maryland into Chesapeake Bay. In 1534, French King Francis I colonized North America, establishing New France, with Jacques Cartier as viceroy in Quebec. The Conoy Creek and Susquehanna River facilitated French trade, connecting the Allegheny, Ohio, Mississippi, and Missouri Rivers and joining the colonies of New France and Louisiana.

Elizabethtown is in Lancaster County, settled by French explorer Étienne Brulé. Between 1612 and 1632, Brulé explored Lakes Huron, Ontario, Erie, and Superior, eventually arriving at Lancaster on Pequea Creek, a 49.2-mile tributary of the Susquehanna River. The French established commercial relations with the Shawanese on Pequea Creek. French and Indian trade expanded with Martin Chartier, Peter Bezaillion, and Jacques Le Tort along the Conestoga River, a 61.6-mile tributary of the Susquehanna.

In 1681, Britain's King Charles II granted William Penn 48,000 square miles of land in America, linking the northern and southern English colonies. In 1686, Penn delegated land agent James Logan to contract coureurs de bois (French fur trappers) for exclusive trading rights and to "urge the Pennsylvania assembly to establish a propriety monopoly in the Indian trade." The French traded New England rum and British-manufactured products for Indian fur pelts and deerskins.

In 1708, Peter Bezaillion settled along the Susquehanna River, building "Old Peter's Road" connecting the Pequea Creek, Conestoga River, and following the Susquehanna River from Conestoga (later Lancaster, the county seat) to Paxtang (later Harrisburg, the state capital). A portion of the road southeast of New Holland still bears his name. The original route followed Chiques Creek, a 31.6-mile tributary of the Susquehanna River, through West Earl, Upper Leacock, Manheim, Warwick, East Hempfield, and Penn Townships, crossing the Little Chiques Creek at Mount Joy. Donegal Springs Road, the other surviving section of Peter's Road, continues along Bainbridge Road to Stackstown, crossing the Conoy Creek and leading to Conoy Town. By 1719, Bezaillion owned 700 acres at Conoy Town; part of this acreage included contemporary Elizabethtown.

The Piscataway Nation lived on the Potomac River in southern Maryland. Members were converted to Christianity by French Jesuit Andrew White. Granted permission in 1701 by Penn to settle on the Susquehanna at Conoy, the tribe built its village, Conoy Town. In 1743, prior to the French and Indian War and based on the advice of the Six Nations, the Piscataway moved from Conoy Town to Shamokin.

French Huguenot refugees, particularly the Ferree, LeFevre, and Dubois families, settled in Lancaster. French settlers in Elizabethtown were ministered to by the French Jesuit mission of St. John Nepomucene in Lancaster. Jesuit father Ferdinand Steinmeyer from Philadelphia, a founding member of the American Philosophical Society, working with Father Robert Molyneux, began serving Elizabethtown in 1741. During 1840–1853, Father Francis X. Marshall, from the Jesuits at Conewago, was the first permanent priest for St. Peter's Roman Catholic Church in Elizabethtown.

Elizabethtown's second attorney and a member of St. Peter's, Henry A. Wade, who graduated from Georgetown University and Harvard Law School, lived with his wife, Maria Flynn, at 130 North Market Street. In February 1857, he attended a dinner hosted by Father Bernard

Keenan of St. Peter's; the guest of honor was president-elect James Buchanan on the eve of his departure for Washington, DC. The Buchanans were among the original Scotch Irish settlers in Elizabethtown.

Aimé LeBreton, a French bookseller from Philadelphia and Lancaster, lived in Elizabethtown. In 1814, LeBreton hosted French Trappist monks, refugees of the French Revolution, en route to their new monastery on the western frontier. Father Charles Guery, one of the Trappists, died in Elizabethtown. His funeral mass was officiated by Jesuit father John William Beschter from Luxembourg, France, who was in charge of St. Peter's.

In 1920, Louis Charleroy of the French firm Charleroy Shoes built the Savoy Shoe Company at 453 West High Street. Charleroy manufactured women's shoes, in 1946 becoming a subsidiary of A.S. Beck, Inc. Today, the building is Savoy Townhouse Apartments. Most former factories in town have been converted into residential properties. After World War II, suburban sprawl in Elizabethtown started with Forest Hills, built by French real estate developers Claude E. and Kathryn D.R. Disney.

The French firms of Martin Chartier, Peter Bezaillion, and Jacques Le Tort conducted their business with Isaac Miranda, a Sephardic Jew with headquarters in the fur trade at Conoy Town. From 1654 through 1720, Jews from Spain and Portugal, such as Isaac Miranda, immigrated to Pennsylvania. A second wave of Jewish migration to America happened from 1709 to 1760, part of the Swiss and German migration from the Palatinate and Holland. In 1710, three thousand Swiss and German immigrants, refugees living in Ireland and England, arrived in New York, then located in the Hudson Valley with commercial contracts for the British military. In 1723, over 100 German families, many who were Jewish, settled along the Susquehanna River in New York and migrated south to Pennsylvania. Led by Conrad Weiser, they established Heidelberg in Lancaster, today's Schaeferstown in Lebanon. The location was chosen because the Lebanon Fur Trading Post had been established by Portuguese Jews led by Isaac Miranda. There, two log cabins have historically been referred to as the "Jew House," or the "Schul." The Hebrew cemetery in Schaefferstown is the third-oldest in America.

In 1740, Joseph Simon, headquartered in Lancaster, was a British Jewish magnate in French and Indian trade. Working closely with the Sephardic and German Jews along the Susquehanna River, Simon and Lazarus Lowrey of Maytown developed Elizabethtown as the gateway for trade routes established through Ohio, Illinois, and the Northwest Territory. Simon coordinated Mennonite gunsmiths, supplying the Continental army with weapons and ammunition. After the American Revolution in 1798, Simon was a commissioner of the Conewago Canal, advancing the economic and transportation significance of Elizabethtown.

In the decades following the Napoleonic Wars, from 1820 to 1850, a new wave of Jewish tobacco merchants immigrated to Pennsylvania from the tobacco port of Bermen, Germany. Merchant Morris Levy and his five sons monopolized the tobacco trade in Lancaster. Between 1849 and 1859, the cultivation of tobacco increased in Lancaster County by 186 percent. In 1859, tobacco yielded in Lancaster was two-thirds of the total crop for the commonwealth. L.L. Engle and Amos L. Harrouf were tobacco dealers in Elizabethtown, where John G. Schwan and Samuel Sharer manufactured cigars.

In 1935, Joseph and Josephine Greenberg opened the Greenberg Garment Factory on West Bainbridge Street, moving to a new factory in 1957 on North Poplar Street. In 1938, Benjamin Weiman and his son-in-law Milton S. Goldstein established the Empire Shoe Company on West Washington Street, making 3,000 pairs of boys' shoes daily. The Weimans and Goldsteins were the first employers in Elizabethtown to provide hospitalization for employees, and they proposed child day care for working mothers. In 1938, Max Hess, a Jewish shirt manufacturer, escaped the Holocaust, moving from Germany to Elizabethtown. With his sons Werner and Gunther and his nephew Fred Stern, he opened the Hestteco Manufacturing Company on West High Street and, in 1972, the subsidiary Hummelstown Manufacturing Company. Hestteco made women's dresses and specialized in children's clothing. In 1957, John B. Greenberg and his son Joel started J.B. Athletic Shoes, manufacturing ice skates and soccer and basketball shoes in Elizabethtown.

Jewish names may be held by persons not of Hebrew heritage, and in a community where German names are common, the definite identification of individuals as Jewish is difficult, unless congregational or burial records provide proof. One observer of the German settlers in Lancaster noted, "Several German Christian families actually returned to the old [Hebrew] dispensation, and with these accessions quite a Jewish community was formed." As some German Christian families returned to the Hebrew faith, others converted from Judaism to Catholicism, such as cattleman Joseph Strouse of Elizabethtown, who became a member of St. Peter's.

The Swiss Mennonites who migrated to Pennsylvania with Jewish settlers purchased land from Martin Chartier in what is today Washington Boro in Manor Township, Lancaster. In 1709, a Swiss Mennonite refugee from the German Palatinate, Melchoir Brenneman, migrated to Philadelphia before settling in Conestoga Manor, along the Conestoga—today's Conestoga Township. Brenneman became the largest landowner in the region, purchasing thousands of acres from Chartier. In 1717, he established New Danville Mennonite Church. In 1728, Brenneman purchased 950 acres on Cony Creek in contemporary Elizabethtown. The Brennemans established a number of gristmills, sawmills, and distilleries along Conoy Creek and operated a ferry for westward transportation across the Susquehanna River at Conoy Town. Melchoir Brenneman established the first Mennonite congregation in Elizabethtown, known today as Goods Mennonite Church.

Beginning in 1719, Scotch Irish Presbyterians from County Donegal, Ireland, began purchasing land from the LeTort and Bezaillion families along the Susquehanna River at Conoy and Conewago Creeks. Thomas Harris and Samuel Smith, Presbyterian members of Donegal Church established gristmills and sawmills along the creeks. In 1801, Mennonite Henry Bates Grubb purchased these mills and built Mount Vernon Furnace, which produced iron in Elizabethtown on Zeager Road. Grubb cleared several acres of woods in Elizabethtown and purchased wood and charcoal from lumber sources across northern Pennsylvania that was shipped on the Susquehanna River.

Along Conoy Creek, a pattern of development emerged: farmers built iron furnaces, mills, and distilleries, then obtained licenses from the courts in Lancaster to sell alcoholic beverages. In this way, they turned their farmhouses into public houses. Trade routes developed along these public houses, and the proprietors subdivided their farmland into lots leased or sold, thus establishing residential hamlets on roads linking the larger cities. The present site of Falmouth was a town created on Conewago Creek as a transfer point for shipping on the Susquehanna River. The towns of Newhaven and Waterford along the Susquehanna were merged into contemporary Marietta. In 1726, John Galbraith raised and malted barley where Mount Joy Turnpike crosses Donegal Run. At his gristmill and distillery, he made whiskey and operated a public house. Samuel Smith built Bossler Road, connecting his homestead on Conoy Creek to his gristmill and sawmill on Conewago Creek. In 1732, Lancaster courts licensed Smith to sell New England rum. In 1735, he was elected to the Pennsylvania Assembly and chosen as sheriff of Lancaster. Thomas and Margaret Shiels Wilson established the town of Wilsonburgh on Conewago Creek in 1811. They operated a public house and leased lots in 1812. Charles O'Donnell established O'Donnellsburg, operating a hotel along the Harrisburg Turnpike. The next year, James Duffy, contractor for the Lancaster, Elizabethtown & Middletown Turnpike, established Irishtown. Duffy and his wife, Catherine Sheridan, named the streets in Irishtown after naval heroes and ships of the War of 1812. Eventually, Irishtown was incorporated into Marietta. Paul Yeuts established the town of Newville, or Yeutstown, with a tavern on the Falmouth & Elizabethtown Turnpike along the Susquehanna River, linking Marietta and Columbia to furnaces and rolling mills manufacturing iron.

In 1738, the commonwealth built a road linking Lancaster to Harrisburg (Harrisburg Pike) in Lancaster, Market Street in Elizabethtown, and Route 230. The road passed the Sign of the Bear Tavern on Conoy Creek. In 1736, the Lancaster courts licensed Thomas and Mary McKinney Harris to sell hard cider and beer at this public house. In 1751, Harris sold the tavern to Lazarus Lowrey, who leased it to Barnabus and Elizabeth Waters Hughes. In 1753, Hughes purchased the Sign of the Bear Tavern before moving to Baltimore in 1761. In 1763, while living in Baltimore, Hughes divided 300 acres surrounding the tavern on Conoy Creek into lots measuring 60 feet wide by 165 feet deep. He laid out a town around a central diamond, naming the streets Market and High while inserting Cherry, Peach, and Rose Alleys. Hughes named Elizabeth Towne to honor his wife. He employed Abraham and Esther Holmes to run the tavern in 1767 and rent the adjacent Hughes farm. Holmes named his youngest daughter Elizabeth Town Holmes.

The Penn family established three counties in Pennsylvania—Philadelphia, Bucks, and Chester. In 1729, Lancaster County was separated from Chester and given its name by John Wright, a native of Lancaster, England. Gradually, six counties were formed out of Lancaster County—York, Cumberland, Berks, Northumberland, Dauphin, and Lebanon. The French, Jewish, Mennonite, Scotch Irish, and Indian settlement at Conoy Town was divided into seven townships—Conoy, Conwego, East Donegal, West Donegal, Rapho, Londonderry, and Mount Joy. Equidistant between Lancaster and Harrisburg along the Harrisburg Turnpike, Elizabethtown on Conoy Creek emerged as the economic, political, and transportation hub of the region.

The Conoy Creek connecting Elizabethtown to the Susquehanna River positioned the community at the center of a rivalry between the port cities of Philadelphia and Baltimore. Established in 1638, Philadelphia was long the commercial capital of Colonial America, eventually becoming the second-largest port city in the United States. Established in 1661, Baltimore rivaled Philadelphia with its 46-mile harbor connecting the Potomac River and Chesapeake Bay. Throughout the nation's development, competition existed between these ports, both of which depended on commercial relations with Lancaster, York, and Carlisle in the backcountry.

Twice, proposals were made to create a new county with Elizabethtown as the county seat. In 1826, state legislator Jacob Gish authored a bill detaching Donegal, Mount Joy, and Rapho Townships from Lancaster County. Gish proposed the creation of Conewago County with Elizabethtown as county seat. In 1831, state legislator James Mackey proposed carving Monroe County out of Lancaster, Dauphin, and Lebanon Counties and establishing Elizabethtown as county seat.

Linking Elizabethtown on Conoy Creek to the interior of Lancaster was the vision of the German Baptist Brethren who migrated to Elizabethtown in 1868 from the Weiseichenland settlement on the Chiques Creek near Manheim. Members of the Church of the Brethren established Elizabethtown as a major industrial manufacturing center with access to the Pennsylvania Canal, the Pennsylvania Railroad, and the Harrisburg Turnpike. The Brethren formed the banks in Elizabethtown, established Elizabethtown College, and developed a number of residential subdivisions. In this way, they attracted the Grand Lodge of Pennsylvania to locate the Masonic Village retirement and children's home and the Thomas Ranken Patton Trade and Industrial School along Conoy Creek. In 1925, Gov. Gifford Pinchot chose Elizabethtown as the site for the Pennsylvania State Hospital for Crippled Children, which, in 1991, became the training academy for the Pennsylvania Department of Corrections. The Church of the Brethren, along with other members of the Historic Peace Churches in Elizabethtown that embraced conscientious objection—such as the Mennonites, United Brethren in Christ, Brethren in Christ, River Brethren, and United Zion Church—defeated plans by the Department of Defense to build major military-industrial bases in Elizabethtown in 1942 and 1951.

By 1922, Klein Chocolate in Elizabethtown was the largest milk chocolate factory in the nation, producing 250,000 bars a day. Owned today by Mars, Inc., the confectionary factory continues contributing to the local economy at 295 Brown Street along Conoy Creek. With access to Amtrak Keystone service connecting New York City and Harrisburg by way of Philadelphia and with proximity to the Pennsylvania Turnpike through Route 283, Elizabethtown has emerged into a commuter community. Suburban subdivisions are growing, the Masonic Village independent retirement cottage community is expanding, and Elizabethtown College's growing enrollment means the inevitable expansion of its residential campus. Residential planning for the future of Elizabethtown has involved sensitivity to preserving historical landmarks while developing land-use laws protecting local agriculture and businesses as suburban sprawl moves toward agricultural and timber areas along the Conoy Creek. This historically significant community moves forward in concert with modern philosophies concerning historic preservation, so the future may learn from the past.

One

CULTURE

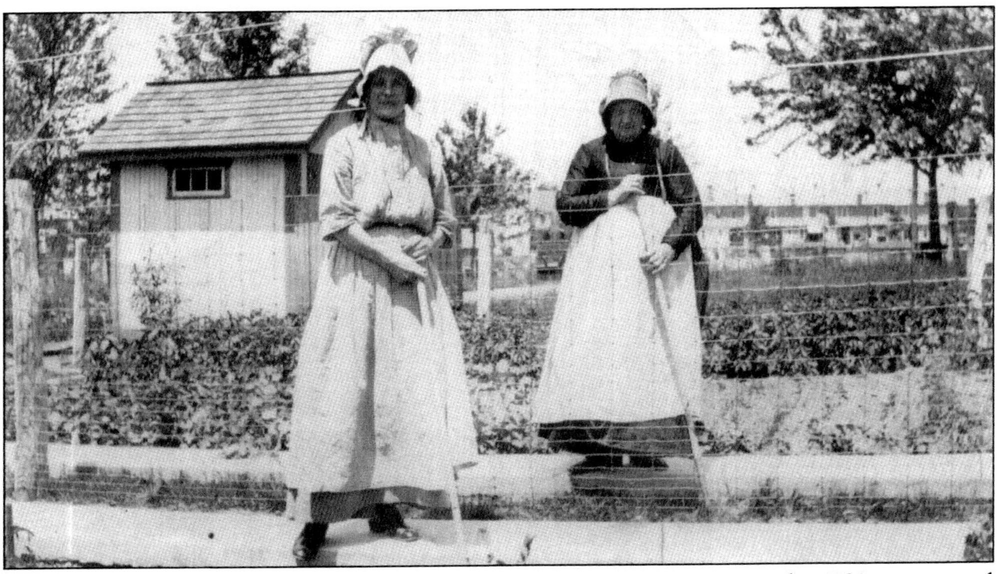

Mennonite women pose in Grandma Rutt's garden in 1920. Beginning in the 1930s, a national fascination with Pennsylvania German or Dutch culture drove the tourist industry in Lancaster County, today a major part of the state's revenue. On the surface, it seems that natives of Elizabethtown identify with Pennsylvania Dutch culture, even if they are of Scotch Irish descent. This popular heritage identification betrays the cultural diversity in Elizabethtown's history.

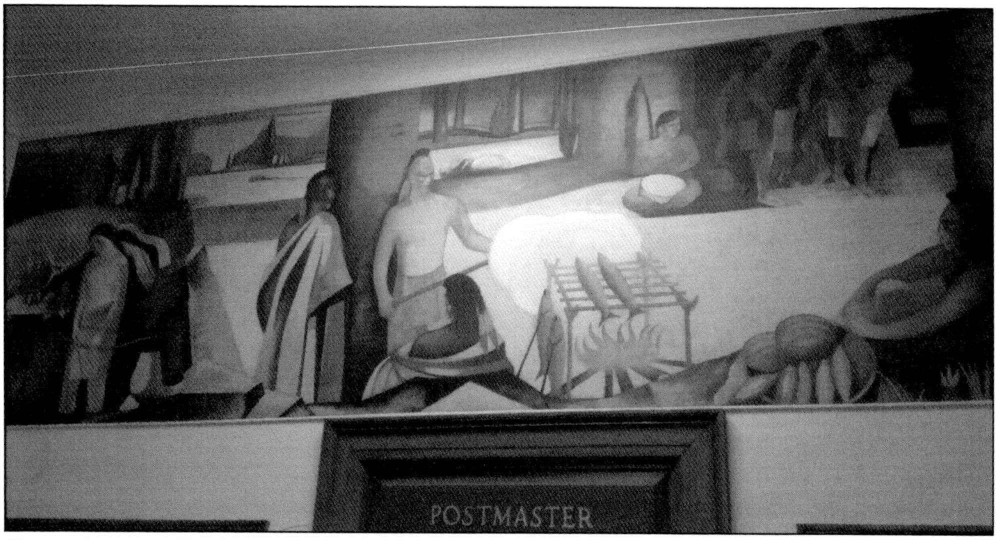

Shown here is a Work Projects Administration mural in the US Post Office in Elizabethtown. In 1942, French-trained artist Henry Lee Gatch painted *Squaw's Rest*, depicting the Conoy Indian village. From 1717 to 1743, the Piscataway Nation lived where the Conoy Creek meets the Susquehanna River. The mural is on display in the post office built by the WPA in 1939 at 137 South Market Street.

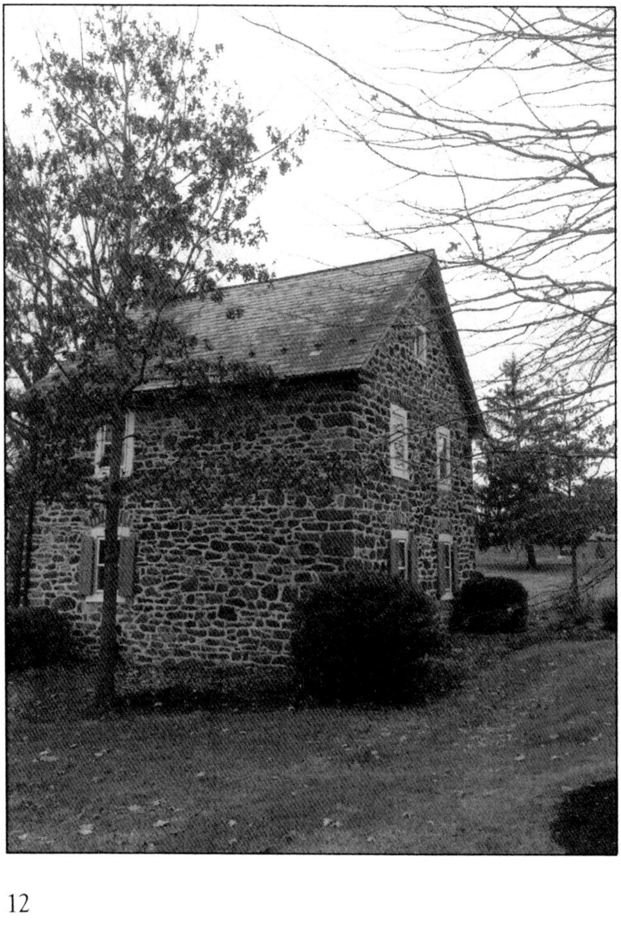

This is perhaps the oldest house in Elizabethtown, built in 1744 by Swiss Mennonite John Nissley. The home is now at Masonic Village. Mennonites maintained strong economic and political power in Elizabethtown, often countercultural. They opposed public education and ecumenical Sunday schools, supporting their own German-language and church-related schools. In 1846, the German Reformed Church advocated catechism classes in response to "fanatic sects around us," preaching "Catechetical instruction is vain."

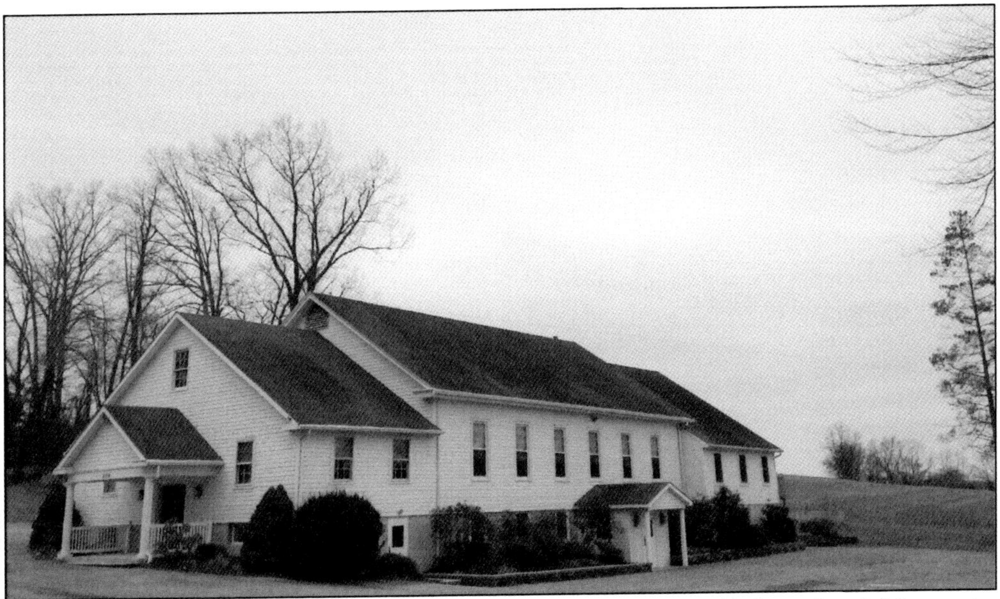

Mennonites settled in Elizabethtown, with Melchoir Brenneman establishing Goods Mennonite Church (pictured). In 1777, the Pennsylvania Assembly passed conscription acts. Conscientious objectors paid a "non-associators" tax. Mennonites influenced Catholics, Lutherans, Presbyterians, and Reformed churches to refuse military service and pay the exemption tax instead. That same year, Elizabethtown's Col. Bartrem Galbraith failed to conscript local men. On one occasion, when he tried to enforce the Militia Act, a dozen men violently resisted.

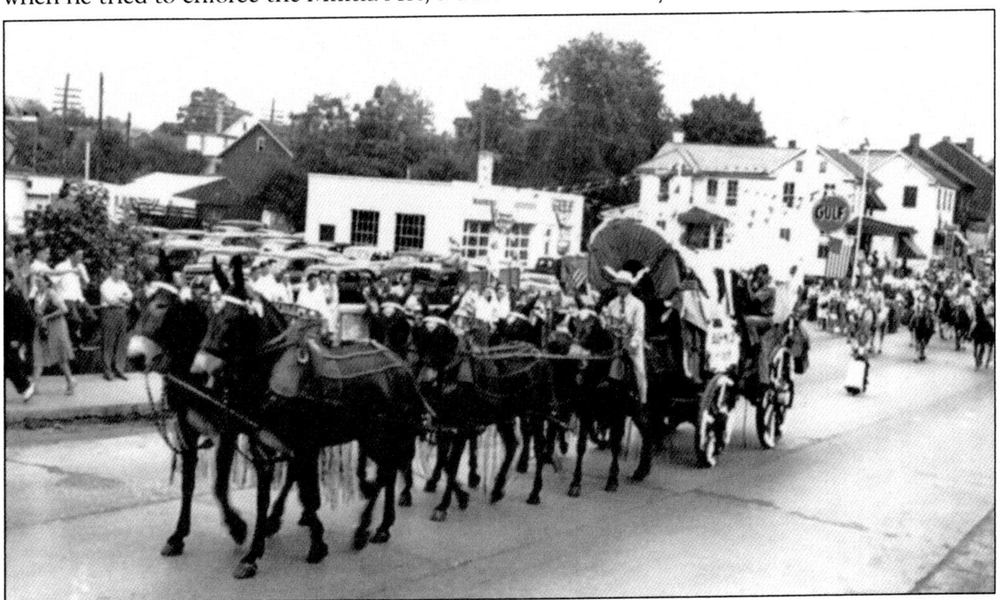

Mennonites with Conestoga wagons, such as the one shown here in a 1945 Victory Parade, supplied militaries while conscientiously objecting to wars. Elizabethtown was a central point for raising militia companies in Lancaster. In 1777, a board was appointed to hear appeals in Elizabethtown against fines for missing militia drills or field days. Historic Peace Churches in Elizabethtown signed an address in 1800 thanking Republican governor Thomas McKean for protecting their constitutional rights as religious pacifists.

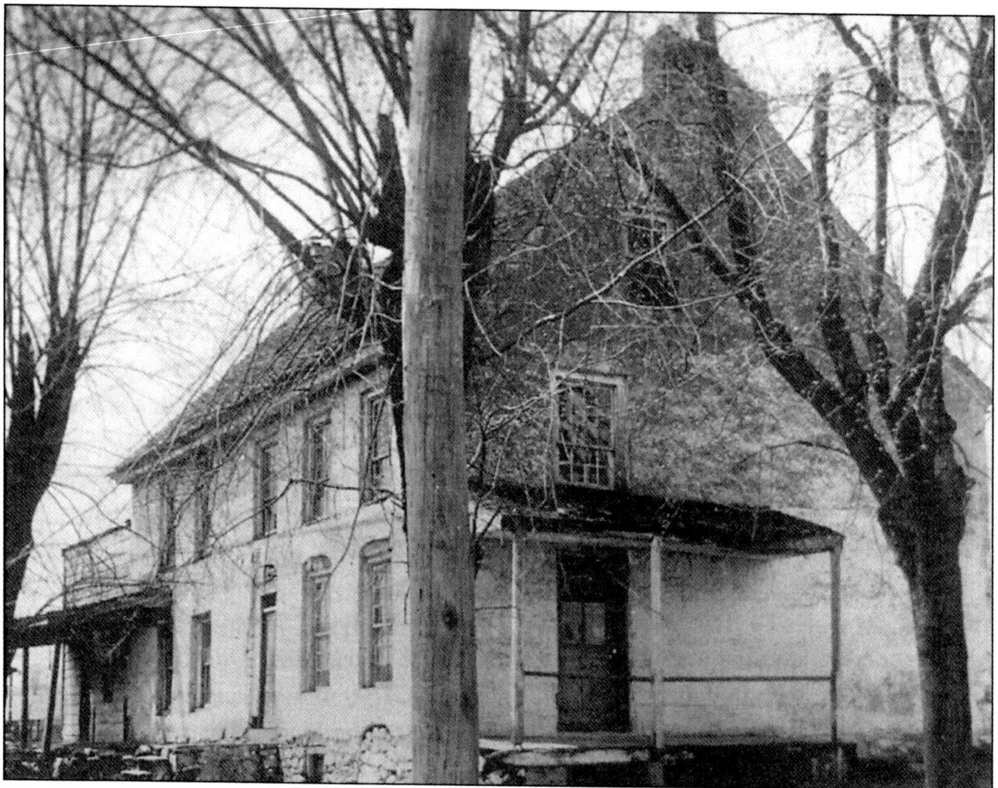

The Sign of the Bear Tavern, shown in these photographs, was built in 1745 and still stands on the corner of Market and Hummelstown Streets. Around 1732, Thomas and Mary McKinney Harris, from Raphoe, County Donegal, Ireland, settled on 230 acres along Conoy Creek. In 1738, they were authorized to operate the Sign of the Bear, paying 22 pounds for indentured servant Andrew Christy. In 1747, anticipating the French and Indian War (1754–1763), Harris was captain of the "Associated Regiment of the West End of Lancaster County on the Susquehanna." In 1751, he sold the Bear to Lazarus Lowrey; Lowrey leased it to Barnabus and Elizabeth Waters Hughes, who purchased it in 1753. Hughes partnered with Quaker merchant and brewer Isaac Whitelock of the Philadelphia firm Baynton, Wharton, and Morgan.

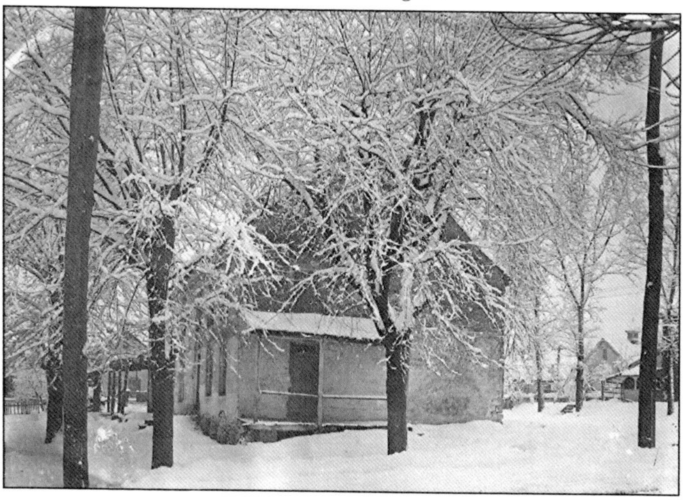

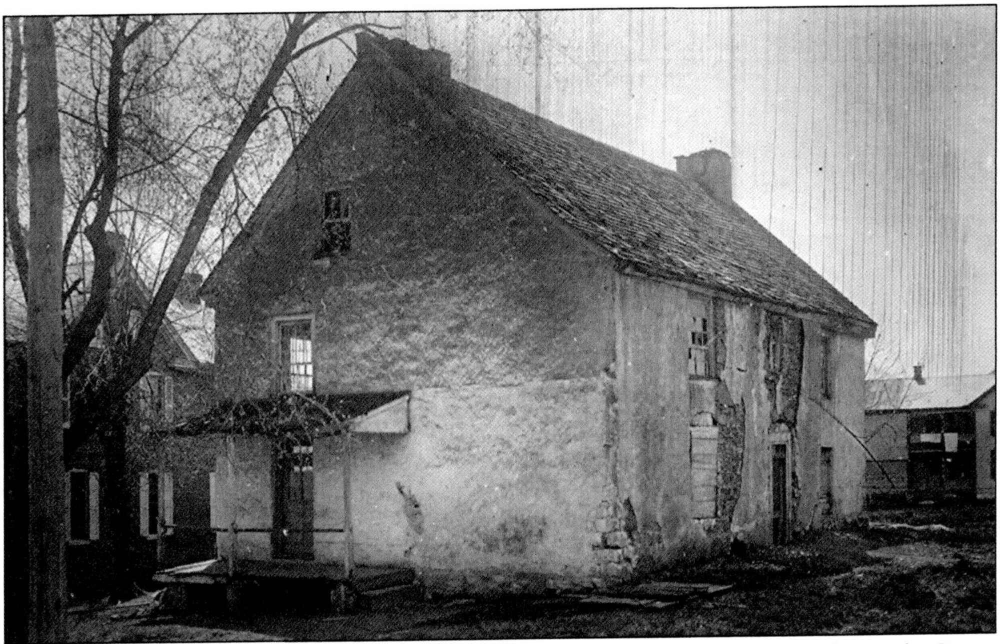

From the Bear, Commissary Captain Hughes supplied Forts Hunter and Swatara during the Seven Years' War. In 1761, he relocated to Baltimore, trading with firms from Belfast and Londonderry. That same year, he leased the Bear (pictured above and below) to Thomas Black, who operated the tavern until 1764. Abraham and Esther Holmes operated the Bear beginning in 1767; they owned one African slave and several Scotch Irish indentured servants. In 1763, Hughes sold lots around a central diamond, calling it Elizabeth Towne. Local farmers purchased lots on condition they build dwellings within two years, or ownership would revert to Hughes. Lots were sold as perpetual leases, and most farmers were rented to immigrants. Visiting Elizabethtown in 1769, Henry Melchior Muhlenberg observed, "The inhabitants of this town are young newcomers and for the most part poor."

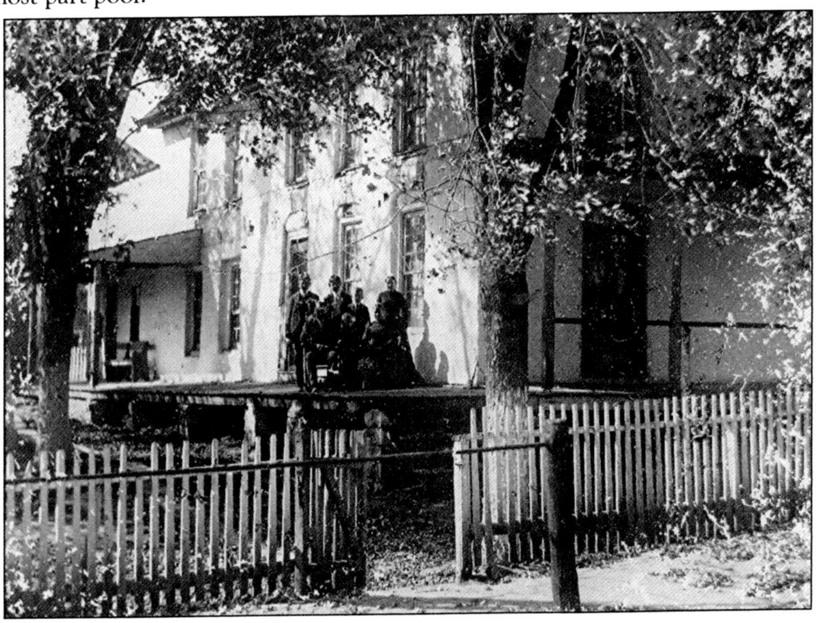

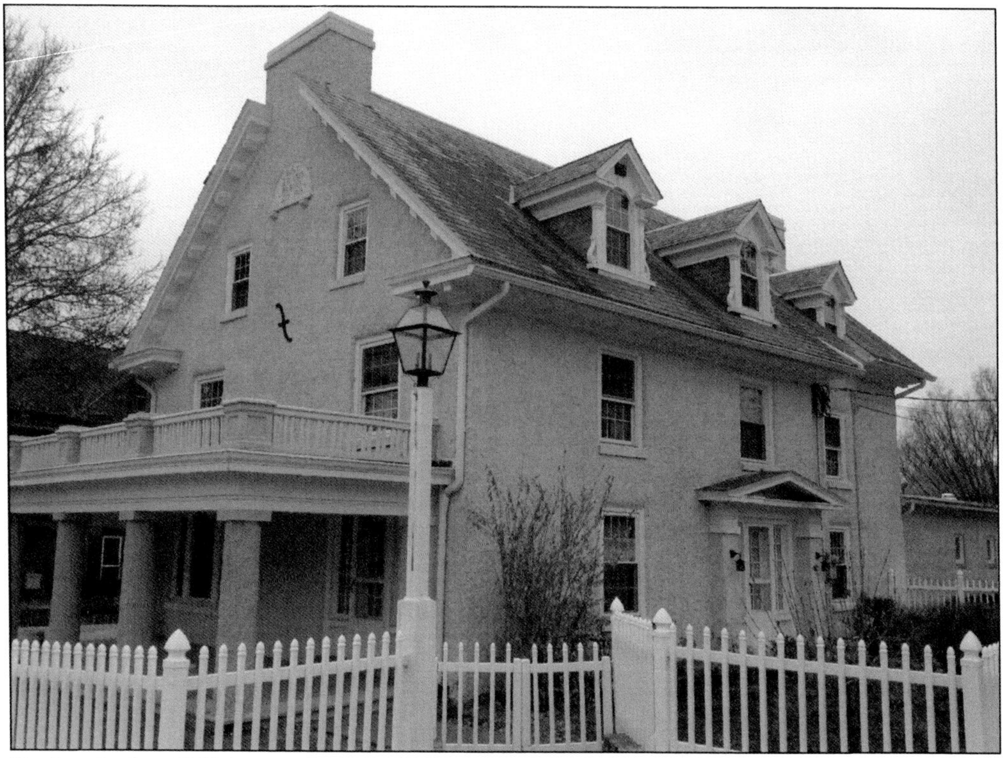

Hughes died in 1765, leaving his iron furnace in Washington County, Maryland, to son Samuel. Underwritten by the British firm Mildred & Roberts, Hughes made cannons for Congress while serving as a delegate to the Maryland Convention (1776) and the House of Delegates (1777–1779), and as a senator (1781–1790). In 1790, Hughes sold the Sign of the Bear (above) to Capt. Andrew Boggs. He operated a tavern in Bainbridge before selling to Valentine Bossler in 1789. In 1801, Boggs leased the Bear to Capt. John Wolfley until 1809, when George Wealand bought it and built a house at 130 North Market Street (below) in 1815. The next year, John Redsecker, owner of the Black Horse Tavern, bought the Bear. Andrew Wade purchased the tavern as a tenant house and lived in the Wealand House (presently the Miller & Sekely Funeral Home). In 1884, cattleman Martin G. Keller bought both properties.

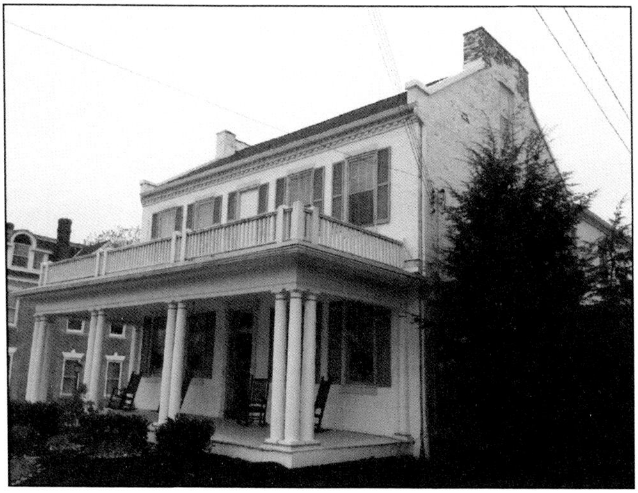

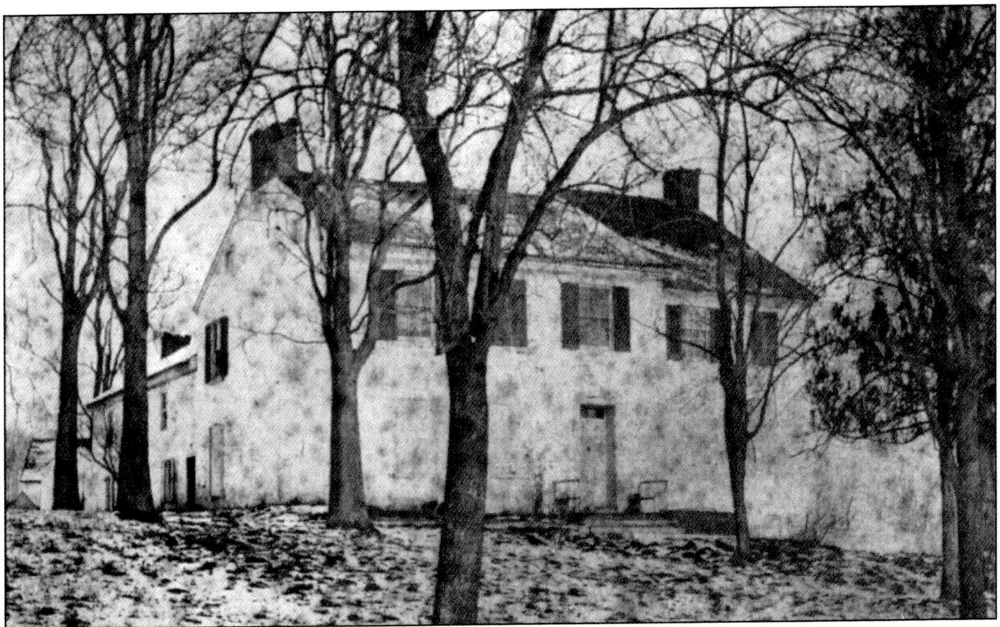

In 1729, Lazarus Lowrey settled in Maytown; his house is pictured here. Lowrey partnered with Joseph Simon, a Jewish fur trader in Lancaster, trading with the Piscataway Nation. In 1775, Lowrey served on committees of the Continental Congress enforcing refusal to trade with London. His son Alexander Lowrey represented Donegal Township at a provincial convention to raise militia units. In 1776, Col. Alexander Lowery commanded the Donegal and Mount Joy militia.

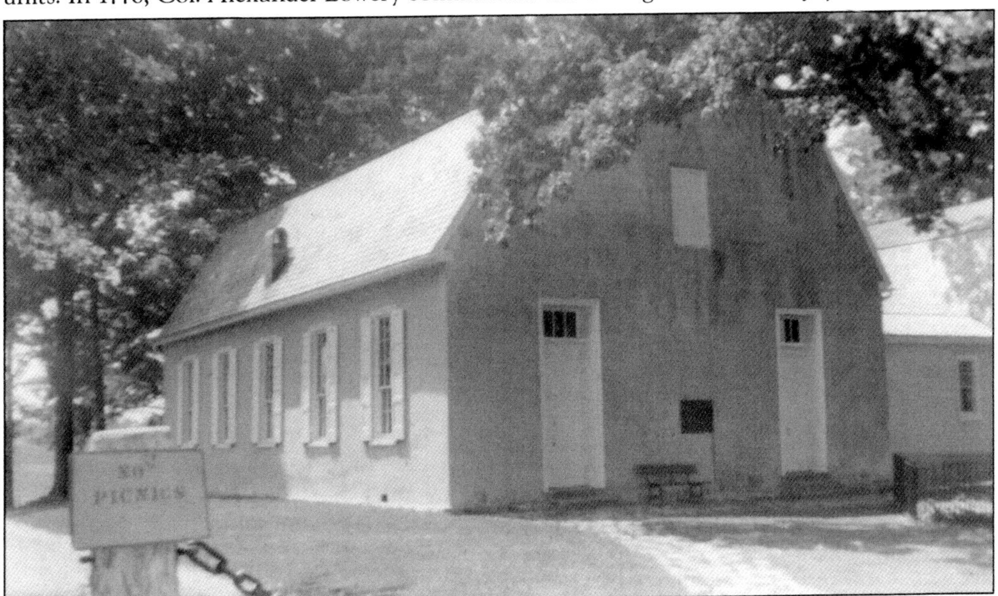

The Donegal Presbyterian Church (pictured) was built in 1726. In 1745, Thomas Harris, of the Bear Tavern, withdrew from Donegal and established Mount Joy Presbyterian Church on Anchor Road under New Brunswick Presbytery, which established Princeton University. In 1756, Harris's sons Robert and John studied medicine at Princeton. Harris joined the Presbyterian exodus to Baltimore in 1751. Eventually, the Mount Joy Presbyterian Church dissolved; there has not been another Presbyterian congregation in Elizabethtown.

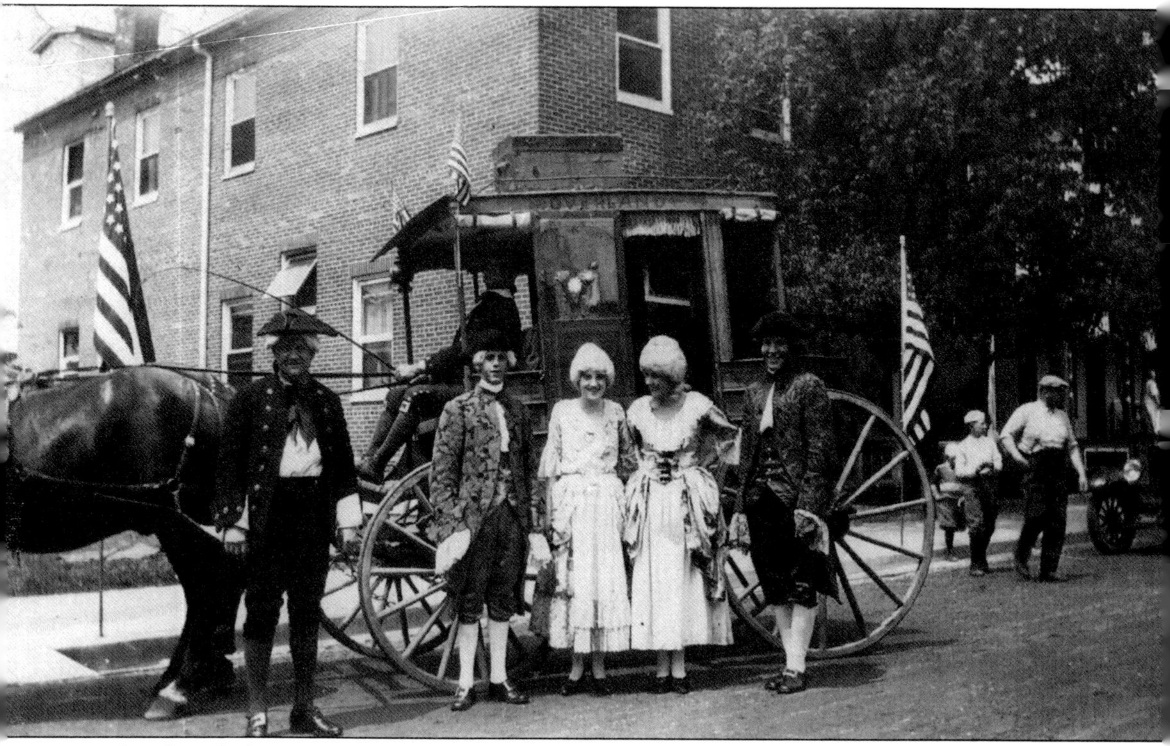

On the 150th anniversary of American independence, celebrated on Saturday, July 3, 1926, Episcopalian brothers Richard and Robert Heistand staged historical reenactments of Revolutionary War battles. Warren Nelson swung a lantern from the bell tower of Christ Reformed Church, and the Church of the Brethren brothers Jacob and Winfield Heisey rode horseback through the borough, announcing, "The British are coming!" The Heistands attended Augusta Military Academy in Fort Defiance, Virginia.

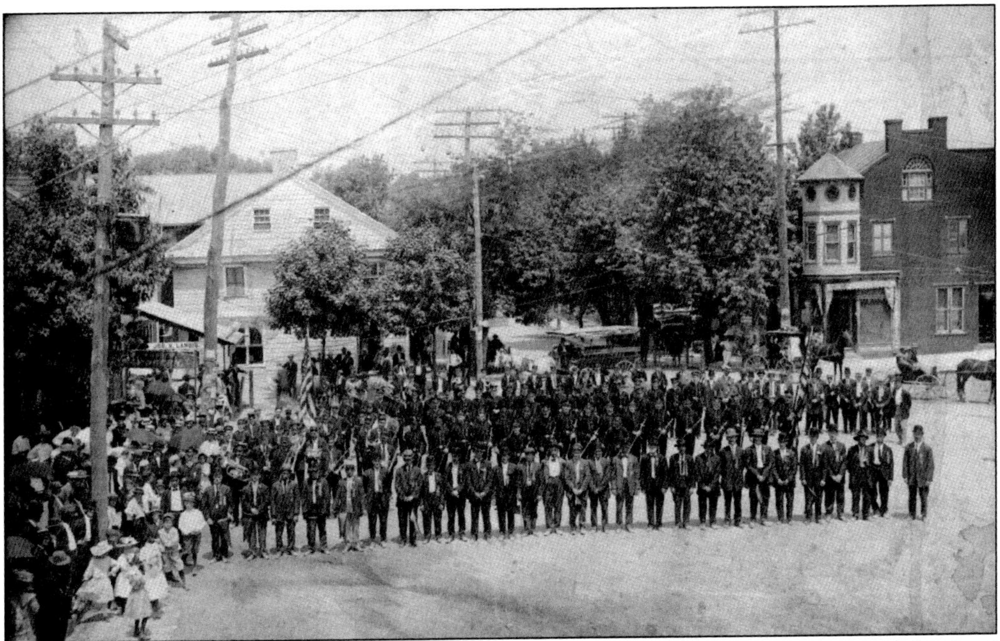

Shown above and below is the 1896 reunion of the Golden Eagles Sons of Veterans of the Civil War. In 1861, Rev. John McCosker of St. Peter's volunteered and served as chaplain of the 55th Pennsylvania at Camp Curtin in Harrisburg. His regiment was sent to Edisto Island on the coast of South Carolina. On June 4, 1862, he died while on leave in a military hospital in Philadelphia. The Friendship Fire Company organized as the Elizabethtown Rangers (later Anderson Cadets) and drilled behind the Benjamin Groff Mill at the corner of South Market and Union Streets. The latter street, named to commemorate the Union cadet drills, was later called College Avenue. As troops converged 55 miles south at Gettysburg and the bridge crossing the Susquehanna linking Columbia to York was burned, hundreds of refugees from Franklin and Cumberland Counties settled in Elizabethtown. Gen. Robert H. Milroy assumed authority, enforcing martial law.

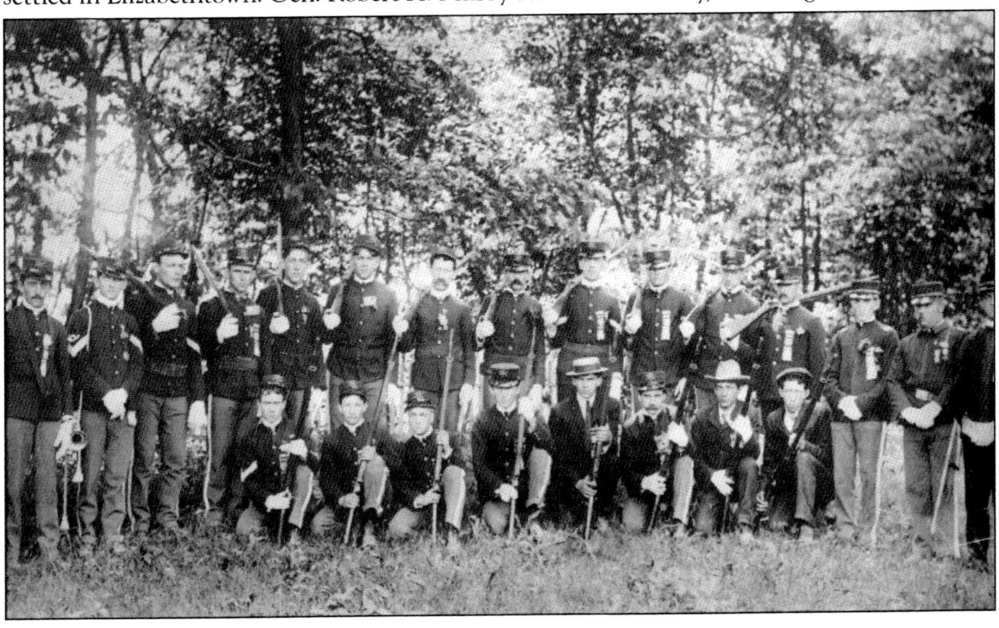

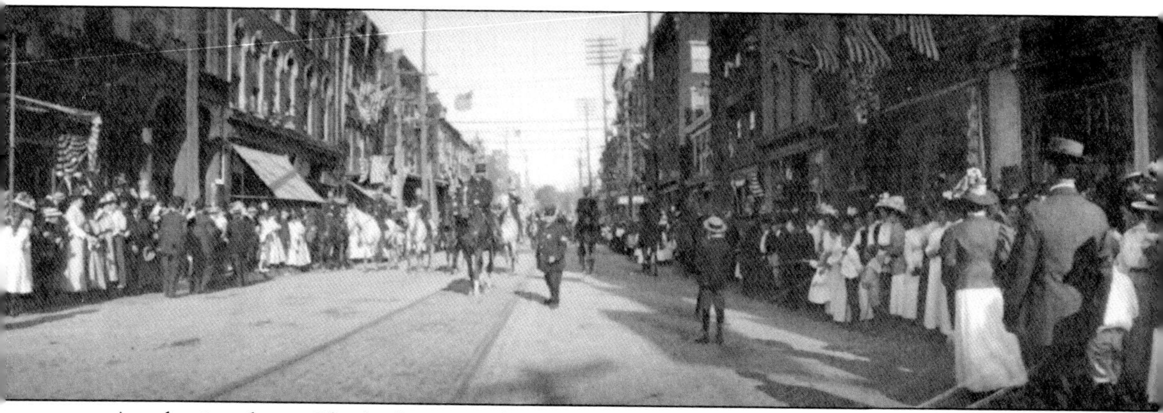

An election day in Elizabethtown is shown here. In Colonial America, residents in areas west of Quaker-controlled Philadelphia were not always granted universal suffrage, particularly the Germans and Scotch Irish. The Constitution of 1776 broadened suffrage, including all freemen over 21 years of age. In 1798, the Pennsylvania General Assembly took favorable action on "a petition from the citizens of Lancaster [County], that they may be permitted to hold their elections in Elizabeth Town." By 1800, the Bear Tavern was the polling place. Lancaster City was a Federalist stronghold despite the decline of the party nationally; Lancaster Federalists maintained political supremacy through the 1820s. Elizabethtown was the exception, with Irish Catholics and German members of the Historic Peace Churches voting Republican. When the voters of Elizabethtown sent native son Republican Samuel Cooke to the Pennsylvania General Assembly in 1801, the editors of the Federalist *Lancaster Journal* charged "Irishmen" at Elizabethtown with casting a "number of illegal votes at the borough box." Republican candidates Maj. Thomas Eagan of St. Peter's and Joseph Gorgas, proprietor of Running Pump Tavern, consistently conceded elections to the Federalist majority of Lancaster.

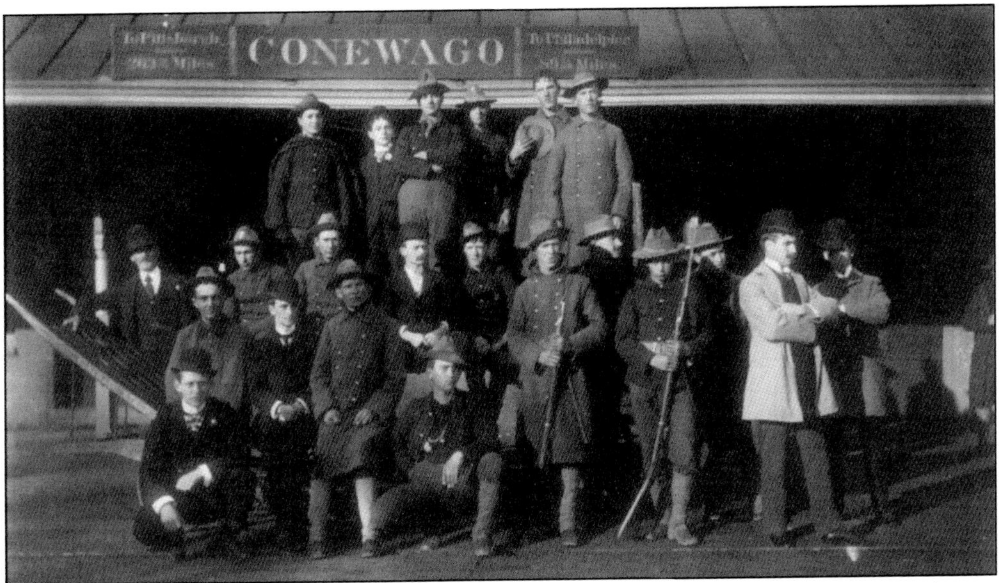

Veterans of the Spanish-American War pose for a photograph. During the American Revolution, the Pennsylvania Assembly purchased "Continental Lot" for a military-supply depot. It was managed by quartermasters from St. Peter's, John Jamison and Timothy Connor. In 1798, America and France prepared for war. The *Lancaster Journal* reported "Handsome volunteer companies of Infantry form in Elizabethtown." During the War of 1812, St. Peter's Terah Jones (16th Regiment Infantry) recruited troops from tents on Market Street.

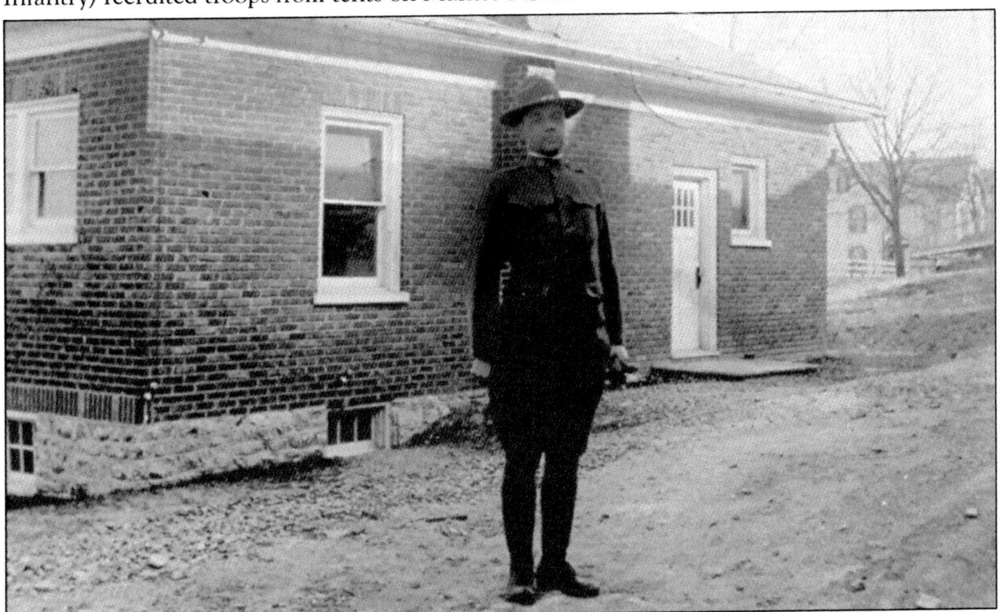

In October 1917, draftees from Elizabethtown attended basic training at Camp Meade. They were assigned to the 316th Infantry serving in France. As a Brethren contentious objector, Walter Eshelman volunteered for noncombatant service, entering Camp Dix in September 1918. Later, on July 4, 1935, Maj. Gen. Smedley Butler, USMC, spoke in Elizabethtown, denouncing "war fomenters" profiting from selling armaments and claiming that Congress represented "munitions makers rather than the people." The man pictured is unidentified.

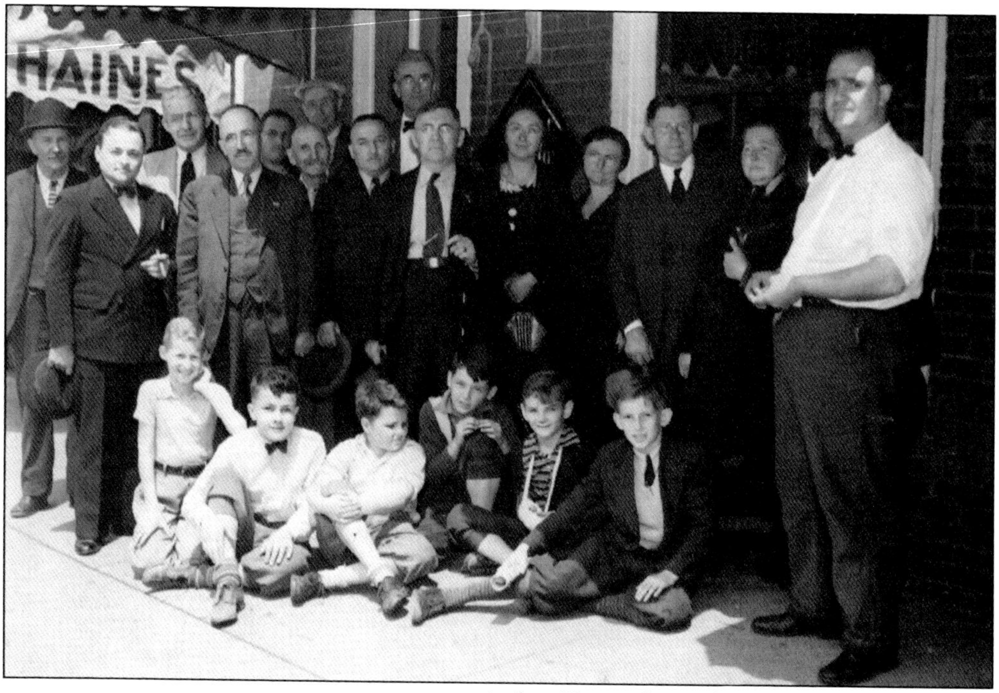

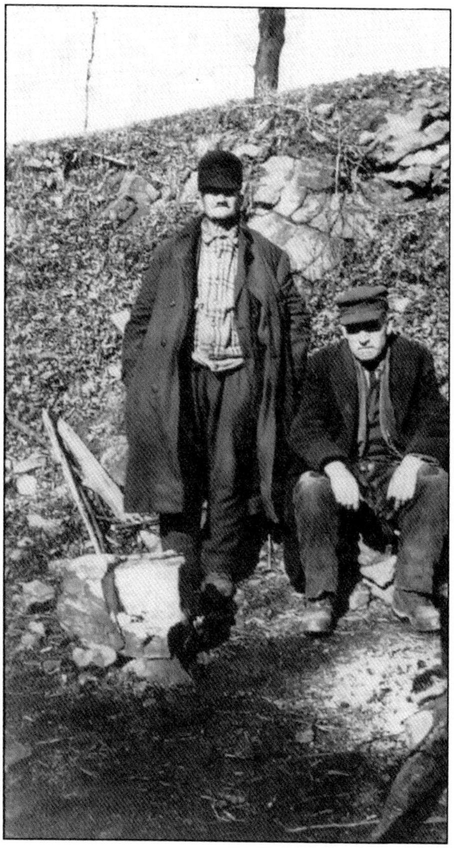

Arthur Horace James (standing, third from right) campaigns in Elizabethtown in 1932. The 14th lieutenant governor (1927–1931) and 31st governor (1939–1943) of Pennsylvania, James was nominated in 1940 as a Republican anti–New Deal presidential candidate. Support for James came from holdovers of the Know Nothing Party in Lancaster, which established the newspaper *Lancaster Inland Weekly* in 1859. Elizabethtown Know Nothings had opposed Democratic governor George Wolf's taxes for state-owned railroads and public schools.

Here, rail riders stop in Elizabethtown during the Great Depression. A transient camp existed on the west side of the railroad embankment near Conoy Creek. At Mount Tunnel Farm, adjacent to the Pennsylvania Railroad, Mrs. Simon Landis fed transients in her kitchen. In 1931, the Elizabethtown Relief Association collected, canned, and distributed produce within the community. Simon Landis was a schoolteacher and pastor of Elizabethtown Mennonite Church.

In 1942, Brethren Paul Grubb, of the Elizabethtown College board of trustees, persuaded Col. J.P. Harris to abandon plans for an ammunitions plant in Elizabethtown. Learning about prayer meetings opposing his plan, Harris said, "Tell the folks their prayers are answered." In 1951, the Pentagon proposed building Elizabethtown-Donegal Air Force Base. Historic Peace Churches defeated the plan. In 1964, Olmstead Air Force Base and the Middletown Air Material Base closed. A 1946 Victory Parade is pictured here.

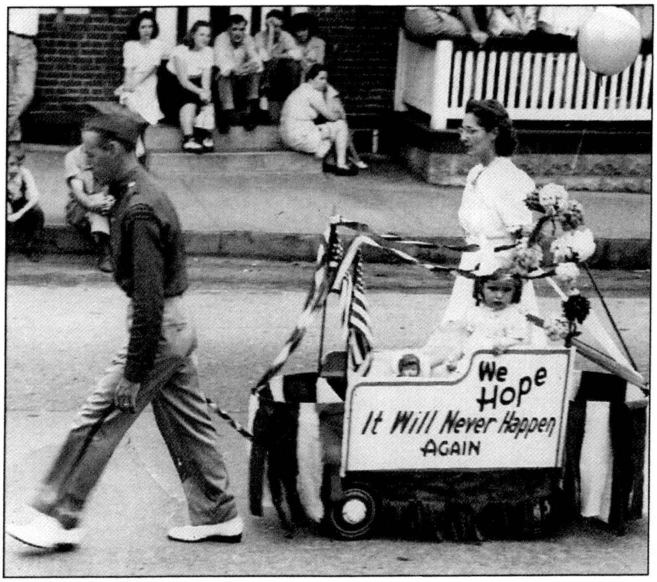

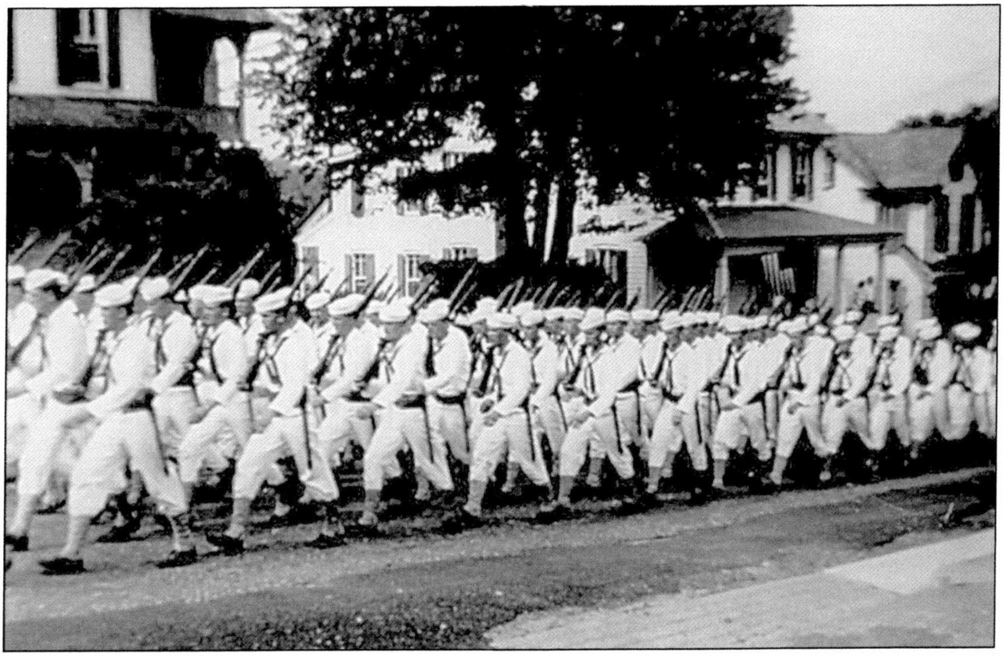

Shown here is the Elizabethtown Homecoming Parade of 1946. By 1953, the Department of Defense was the largest single employer of Elizabethtown residents, with 242 households headed by persons in civilian positions working at local Air Force and Navy bases. In 1952, the Capitron division of the electronics connector manufacturer AMP, Inc., opened a plant on East Park Street. The firm made components for radar systems in military aircraft. AMP moved to the Elcor Industrial Park in 1967.

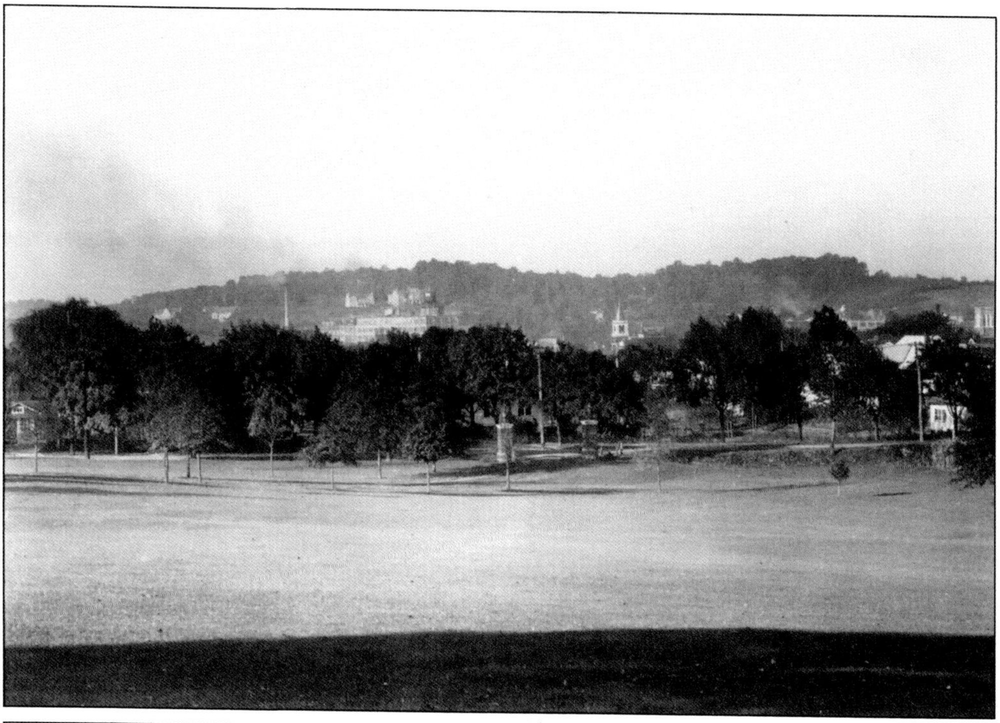

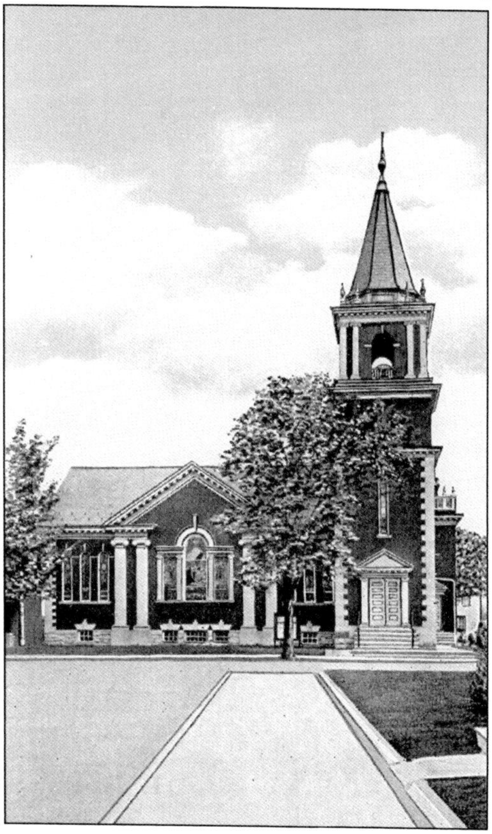

This 1930 photograph of the Elizabethtown skyline was taken from Elizabethtown College's Rider Hall. On the left beyond the trees is Klein's Chocolate Factory. On the hill behind the factory are buildings of the Masonic Village. Right of center is the steeple of Christ Church United Church of Christ. In 1752, Blaser's German Reformed Church started on the farm of Peter and Magdalena Blaser. In 1815, the congregation built Christ Reformed Church on South Market Street.

Christ Church United Church of Christ was built in 1909. In 1957, Evangelical, Reformed, and Congregational churches formed the United Church of Christ. Capt. John Bucher had pastored this church in 1767. A theologian at the University of Marburg, he joined the Dutch military in 1755, coming to Lancaster while fighting for Col. James Armstrong. In 1758, he fought with Gen. John Forbes at Fort Duquesne. From 1759 to 1761, Bucher was commissary at Carlisle.

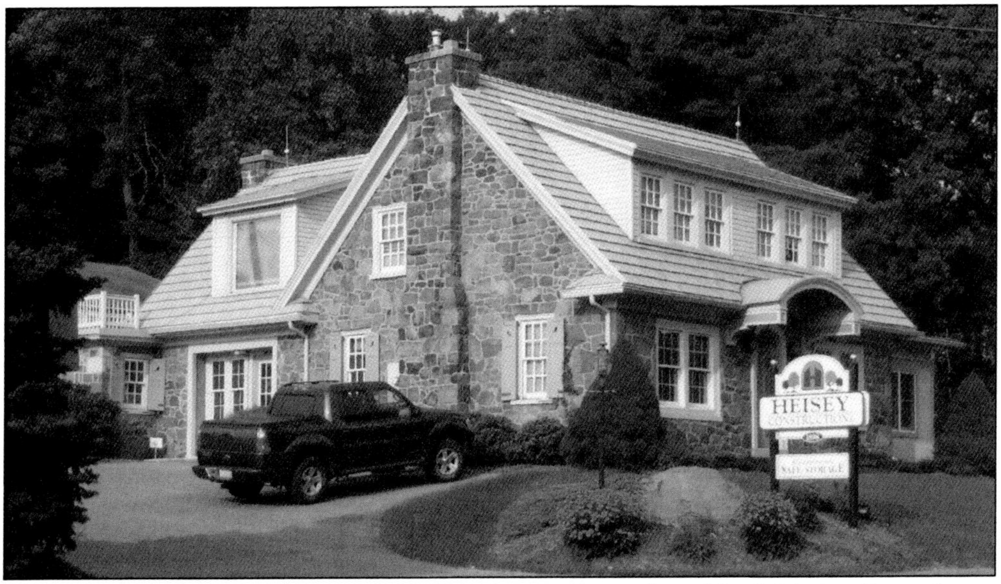

Ober School House, adjacent to Mount Ober Cemetery, stands on North Market Street. It was also known as Ober Meetinghouse, and many congregations formed here due to denominational schisms. In 1932, Henry K. Ober was a Republican candidate for state senate. He pastored Elizabethtown Church of the Brethren from 1928 to 1939 and was president of Elizabethtown College (1918–1928). Ober authored the motto on the college seal, "God, Light, and Truth," as well as the college motto, "Make Jesus King."

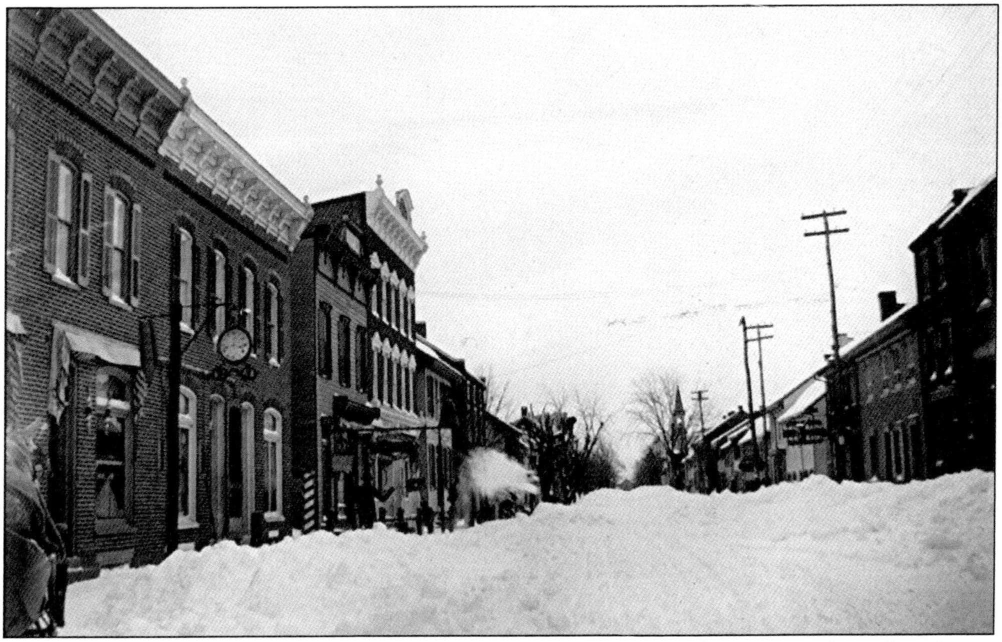

South Market Street is seen here in a photograph taken at Diamond Square. Today referred to as Center Square, the intersection of High and Market Streets is described in historical documents as "Diamond Square." On the right in the distance is the steeple of the Church of God, Bethel, built in 1853. The church was erected on South Market Street on land deeded by the Redsecker family, where their Black Horse Tavern was located.

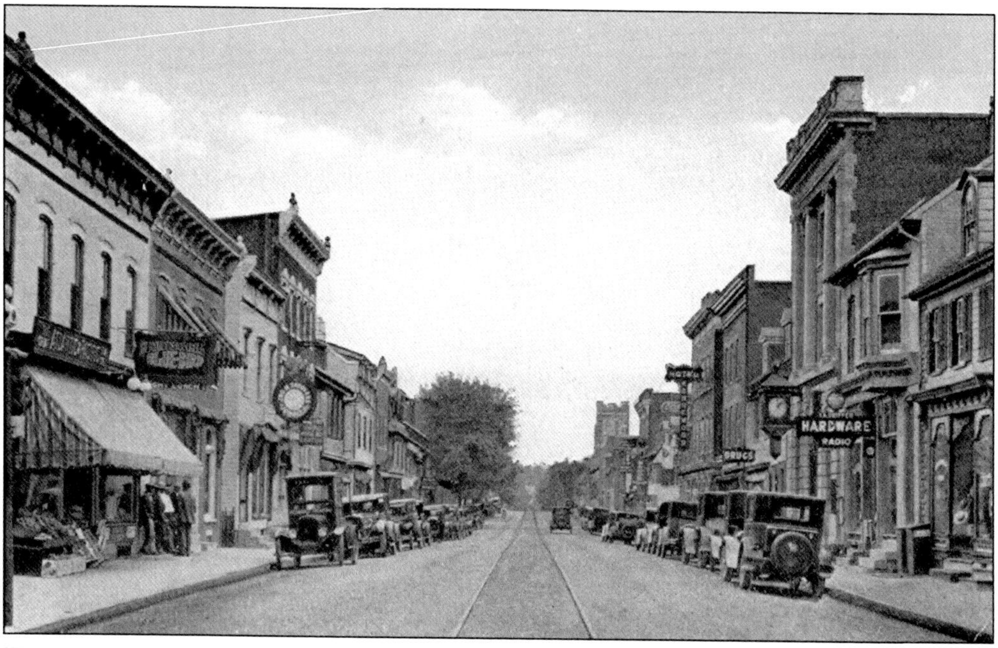

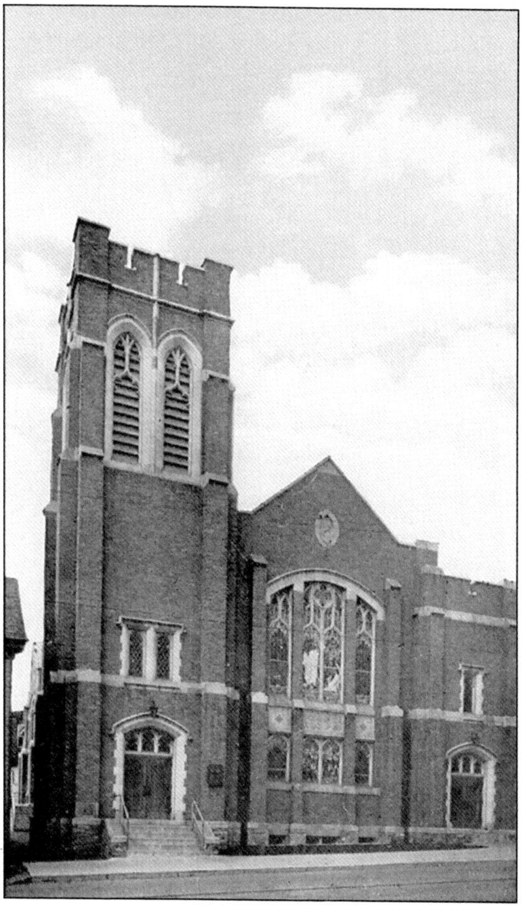

South Market Street is shown here in another photograph taken from Diamond Square. On the right is the steeple of the present Church of God, Bethel, built in 1918. Major Brenneman's family established the Church of God in Elizabethtown. In 1843, the first church building, Bethel, was erected on Brenneman land on East High Street. The land was sold to the United Brethren Church in 1853. The present Church of God was dedicated on March 24, 1918.

The Reverend John Winebrenner, pastor of Salem German Reformed Church in Harrisburg, was expelled in 1827 from the Lebanon Classis for advocating adult baptism, evangelism, and social reform movements. The Lebanon Classis held annual regional ministerial association meetings in the Christ Reformed Church of Elizabethtown. In 1826, Winebrenner began preaching at Ober's Meetinghouse. In Elizabethtown, he established the Church of God (pictured) denomination in 1829.

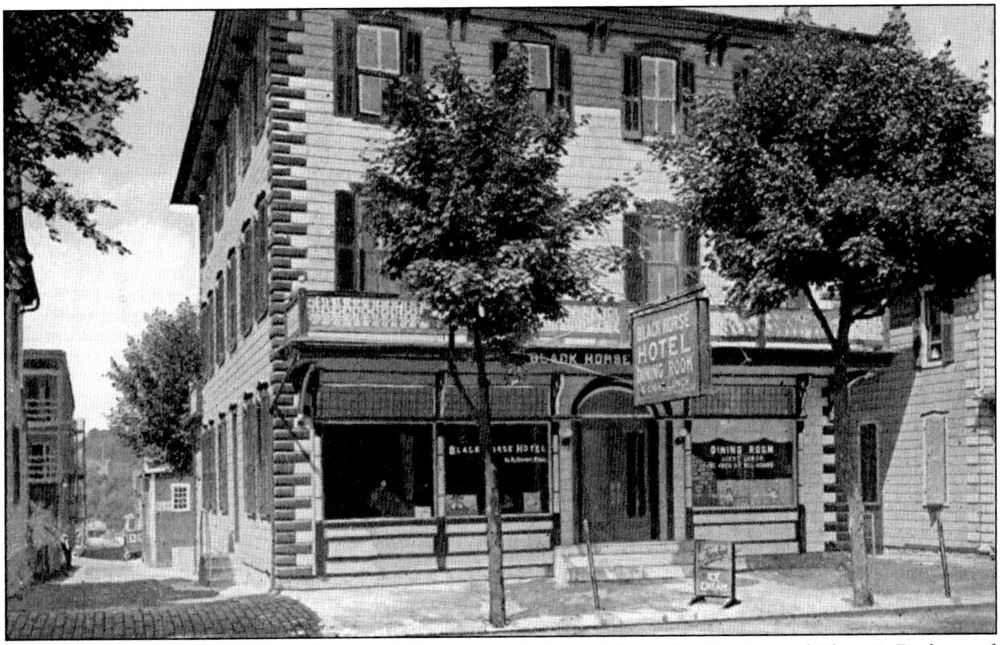

In 1766, the Lancaster courts licensed George and Anna Maria Redsecker, of Blaser's Reformed Church, to retail spirituous liquors at their Black Horse Tavern on South Market Street. Black Horse, Greenawalt House, Railroad House, Washington House, and Golden Star were all taverns supplied by local mills, distilleries, and breweries and serving travelers on the Harrisburg Turnpike and Pennsylvania Railroad. As early as 1839, the Lebanon Classis of the German Reformed Church, held at Christ Reformed Church in Elizabethtown, adopted resolutions declaring the use, manufacture, and sale of alcoholic beverages and intoxicating liquors a sin. In the 1930s, a Woman's Temperance water fountain was installed in the community park. In 1985, fire destroyed the Black Horse Tavern (shown above and below). It was demolished to provide a car park for the Bethel Church of God, which had formed from a schism in the Reformed Church in 1829.

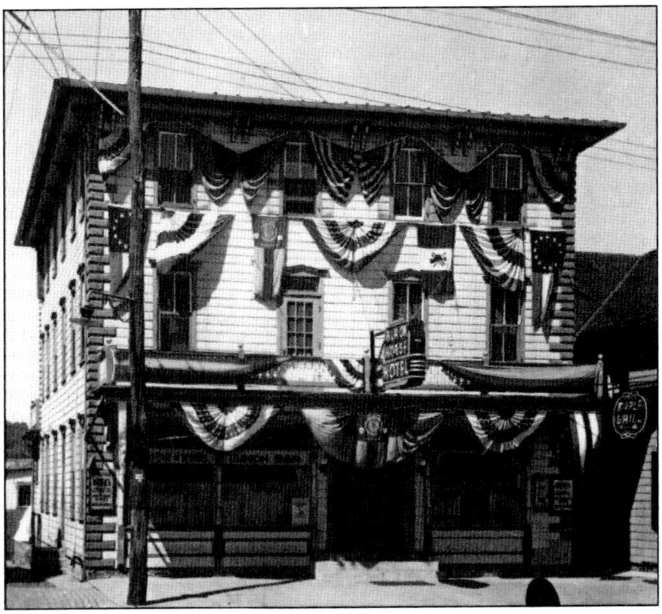

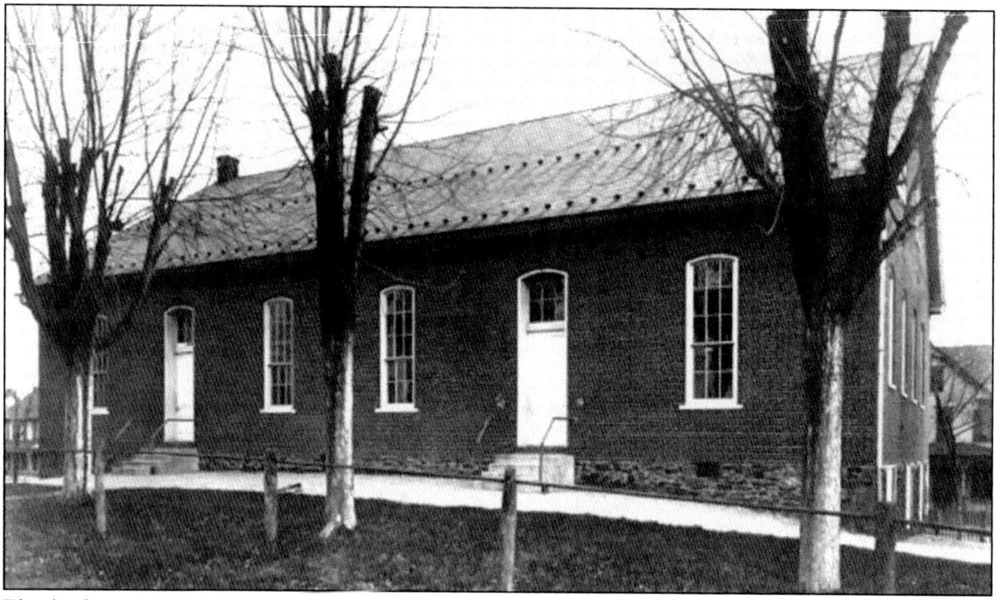

Elizabethtown Church of the Brethren (pictured), on Washington Street, was built in 1888. In 1874, Addison Buch, Jonathan Buch, Benjamin Groff, Joseph Heisey, Jacob Hoffer, and Joseph Rider, from White Oak and Chiques Brethren congregations in Manheim, purchased Mechanic Street School. They established a Brethren church, with Jacob Rider and Samuel Zug as clergy. Rider was the first president of Elizabethtown Exchange Bank. Zug was on the board of directors of Elizabethtown National Bank.

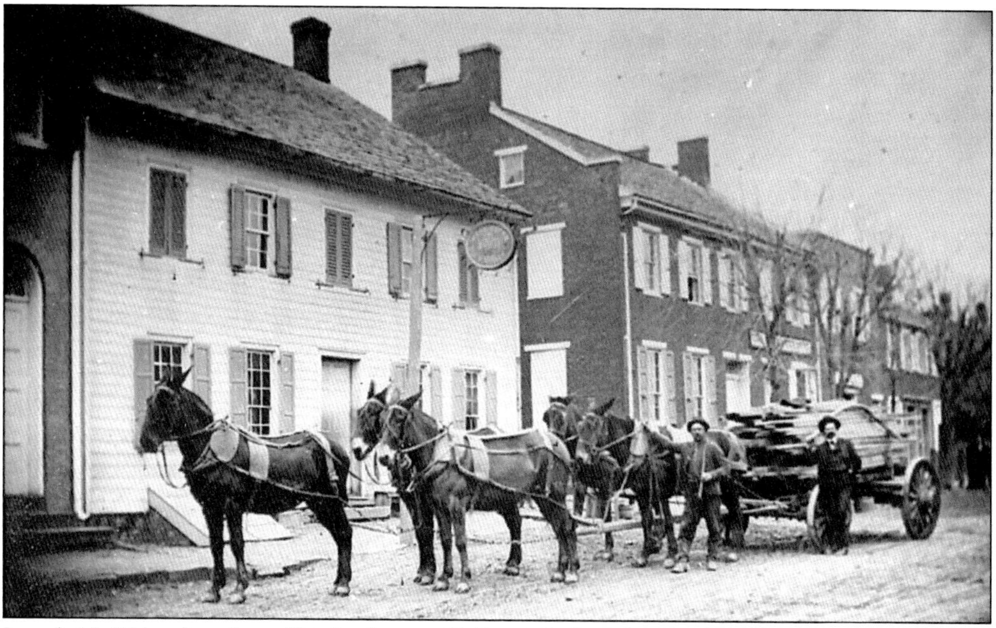

Joseph H. Rider, for whom Elizabethtown College's Rider Memorial Hall was named, was vice president of the college's board of trustees. His hardware store and family residence (on the right) stood side by side on South Market Street (now the site of the post office built by the WPA in 1939). In a crusade to close all the taverns in Elizabethtown, in 1886, Rider bought the Washington House Hotel (built in 1798 and pictured on the left) next door.

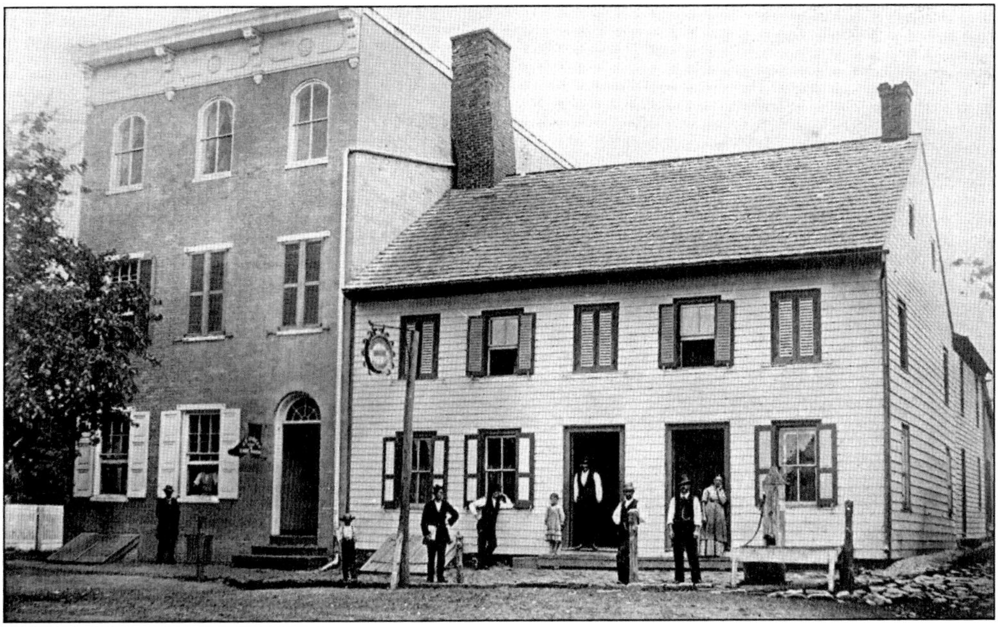

The Washington House on South Market Street belonged to attorney John R. Montgomery. This was the meeting hall of the Elizabethtown Lodge No. 128, Independent Order of Odd Fellows, instituted in 1845 by Jacob Redsecker, Jackson Sheaffer, Joseph Buchanan, and Sebastian Keller. The IOOF first met at George Redsecker's home at 244 South Market Street. In 1862, it moved to Benjamin Sheaffer's home, on the corner of South Market and Washington Streets.

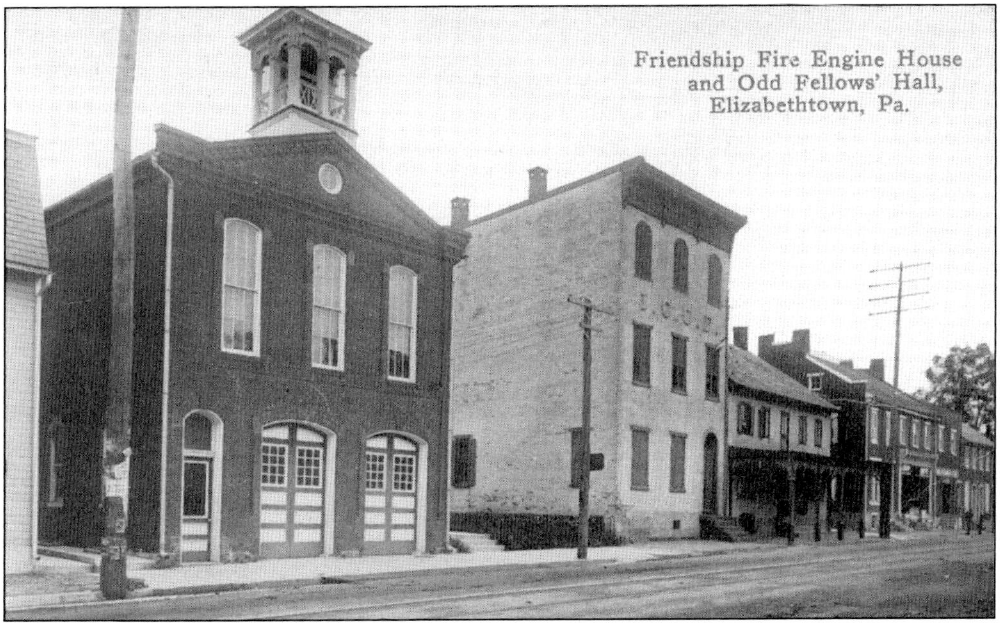

The IOOF moved to a brick building (right) next to the current post office, remaining there until 1921. The Unity Castle and Knights of the Golden Eagle also met at this location. In 1935, the women's division of IOOF, Betsy Ross Rebekah Lodge No. 129, was chartered. The Elizabethtown Democratic Club held meetings in the Friendship Fire Engine House (left), next to the IOOF Building, in 1867.

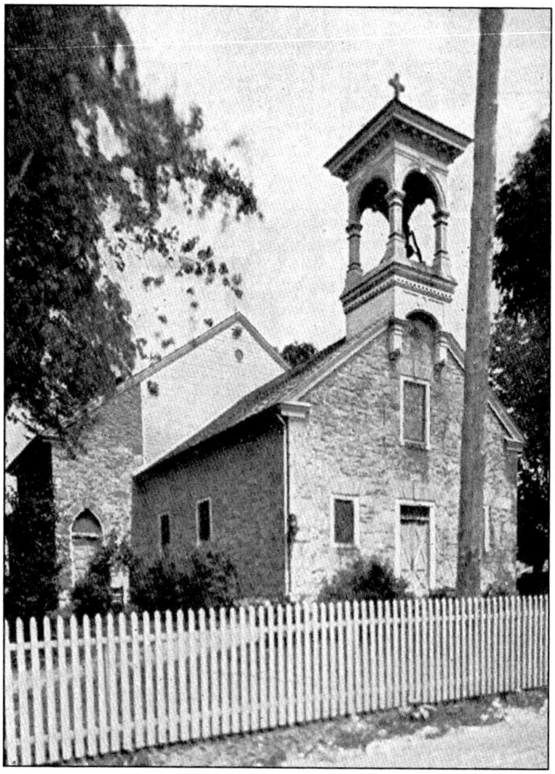

In 1752, Roman Catholic services were held in the home of Henry Eckenroth. Later, during the French and Indian War, arsonists destroyed St. Mary's in Lancaster. Many in Lancaster suspected that French Jesuit missionaries were spies. Catholics in Elizabethtown waited until 1768 to build St. Mary's of the Assumption. In 1799, Eckenroth built St. Peter's Catholic Church (pictured) and expanded it in 1834. The present church on Marshall Drive was completed in 1999.

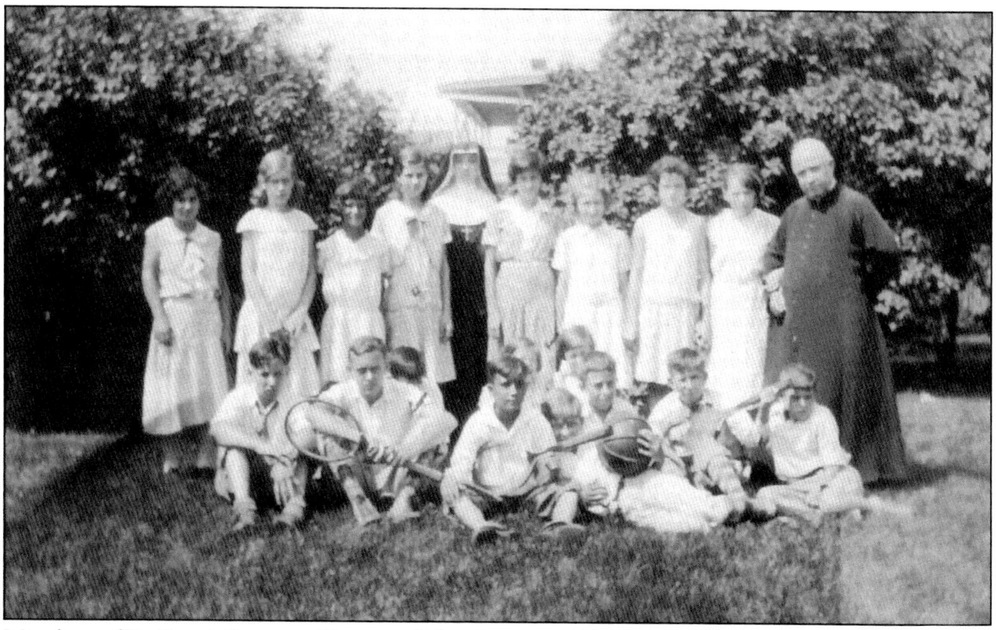

Members of St. Peter's Summer Vacation School pose in 1936. Rev. William Howard (far right) was in charge of St. Peter's from 1924 to 1939. The chamber of commerce and WPA built a community park in 1932. Father Howard and St. Peter's ran a summer playground program in the park. This led in 1949 to Elizabethtown Borough and public schools running a summer playground program in the park for five days a week, enrolling 1,250 children.

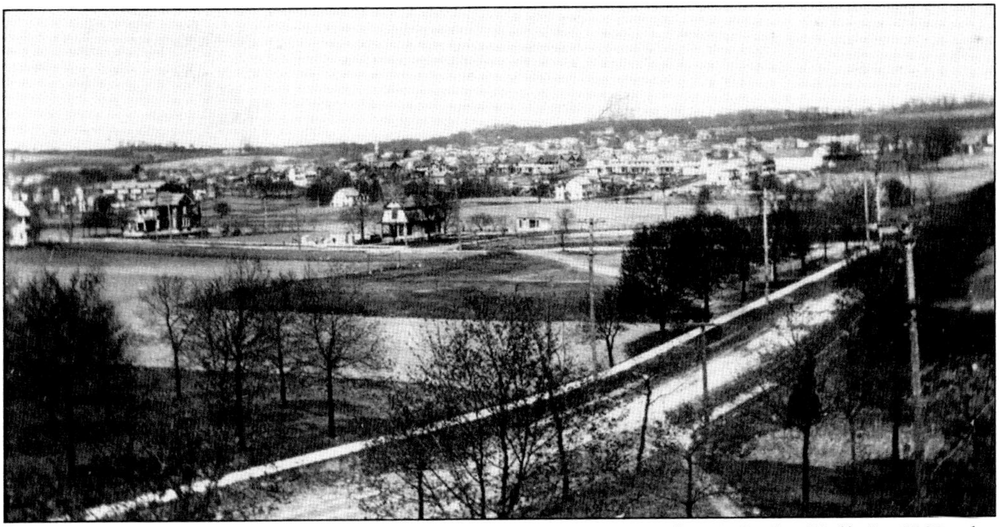

This is a view of the community park from Elizabethtown College's Rider Hall. In 1932, the chamber of commerce and Elizabethtown Business and Professional Women's Club purchased land from the Kalbach and Heisey families to build a park. The Chamber of Commerce Park and Playground Committee administered the park and athletic field until transferring responsibility to the borough in 1950. On summer nights in the park, St. Elizabeth's Episcopal Church offered free concerts and films.

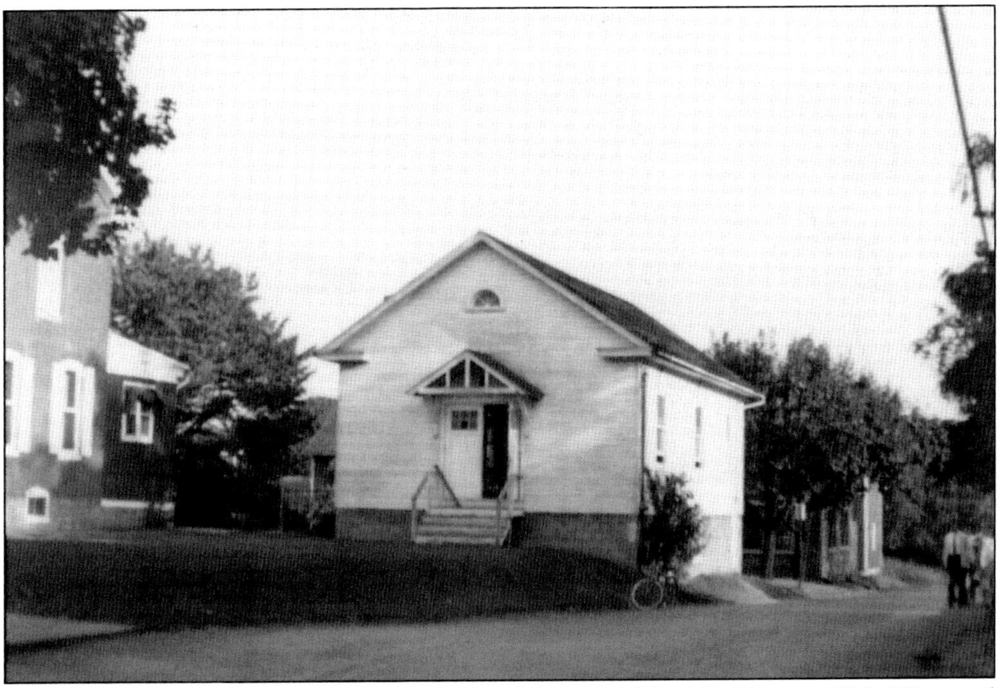

In 1911, St. Elizabeth's Protestant Episcopal Church was established by Oliver and Ethel Heistand of Heistand Brothers Mills (originally, and currently, Union Mill). The Heistands descended from the Swiss Mennonite founders of Elizabethtown. Their son, Rev. Thomas Heistand, was later bishop of the Episcopal Diocese of Central Pennsylvania in Harrisburg. St. Elizabeth's (pictured) was built in 1927 at the corner of Park and Spruce Streets.

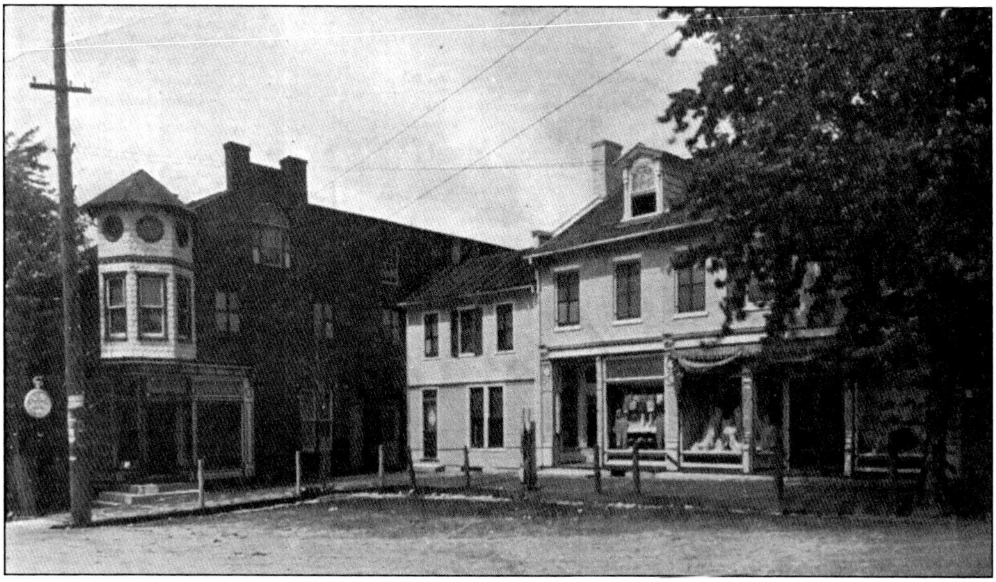

This is the northeast corner of Diamond Square. The buildings shown here are the Coble residence (left) and Hertzler Brothers Department Store. In 1859, African Americans George Harris and his son Nathaniel operated a barber and hairdressing shop on Diamond Square. The Harrises were not slaves (a Pennsylvania law deemed free all children born to slaves after March 1, 1780). Harris lived in the Bear Tavern tenant house and sheltered fugitive slaves.

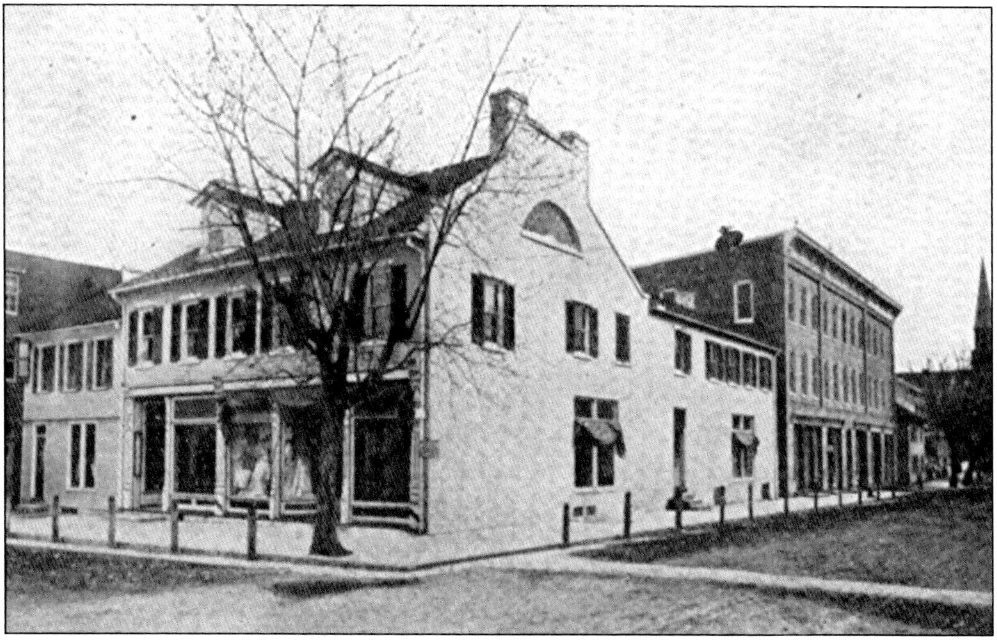

In 1815, Adams Campbell built this Federal-style house at 5 Diamond Square. Robert McClure operated a general store here from 1822 to 1829. In 1884, Church of the Brethren brothers Aaron and Isaac Hertzler opened a department store (pictured). They were joined in 1891 by their brother Samuel. Rev. Samuel Hertzler was a minister in the Church of the Brethren and treasurer of the first board of trustees for Elizabethtown College.

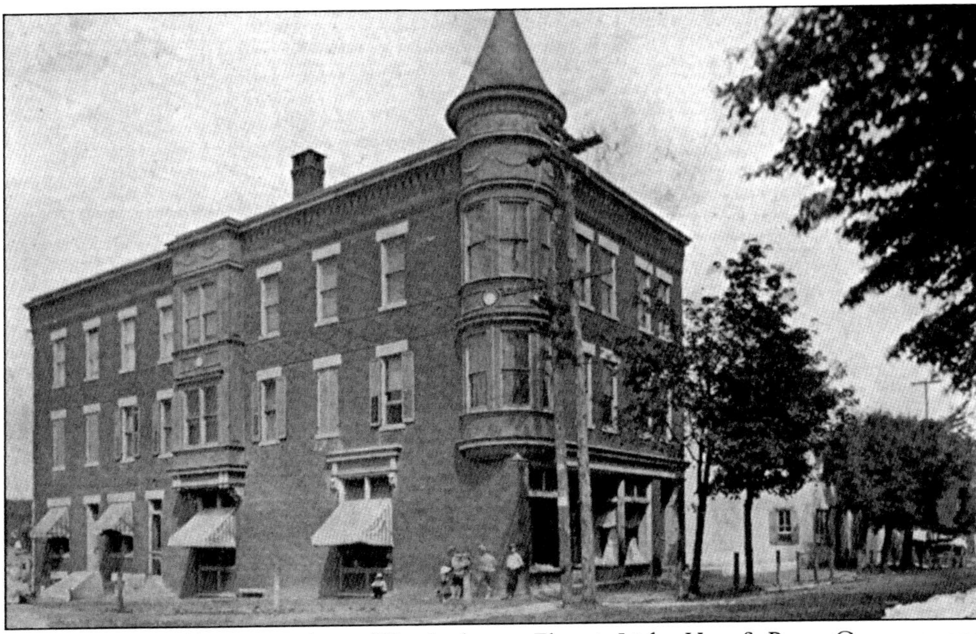

In 1890, Isaac Hoffman, president of Elizabethtown Electric Light, Heat & Power Company, and Abraham Heisey, treasurer of the Elizabethtown Water Company, operated the Elizabethtown Creamery near their homes on South Market Street. Heisey built this three-story brick building at 256 South Market Street. Heisey Hall, on the third floor, was a public meeting venue. Simon Engle had a grocery store on the first floor in 1900.

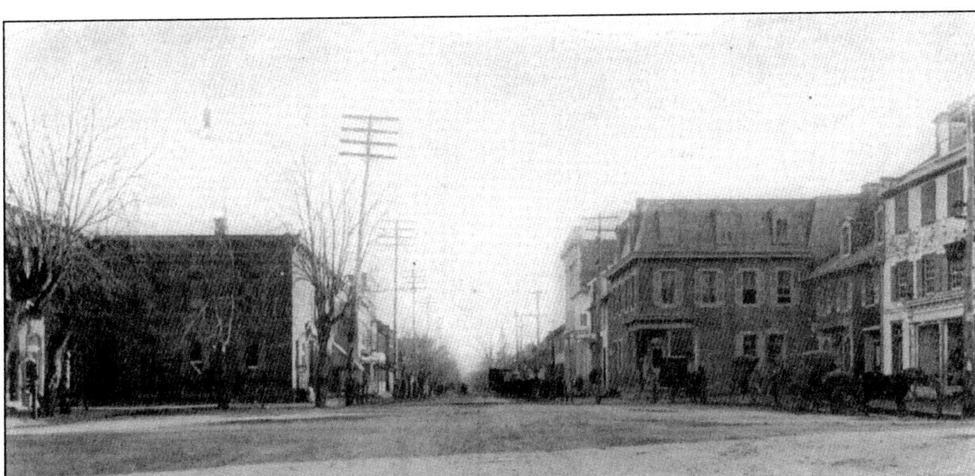

Telephone lines are seen running along South Market Street. In March 1897, Elizabethtown Borough Council authorized Pennsylvania Telephone Company, a subsidiary of Bell Telephone Company, to establish service in Elizabethtown. In 1898, an independent firm, the Columbia Telephone Company, later acquired by United Telephone & Telegraph, offered service in the borough. The Independent Telephone Company was established in Elizabethtown in 1914. On the right side of Diamond Square is the Horst Building.

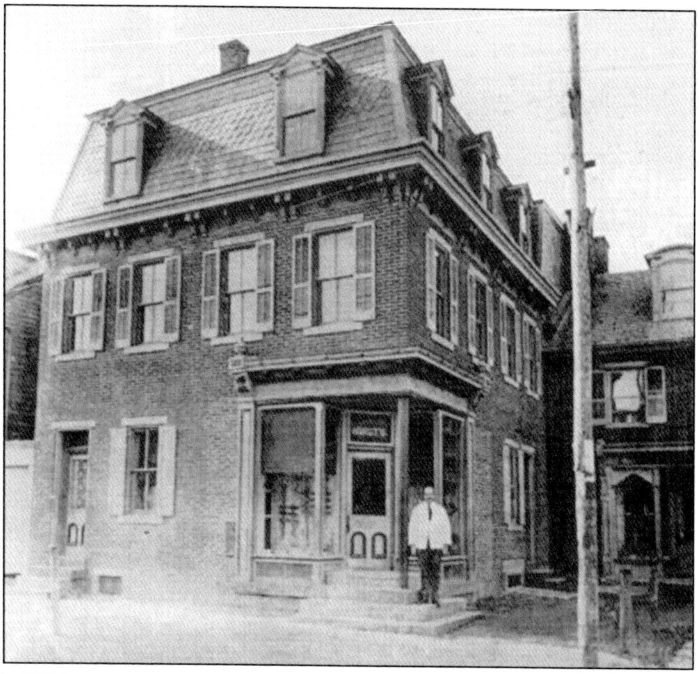

In December 1878, Anthony Harchenrader of St. Peter's sold his house at 17 Diamond Square to John Horst, who opened a restaurant and ice-cream parlor. Washington Camp, Patriotic Sons of America, and Knights of the Mystic Chain met in Horst Hall. In 1894, Horst installed electric lights. Electricity was purchased from Elizabethtown Electric Company, established in 1894 by John Redsecker with a power plant on Brown Street.

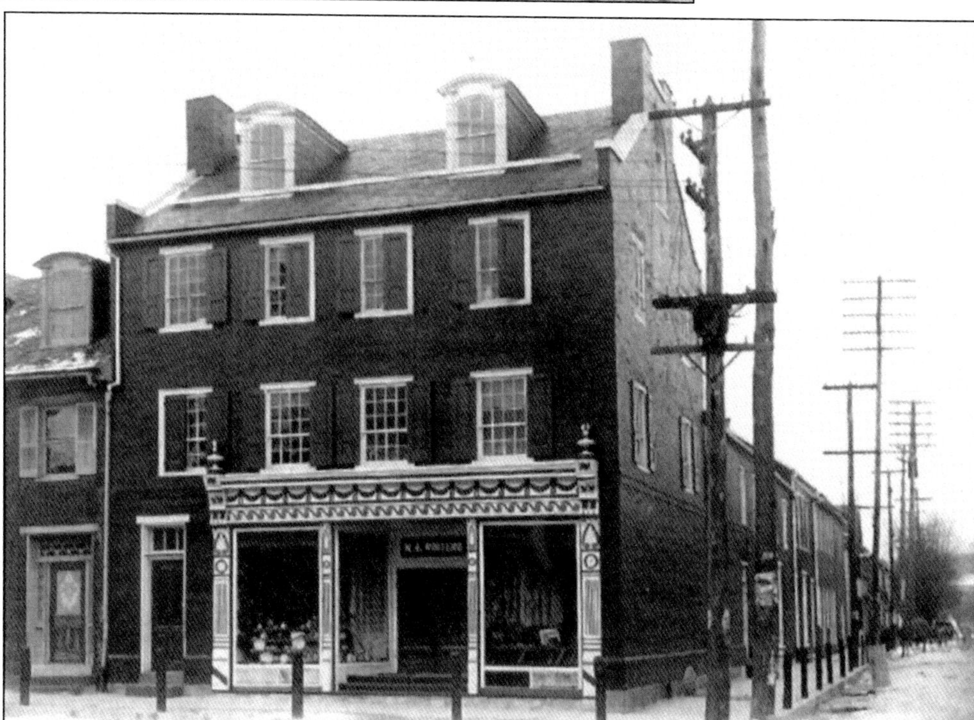

As early as 1859, the brothers Aaron and Henry Dissinger, of Christ Evangelical Lutheran Church, operated a general store on the southwest corner of Diamond Square. The Elizabethtown *Weekly Trumpet* advertised "Dissinger's Cheap Store" featuring "dry goods, clothing, fresh mackerel, alum, salt, and cider vinegar." The John Wanamaker Republican Club met on the first Tuesday of every month in a back room above Dissinger's store on West High Street.

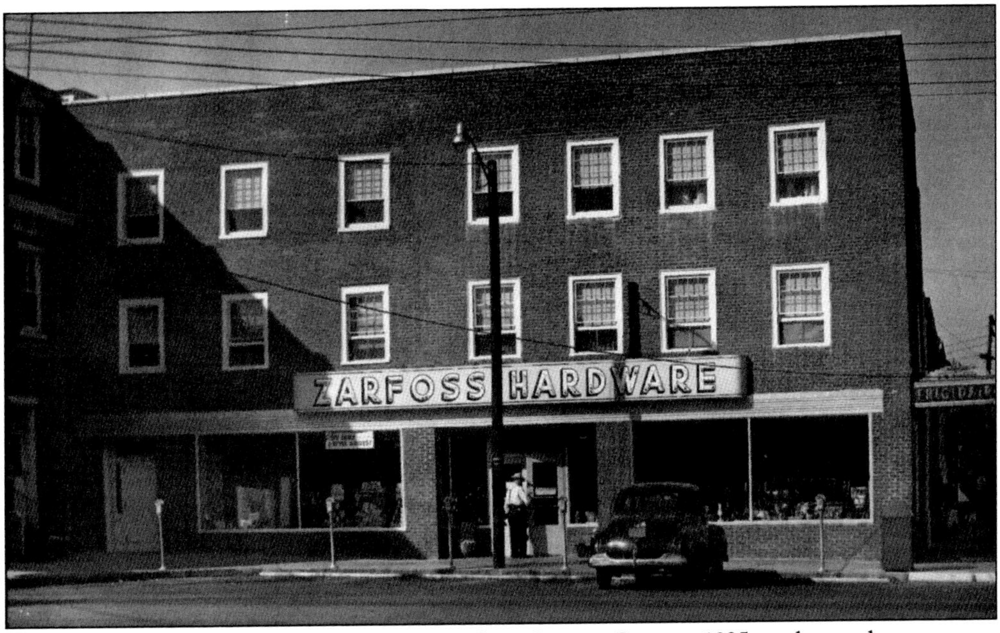

Melvin and John Wenger opened Wenger Brothers Grocery Store in 1935 on the southwest corner of Diamond Square in the Horst and Dissinger Buildings. Wenger Brothers claimed to be the first grocer in the nation to sell dog food. In 1945, Melvin purchased Wolgemuth Mills and sold the grocery store to Arthur, Henry, and Robert Greiner. Later, Howard and James Zarfoss bought the properties, establishing a hardware store.

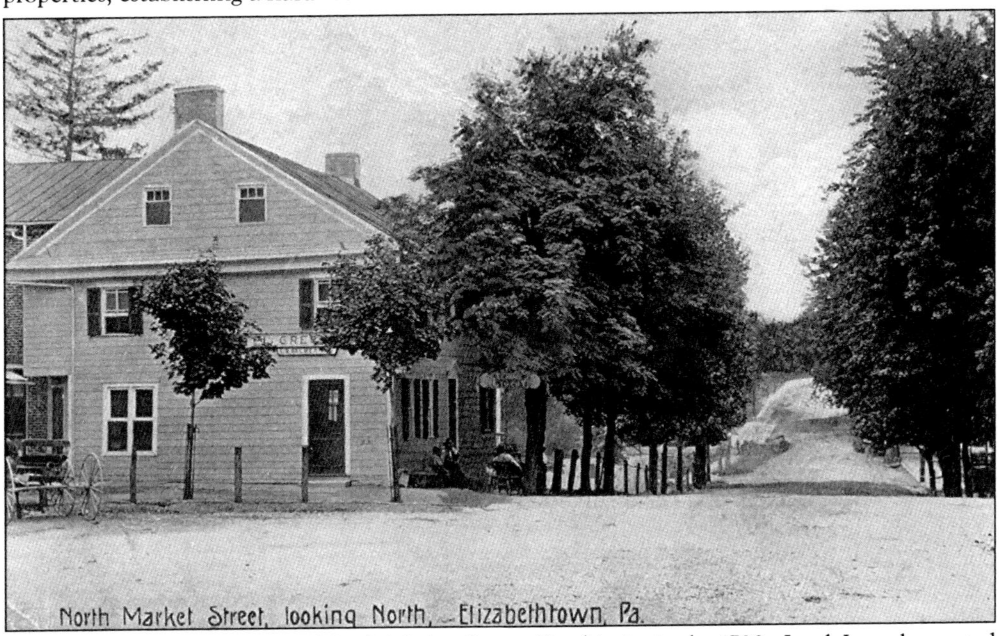

This is Greenawalt House at 18 North Market Street. On this site in the 1700s, Jacob Immel operated a tavern. In 1822, Jacob Coble, of St. Peter's, continued the tavern before moving to 103 North Market Street. The following year, Maj. Michael Brenneman, a Mennonite, opened Brenneman's Inn. Brenneman died in 1826, and, the next year, his widow, Elizabeth, married Col. Abraham Greenawalt. In 1828, this became Greenawalt House, and, in 1836, the Union Hotel.

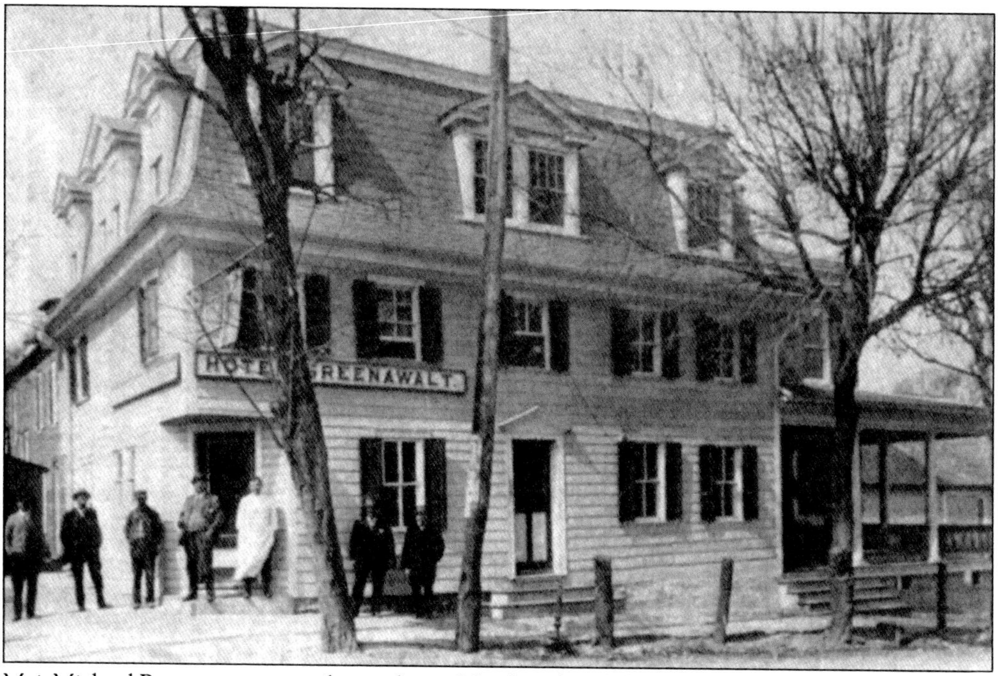

Maj. Michael Brenneman was a descendant of the founder of Elizabethtown and Goods Mennonite Church, Melchoir Brenneman. Michael's wife, Elizabeth Elliott Coble, was related to the previous owners of the tavern, Jacob and Michael Coble. When she married widower Col. Abraham Greenawalt in 1827, he was the owner of Running Pump Tavern on the turnpike to Harrisburg. Joseph Gorgas operated Running Pump in 1810, before John Probst took over in 1814. Michael Coble served as postmaster.

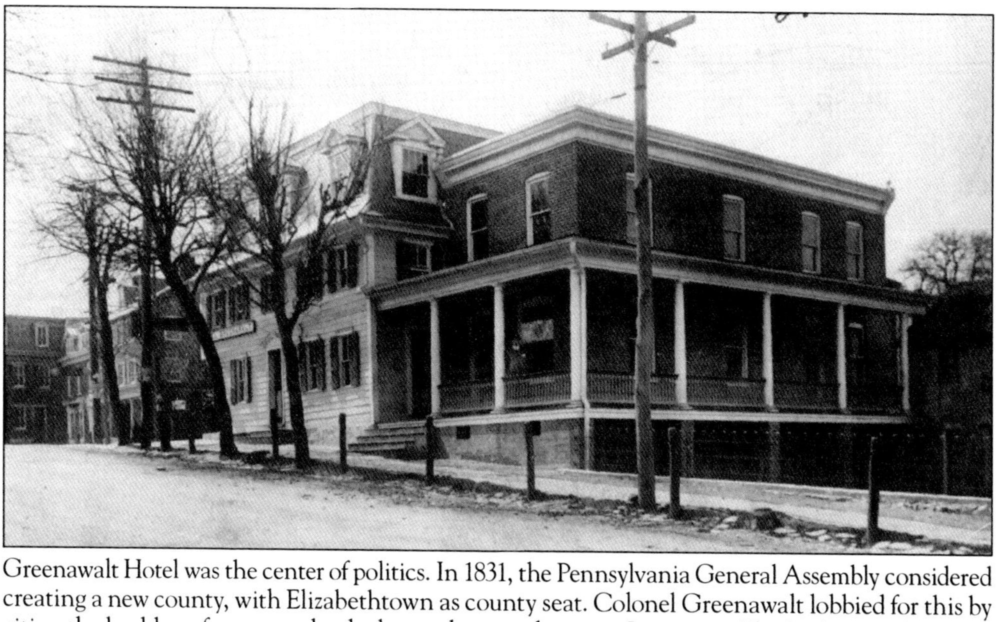

Greenawalt Hotel was the center of politics. In 1831, the Pennsylvania General Assembly considered creating a new county, with Elizabethtown as county seat. Colonel Greenawalt lobbied for this by citing the backlog of cases on the docket at the courthouse in Lancaster. Elizabethtown deposited $10,000 to meet the cost of erecting a courthouse and a jail. In 1840, Greenawalt was a delegate to the nominating convention in Baltimore for William Henry Harrison and John Tyler.

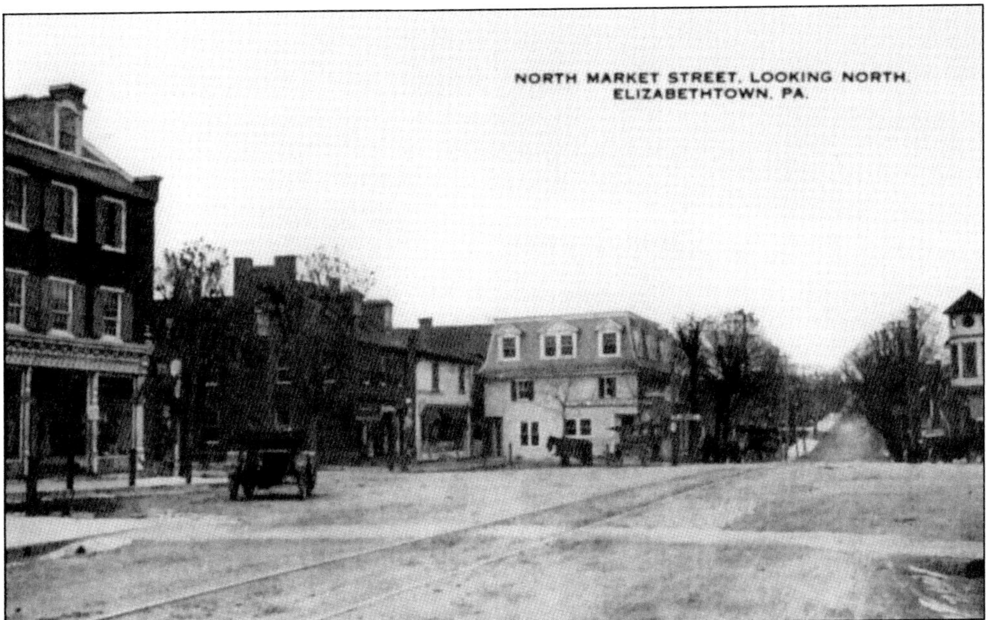

Beginning in 1792, Samuel Grimes operated an inn (second from left) on the northwest corner of Diamond Square. Thomas Masterson, of St. Peter's, operated a store there starting in 1801. In 1822, Mennonite Jacob Kauffman, the turnpike manager, bought this store. From 1839 to 1840, this was the site of a silk factory. In 1832, the Pennsylvania General Assembly encouraged farmers to plant mulberry trees and harvest silkworms. Elizabethtown farmers and business investors belonged to the Lancaster Silk Society.

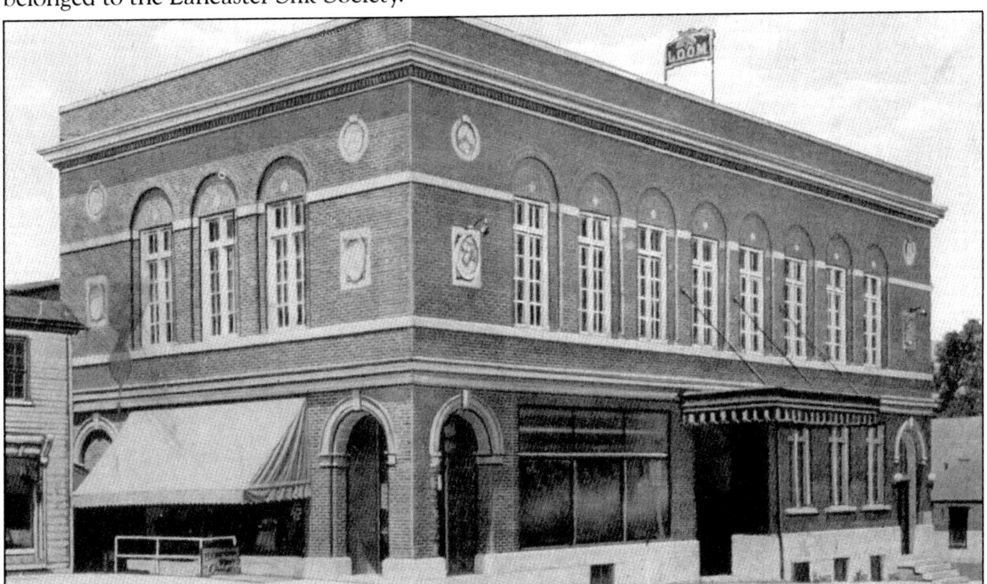

In 1911, Elizabethtown Lodge No. 596, Loyal Order of the Moose, was chartered in Horst Hall. It moved to 43 West High Street two years later. In 1922, the Moose lodge purchased and razed the Greenawalt Hotel. Moose Theater (pictured), designed by Lancaster architect C. Emlen Urban, was completed in 1928. Prior to the existence of Moose Theater, William Rogers screened films at the Hertzler Building beginning in 1908. John Ulrich opened the Majestic Theatre in 1913.

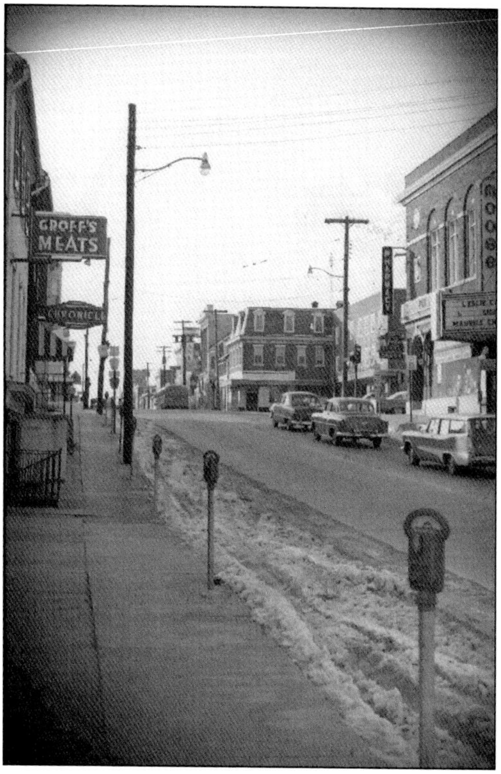

Herdsmen James Close, Owen Gorman, and William Wallace of St. Peter's operated stockyards, making Elizabethtown a major intersection for driving cattle to Philadelphia and Baltimore. In 1875, the brothers Joseph and John Groff, of Benjamin Groff Mills and members of Church of the Brethren, bought cattle dealer John Hildebrand's butcher shop and opened Groff's Meats at 13 North Market Street. In 1987, the store moved to 33 North Market Street.

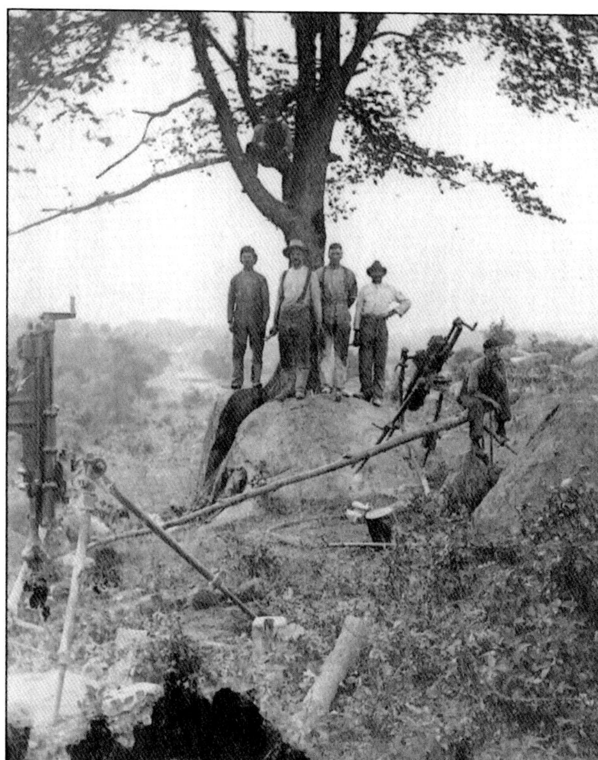

Throughout Lancaster, the Native American Party, viewing immigrants and Catholics as threats to democracy, gained support. Elizabethtown was an exception, counting for only two percent of this vote in 1844. Elizabethtown supported Catholic immigrants, despite the fact that, in 1837, Irish railway workers murdered 19-year-old Michael Ellentin of Christ Evangelical Lutheran Church. The Know Nothing Party won 20 percent of the vote in 1854 and 40 percent in 1856. This 1898–1899 image shows a group of Irish railway workers.

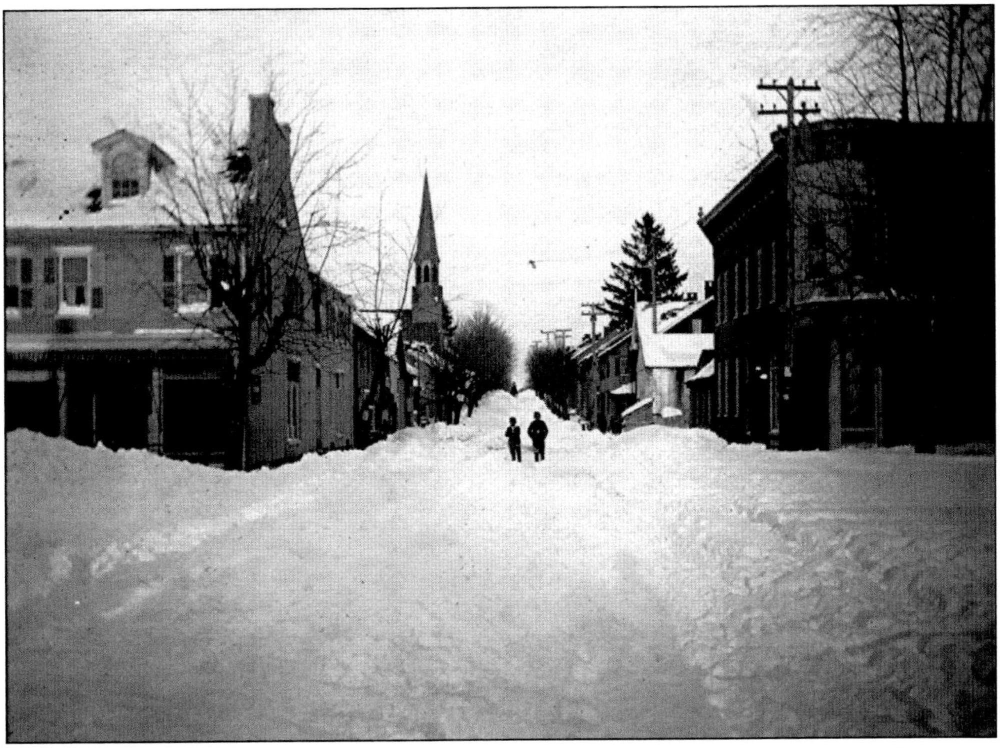

East High Street is seen here from Diamond Square. Left of center is the steeple of Christ Lutheran Church, built in 1771 and rebuilt in 1807 and again in 1887. Lutherans worshipped on William Bischof's farm. In 1769, the synod at Philadelphia sent John Enderlin as their pastor. The 1946 merging of the Hauge and Norwegian Synods with the United Norwegian Lutheran Church of America resulted in the Evangelical Lutheran Church and, in Elizabethtown, Christ Evangelical Lutheran Church.

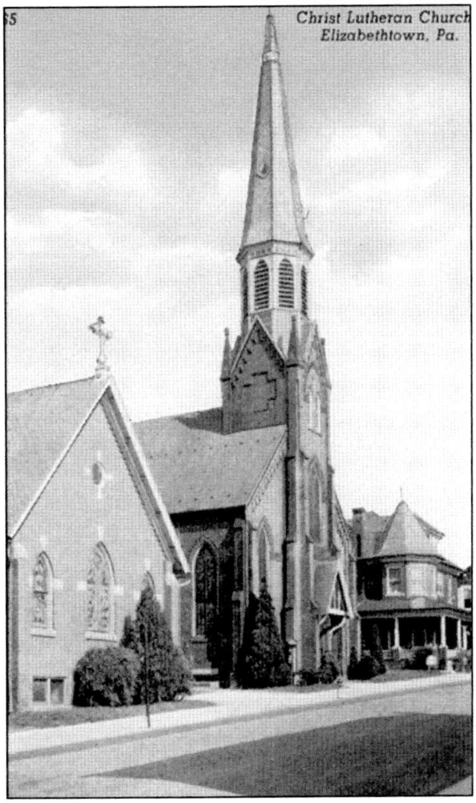

Beginning in 1783, Christ Lutheran Church was pastored by Frederick Melsheimer. He had been chaplain in 1776 to the Brunswick Dragoons, part of General Burgoyne's British and Hessian army that surrendered at Saratoga in 1777. While a prisoner of war, Melsheimer collected and classified insects according to his own system. In 1787, he taught German at Franklin and Marshall College, eventually becoming president. His extensive insect collection was donated to the Louis Agassiz Museum of Comparative Zoology at Harvard University.

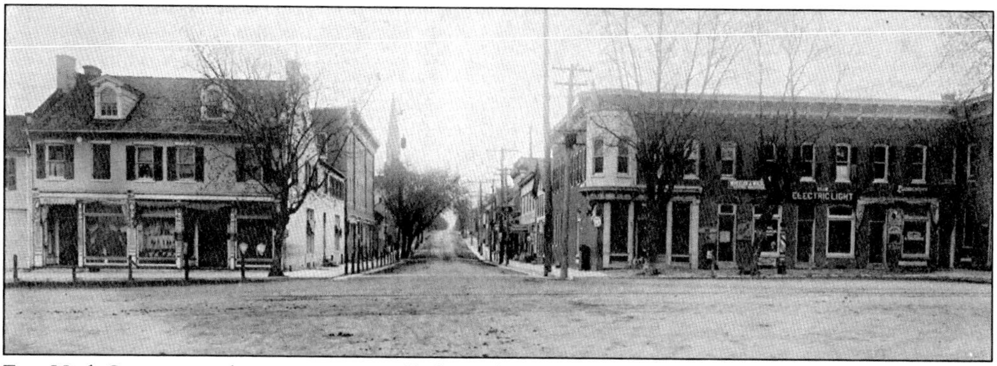

East High Street, seen here, was once called Manheim Road. In 1814 Henry Brubaker and Mahlon Roberts from Manheim advertised "Elizabethtown Continued." They laid out Locust, Mount Joy, Chestnut, and Mechanics Streets on a square turned as a diamond at the intersection of East High and Mount Joy Streets. This increased commercial relations between Elizabethtown and Manheim. Simultaneously, the towns of Florin, Richland, and Mount Joy formed, linking Manheim to trade along the Susquehanna River.

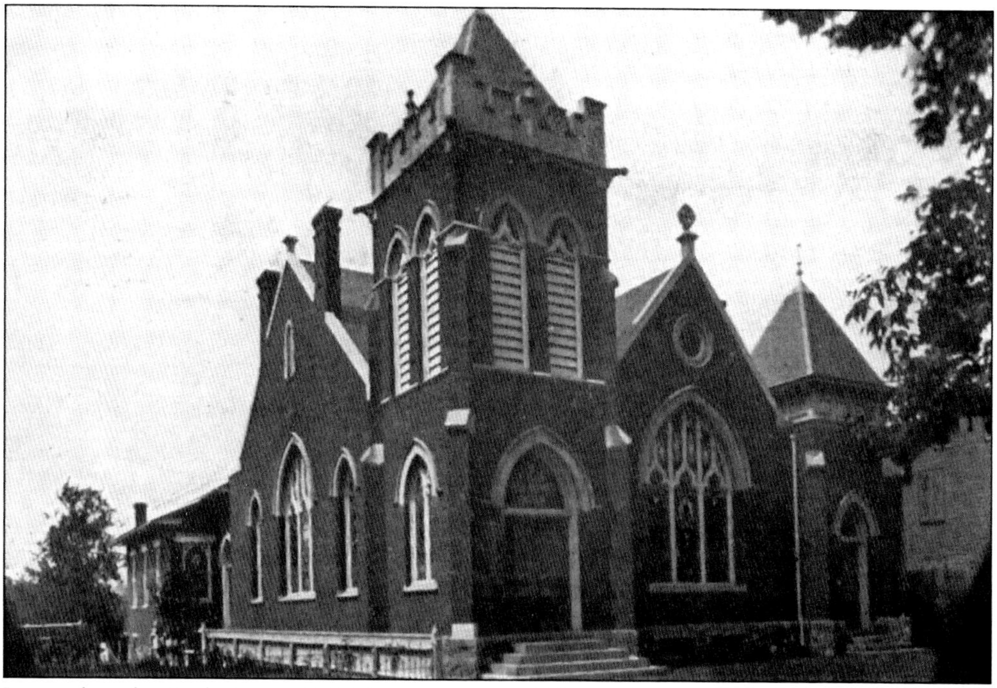

Located in the Brubaker and Mahlon extension of Elizabethtown, St. Paul's United Brethren Church was built in 1903. In 1816, schisms in the Reformed and Mennonite Churches—led by Philip William Otterbein and Martin Boehm, respectively—created the United Brethren in Christ Church. In 1956, a new church was built between North and Spruce Streets. Since the 1968 merger of Methodist and Evangelical United Brethren Churches, it has been St. Paul's United Methodist.

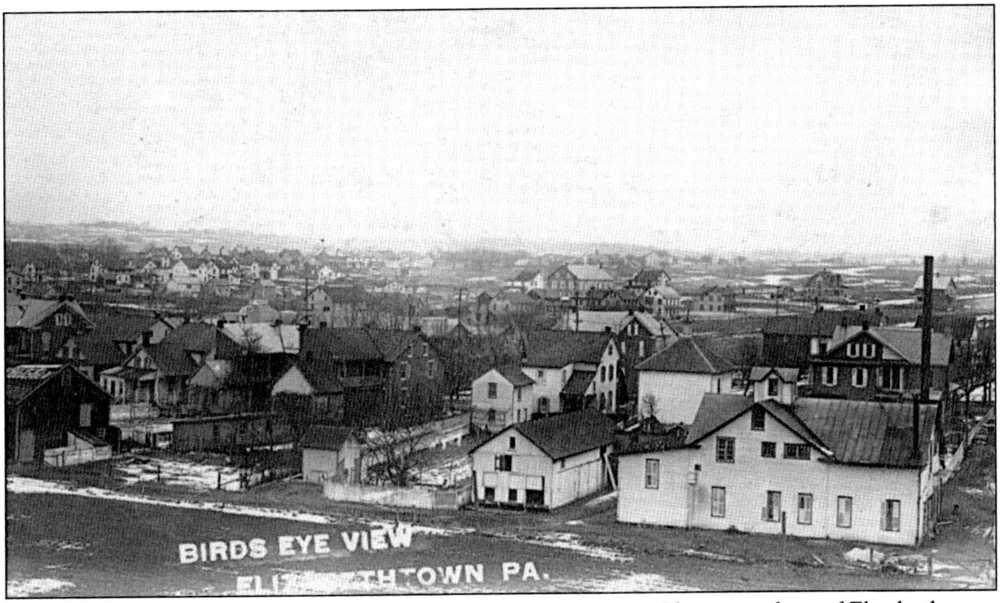

This is a 1908 bird's-eye view of College Heights. Rev. Henry Ober, president of Elizabethtown College, designed a residential subdivision around the campus. College Heights Development Company sold lots through Buch-Hoffman Realty. In 1909, J. Harvey Buch and Isaac W. Hoffman formed the company. Their advertising, targeting parents "who have young men and women to educate," asked them to consider Elizabethtown College and "this College Heights tract to build and live near this institution."

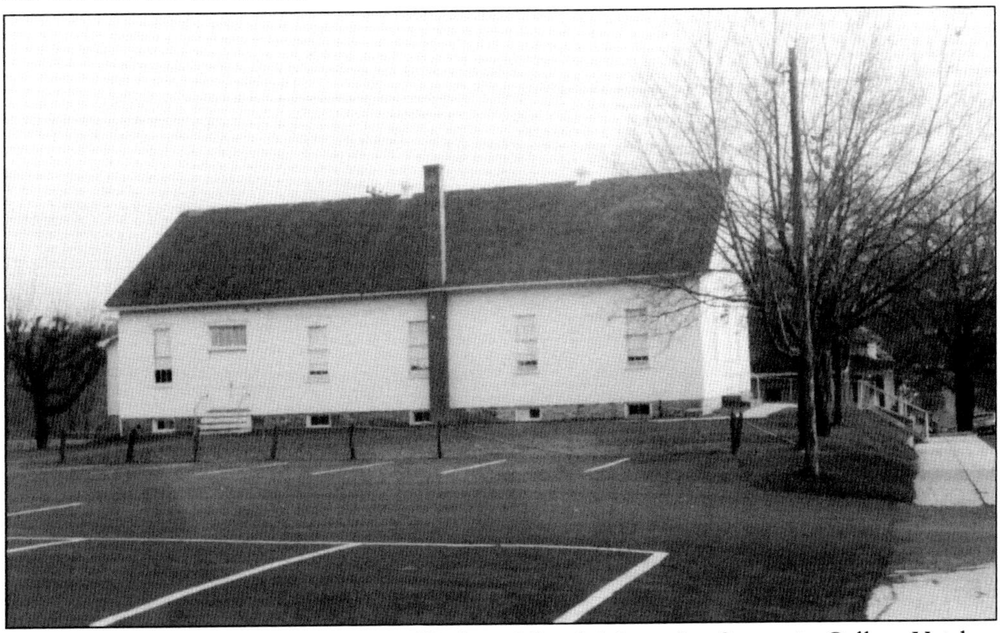

United Zion's Church, on the corner of Park and South Mount Joy Streets in College Heights, was built in 1887, enlarged in 1908, and rebuilt in 1971. Schisms among Mennonites created the River Brethren (now Brethren in Christ) and United Zion's Children. When Matthias G. Brinser and Matthias C. Brinser were excommunicated from the River Brethren, they started a new denomination, meeting at Ober's School and at the United Brethren Church.

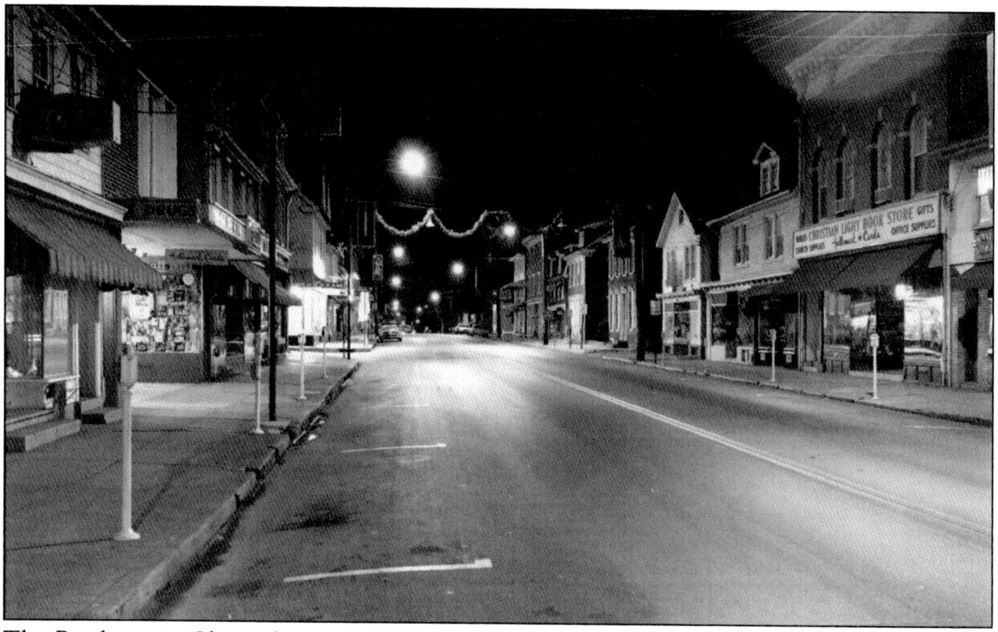

The Brethren in Christ denomination resulted from a schism among the Mennonites. The Brethren in Christ Mission Board and national denominational offices, with headquarters for its Evangelical Publishing House and Bookstore (later Christian Light Book Store, pictured on the right in 1962), were located in Elizabethtown at 24 East High Street in 1942, 20 South Market Street (1943), 48 Market Street (1962), and at 1575 South Market Street (1997).

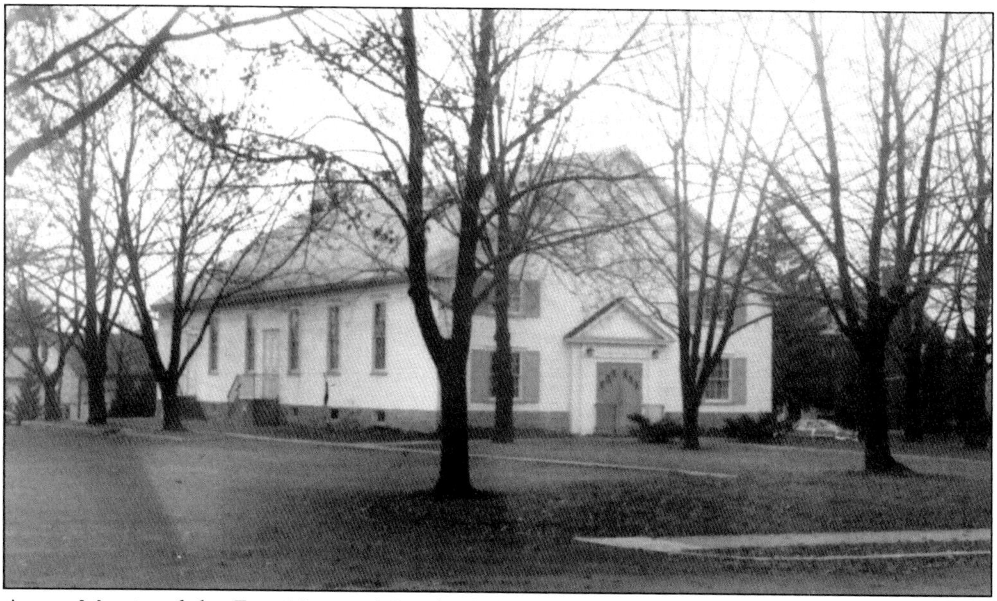

Aaron Martin of the First National Bank of Elizabethtown was pastor of the Elizabethtown Brethren in Christ Church (pictured) when it was built at Arch and South Streets in 1910. Located in College Heights and supporting the local Historic Peace Church Elizabethtown College, this congregation formed from Cross Roads Church in Mount Joy, Maytown Brethren in Christ Church, and Conoy Brethren in Christ Church, Elizabethtown. The building became Elizabethtown Borough Offices in 1985.

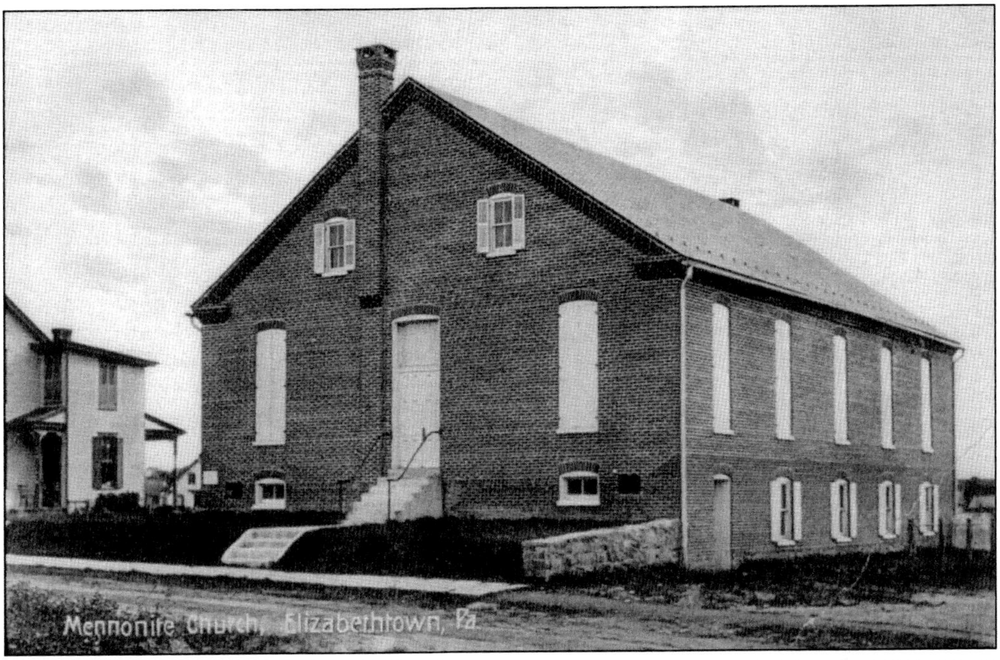

Supporting the local college founded by the Historic Peace Churches, Mennonite bishop Martin Rutt established the Elizabethtown Mennonite Church, near Elizabethtown College, on Bainbridge and South Spruce Streets in the College Heights development. This congregation was formed from members of the Rissers and Goods Mennonite meetinghouses. Services began on Thanksgiving Day, November 30, 1905.

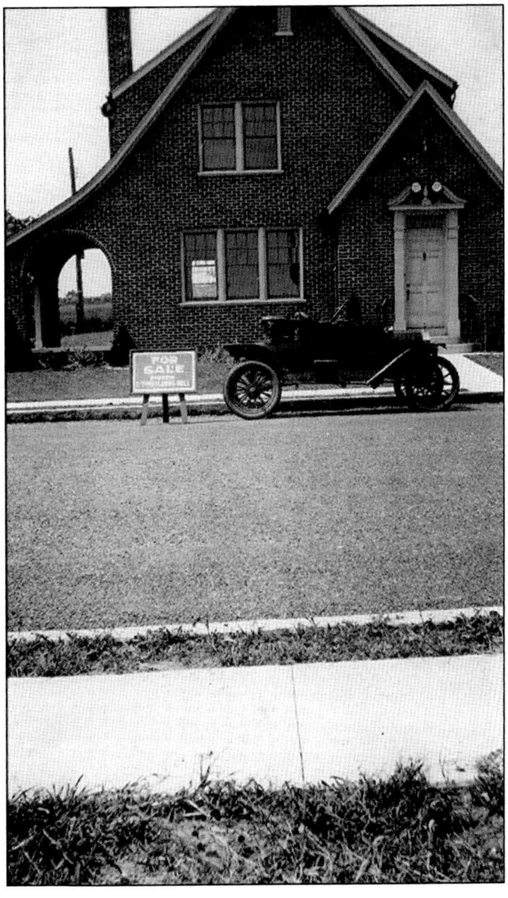

This home, at 15 Linden Avenue, was built in 1930 and still stands. Suburban encroachment into the neighboring farmland began in the 1930s. Expanded residential communities farther away from Central Diamond brought new families to Elizabethtown, diversifying the local culture. Commuters using the Pennsylvania Railroad found Elizabethtown an attractive bedroom community with proximity to Philadelphia, Lancaster, and Harrisburg.

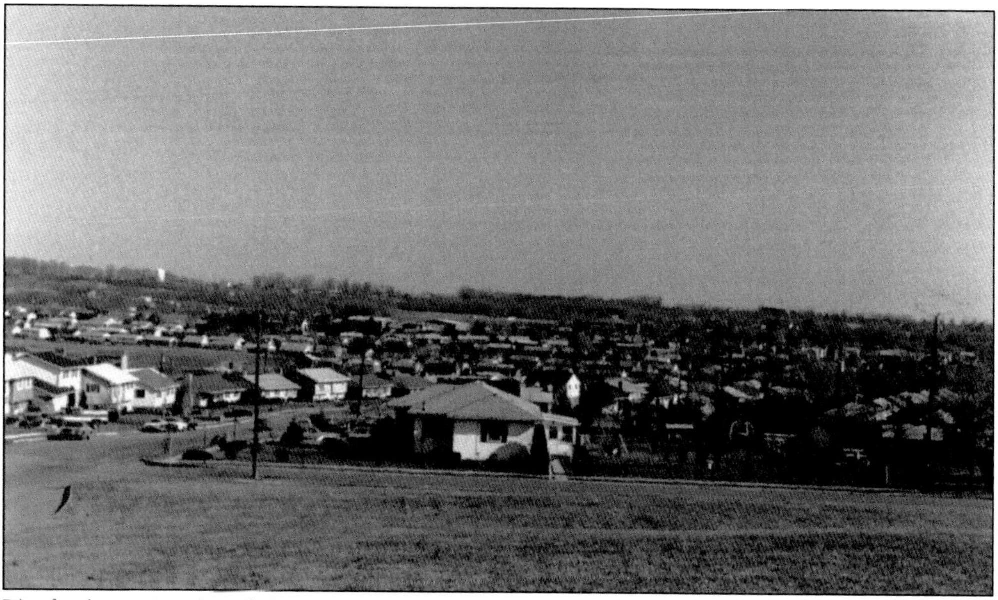

Elizabethtown's cultural diversity augmented post–World War II suburban development. The following residential communities were built: Maple Hills (1941), Sunnyside Heights (1941), Forest Hills (1945), Highlawn Acres (1947), Snyder-Hess Development (1952), and Valley View (1965). In 1980, Elizabethtown Borough introduced Planned Residential Developments. Suburban development since the 1980s has increased substantially. Rather than building consecutive blocks of single-family detached homes, builders could add duplex and multifamily dwellings.

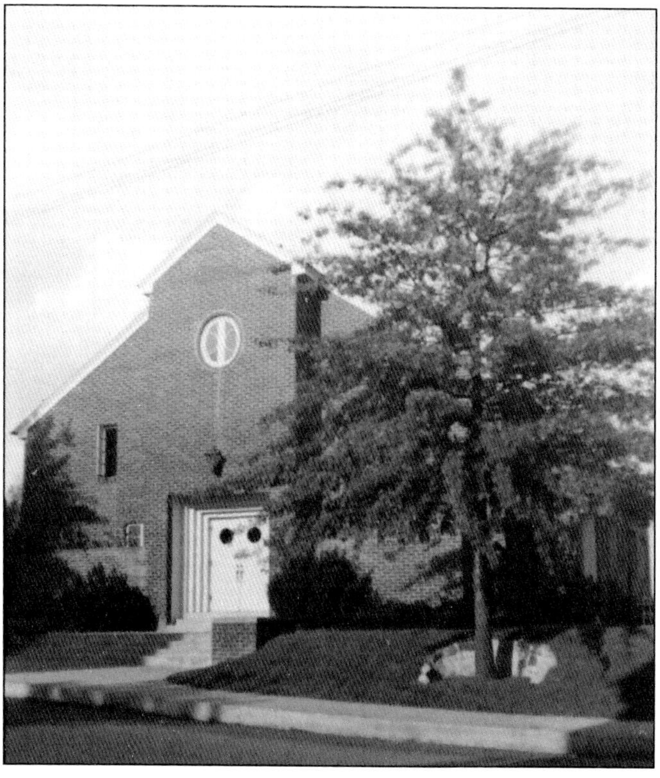

Within the growing suburbs, new congregations developed. In 1920, Rev. Charles Fahl of the Church of God, with the Brethren in Christ and Mennonites, held Bible conferences at Mennonite pastor Benjamin Keener's Beulah Heights conference grounds. A nondenominational fundamentalist congregation formed the Gospel Tabernacle. Former Anabaptist pastor Hiram Lefever, a founder of Lancaster Bible College, led the Mount Calvary congregation and built a church (pictured) at 399 North Hanover Street.

On April 28, 1970, the Elizabethtown Historical Society was incorporated "to encourage the study and understanding of the historical heritage of Elizabethtown." Ann O. Needham willed Peach Alley Schoolhouse to the historical society. The Kiwanis Club restored the schoolhouse, and it was dedicated on May 31, 1971. In 1999, a new building was dedicated for community meetings, and the schoolhouse was designated as a museum.

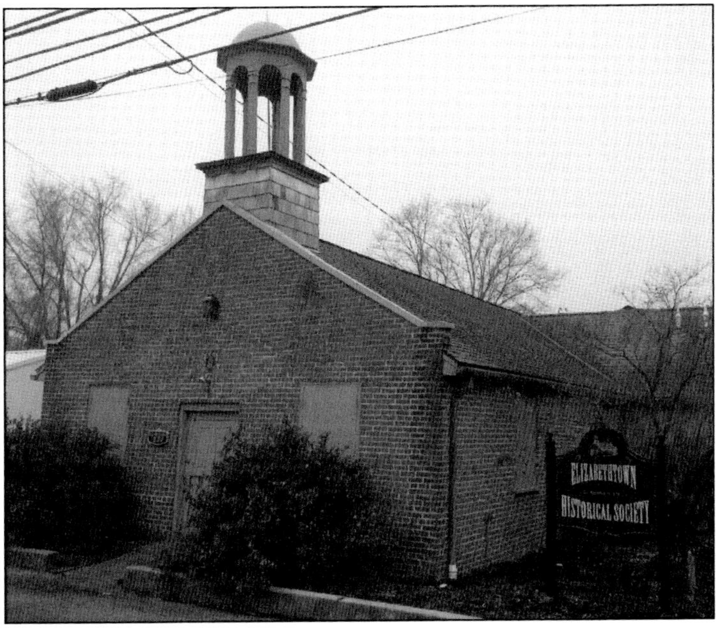

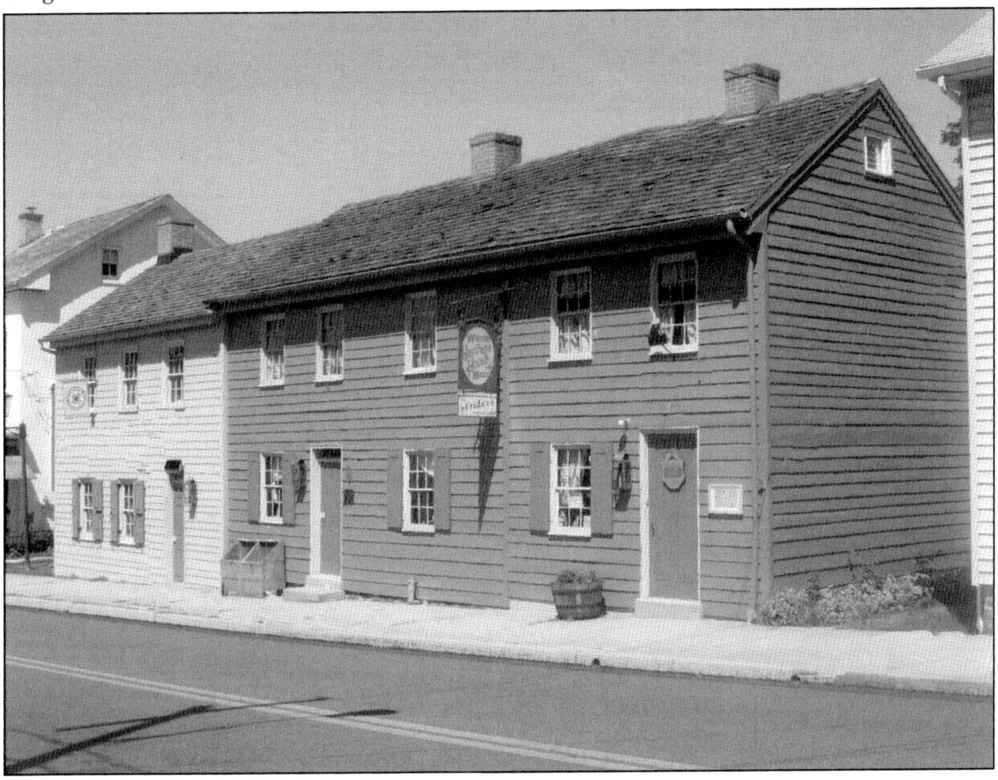

In May 1988, Elizabethtown Preservation Associates was organized to save a historic property at 43 East High Street (right). The structure was restored and opened to the public in 1991 as the Elizabethtown Heritage House. The facility, which includes a genealogical library, offers historical, educational, and cultural programming. In 1995, Esther (Mrs. William K.) Winters deeded the log building next door (left), which has served as the Winters Heritage House Museum.

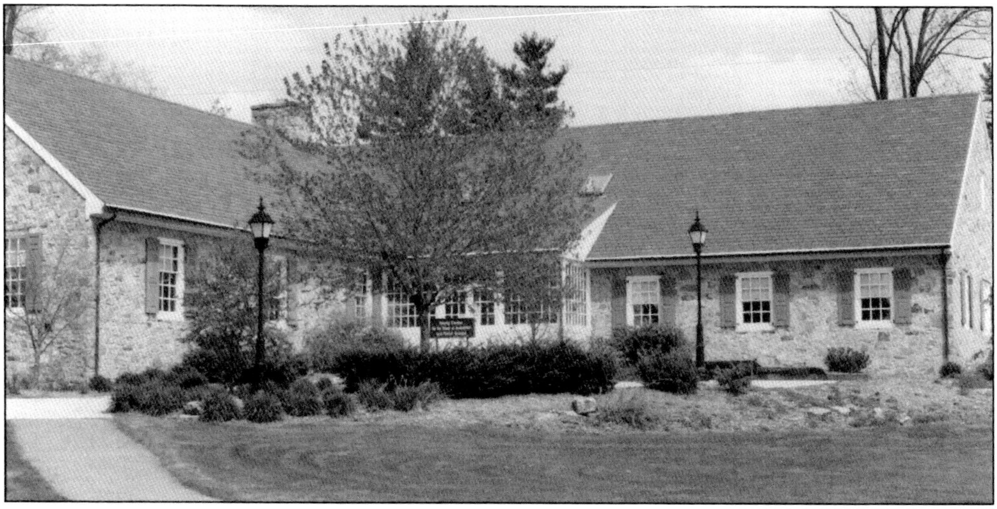

The history and culture of Elizabethtown is preserved and studied at the Young Center for Anabaptist and Pietist Studies. This research center at Elizabethtown College hosts nationally recognized visiting scholars, who interpret the cultural and religious heritage of Anabaptist and Pietist communities to the general public through lectures, seminars, exhibits, and conferences.

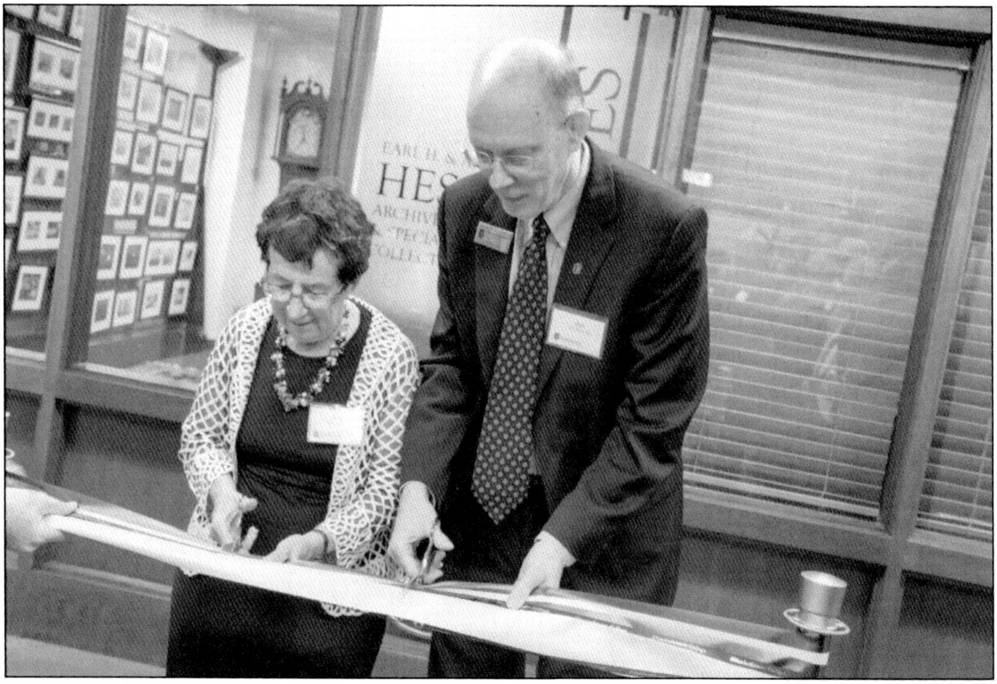

On November 5, 2014, Anita Hess (left) and historian Dr. Carl Strikwerda (right), president of Elizabethtown College, cut the ribbon dedicating the Earl and Anita Hess Archives and Special Collections of the college's High Library. President Strikwerda said, "History is a precious teacher." This facility serves the college's Young Center for Anabaptist and Pietist Studies, the college's archival and Brethren history collections, thus preserving Elizabethtown's culture and history.

Two

COMMERCE

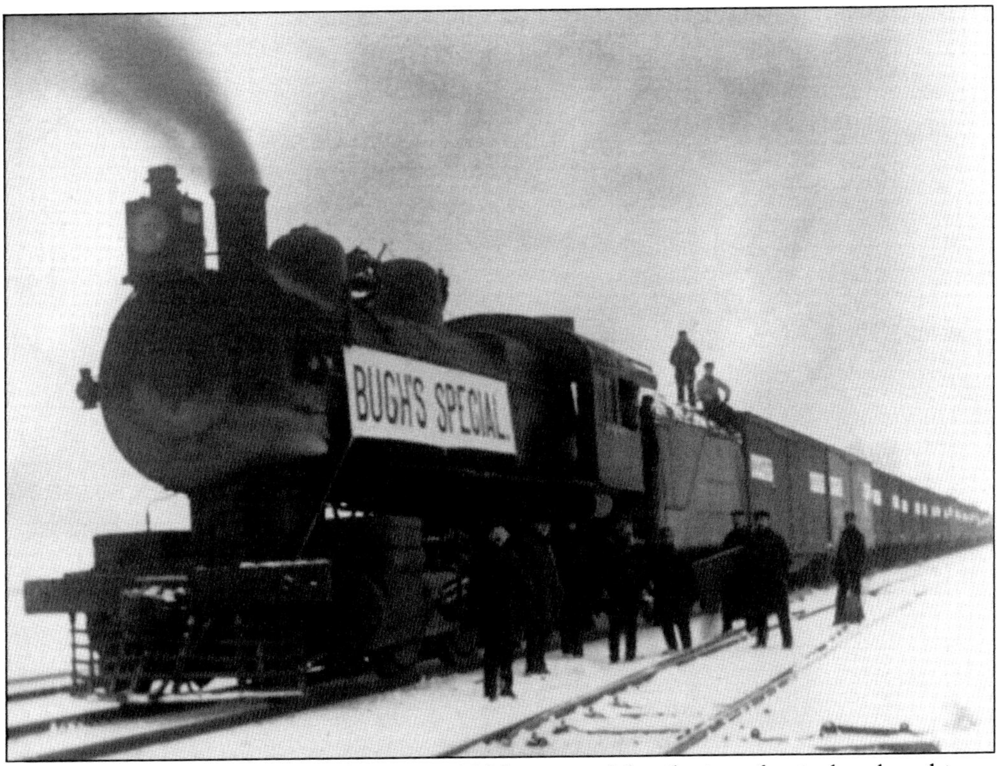

This 20-car train was headed to Chicago in 1906 for national distribution of agricultural machinery produced by Buch Manufacturing. Agricultural production for the military during the French and Indian War and the American Revolution built the local economy. Factories making wagons and farm equipment converted to the manufacture of shoes and garments. By the 1960s, with the presence of nearby military bases, the Department of Defense was the largest employer. Local industries relied on military contracts.

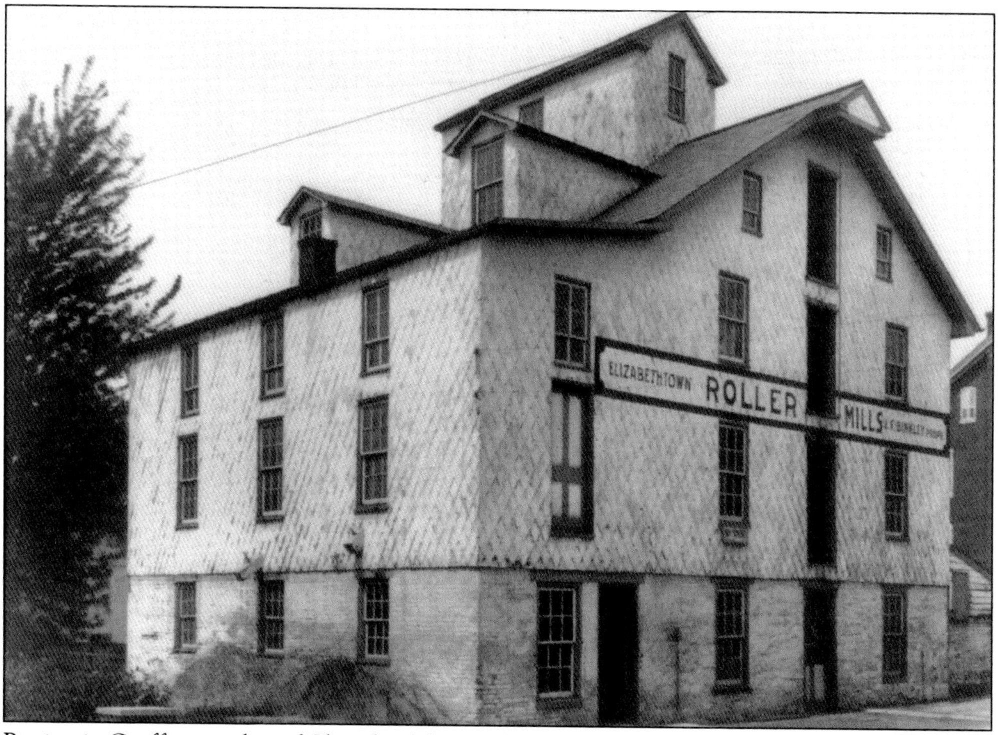

Benjamin Groff, a member of Church of the Brethren, established a gristmill on Conoy Creek at the intersection of College Avenue and South Market Streets. In 1877, Groff's sons sold the mill to Jacob Stauffer, who in turn sold it to his son-in-law J.F. Binkley in 1898. Binkley's grandson Jacob began custom milling for area farmers in 1917, producing Silver Cloud Flour, Blue Ribbon Corn Meal, and a variety of poultry feeds.

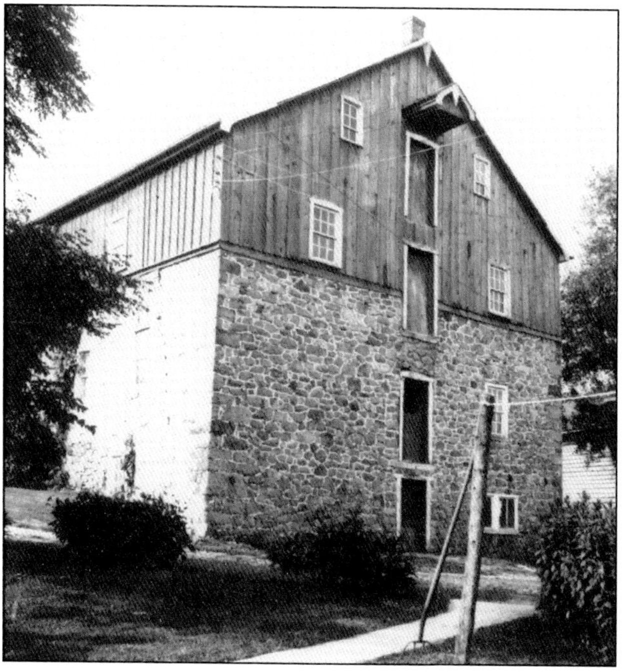

Union Mill, built in 1817 on Chiques Creek, was purchased in 1870 by the Daniel Heistand family. Descendants of Swiss Mennonites, the Heistands were charter members of St. Elizabeth's Episcopal Church in Elizabethtown. The Heistand family has produced several generations of Episcopal clergy and bishops. Today, the property and mill are known as Union Mill Acres. The current owners grow and retail flowers, pumpkins, and Christmas trees.

Aberdeen Mill was built in 1774 on the Conewago Creek by Ulrich and Barbara Stauffer. It was owned by the George Redsecker family. An excellent example of the mills that operated along Conoy and Conewago Creeks, this mill and distillery operated until the 1960s. The present owners have plans to develop the mill for the benefit of the community, employ sustainable agricultural methods, and emphasize the property's historical significance. (Courtesy Lancasterhistory.org.)

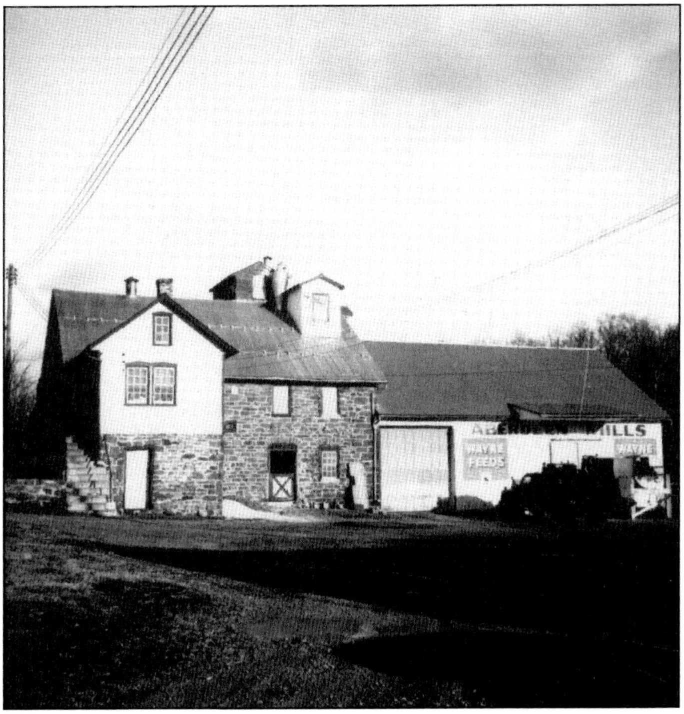

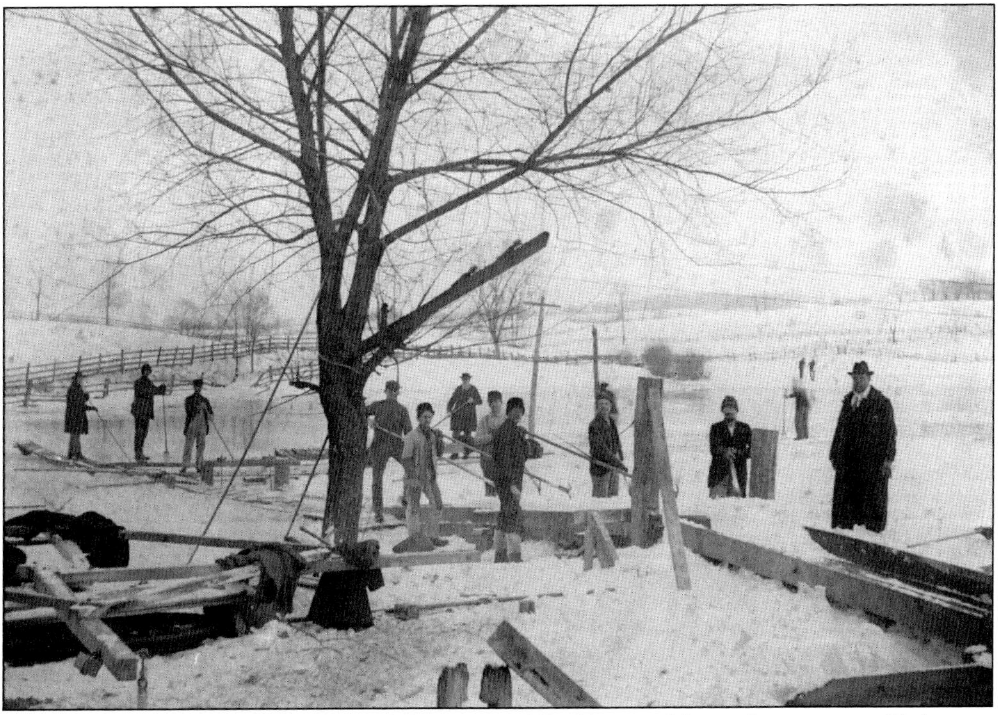

Charles B. Stephan, vice president of the National Building and Loan Association of Lebanon, emigrated from Germany to Elizabethtown in 1884. He opened a produce and poultry shop in the former Washington Hotel on Market Street. In 1890, Stephan created Stephan's Ice Pond (today, the community park), built an icehouse, and started an ice-delivery business.

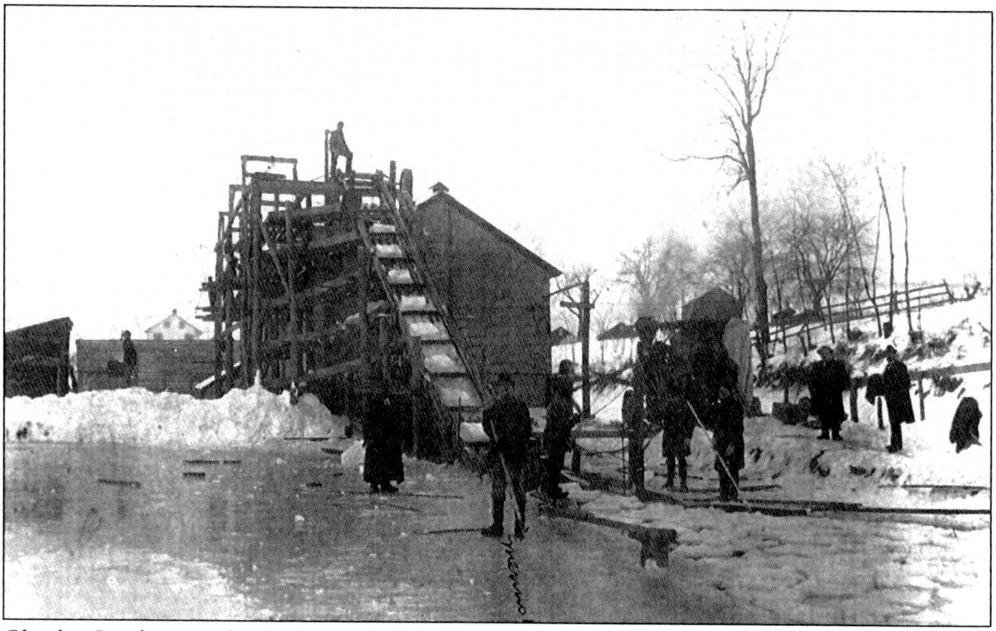

Charles Stephan made Elizabethtown the center of egg production in central Pennsylvania. Launching into the egg business, he gained a reputation for superior eggs in the New York and Philadelphia markets. He established a wholesale and retail egg, poultry, and produce branch called Anchor Produce Company, in Atlantic City, New Jersey. Stephan turned Elizabethtown into the principle produce shipping point between Harrisburg and Philadelphia.

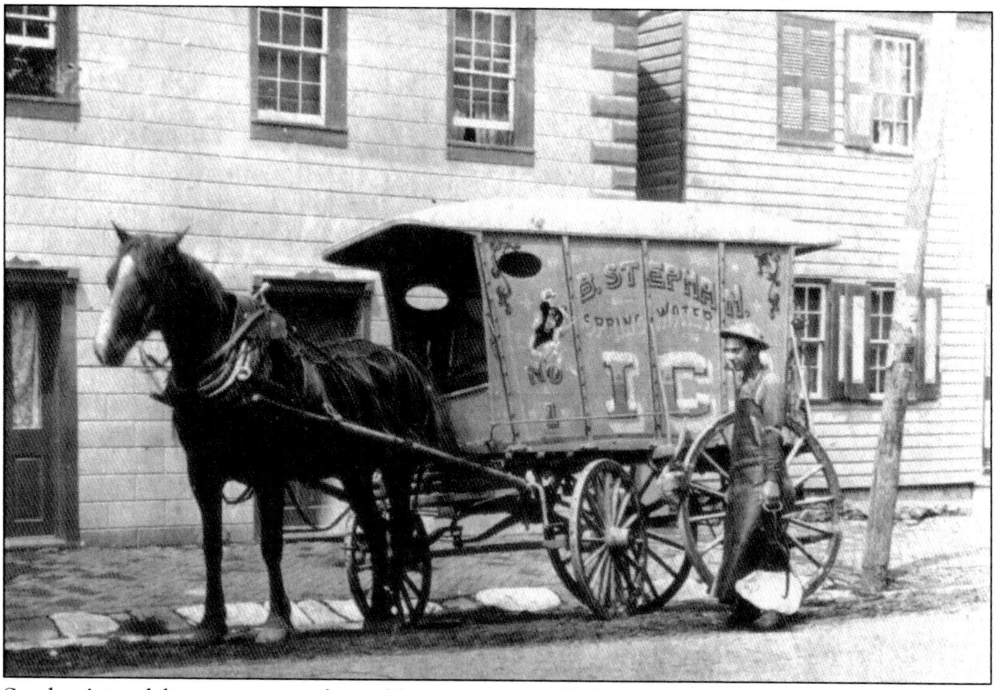

Stephan's ice-delivery teams made weekly runs to over 400 farms in the Elizabethtown area. He was the first dressed-calf shipper to New York between Harrisburg and Philadelphia. Stephan was an active member of St. Peter's, the Catholic Benevolent League, and Democratic Party politics.

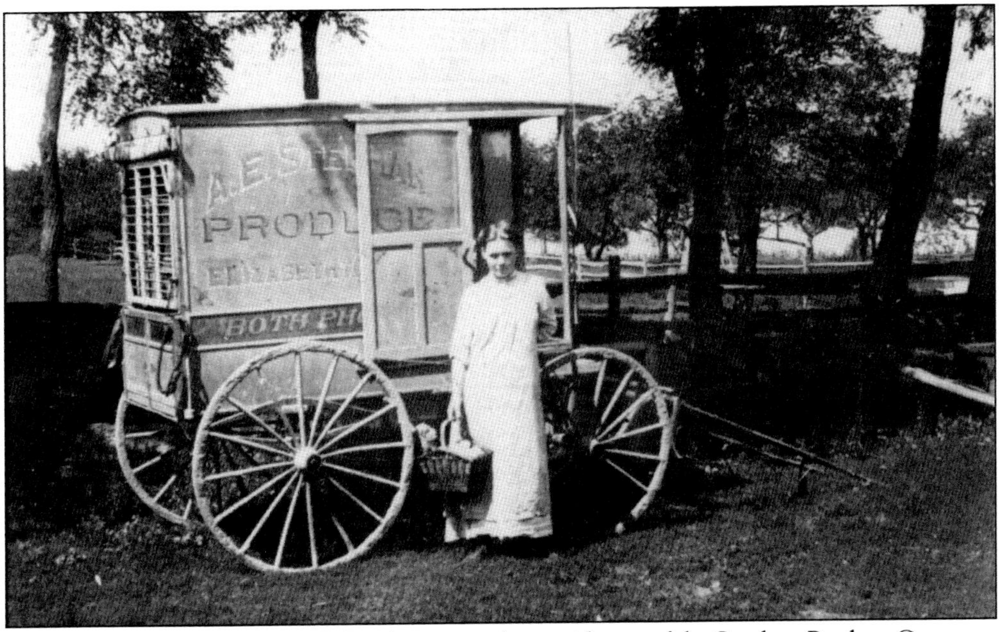

Charles Stephan's wife, Anna E. Stephan, poses here with one of the Stephan Produce Company wagons in 1909. She was born on June 16, 1854, in Lancaster to Frank and Margaretha (Herzog) Morck. Her paternal grandfather, Andrew Morck, emigrated from Germany to Lancaster in 1840 and was a charter member of St. Joseph Roman Catholic Church. Charles and Anna were married on September 23, 1880. (Courtesy LancasterHistory.org.)

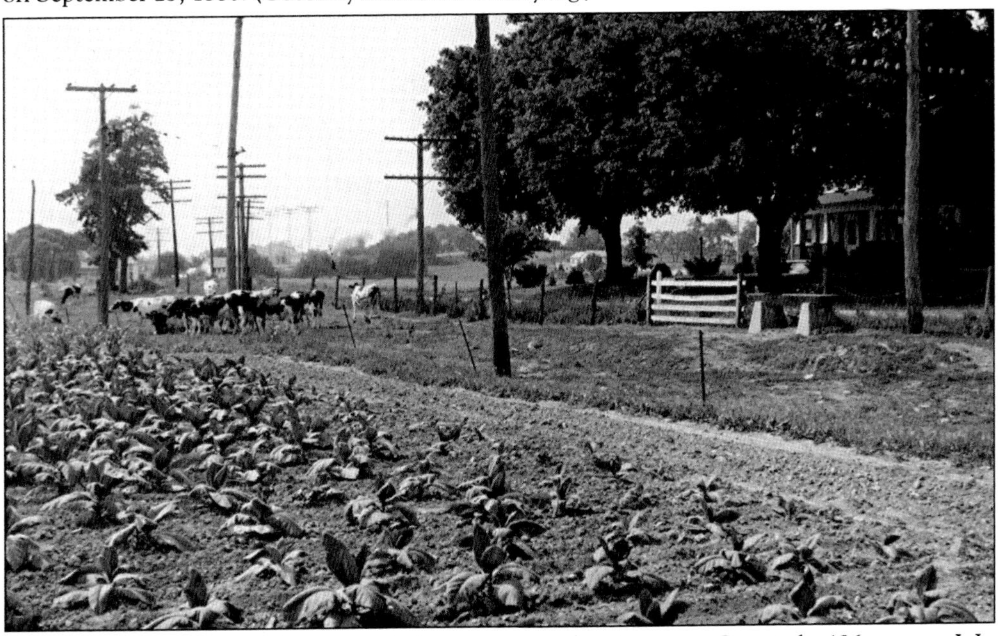

Between 1849 and 1859, cultivation of tobacco increased in Lancaster County by 186 percent. L.L. Engle, Amos Harrouf, Ambrose Ulrich, and Simon Nissley were tobacco dealers with warehouses on Bainbridge Street. Frank Keller manufactured cigars on South Market Street beginning in 1885. Samuel Sharer made cigars on East High Street. Joseph Gross, James Doyle, John Brandt, and John Ulrich started operating cigar factories in Elizabethtown in 1890.

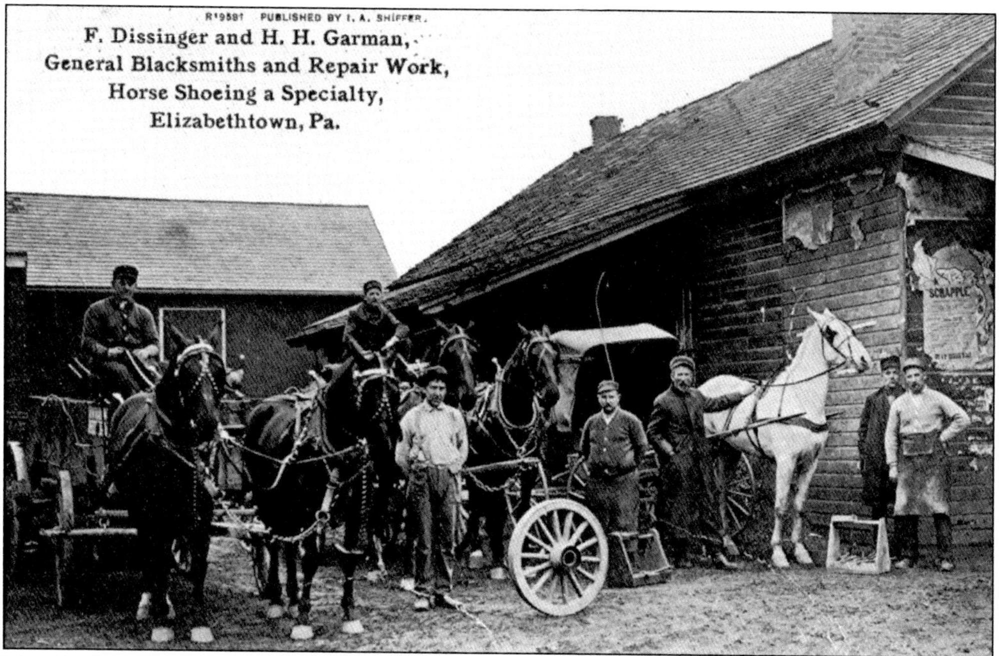

The Dissinger and Garman Blacksmith Shop, seen here in 1908, was located at 33 North Market Street. With a strategic location at the intersection of trade and transportation routes, Dissinger and Garman played an important role in Elizabethtown. In a related industry, beginning in 1868, Albert and Lewis Leicht made carriages and wagons at 412–414 South Market Street. After a fire in 1876, the company moved to the rear of 311 South Market Street.

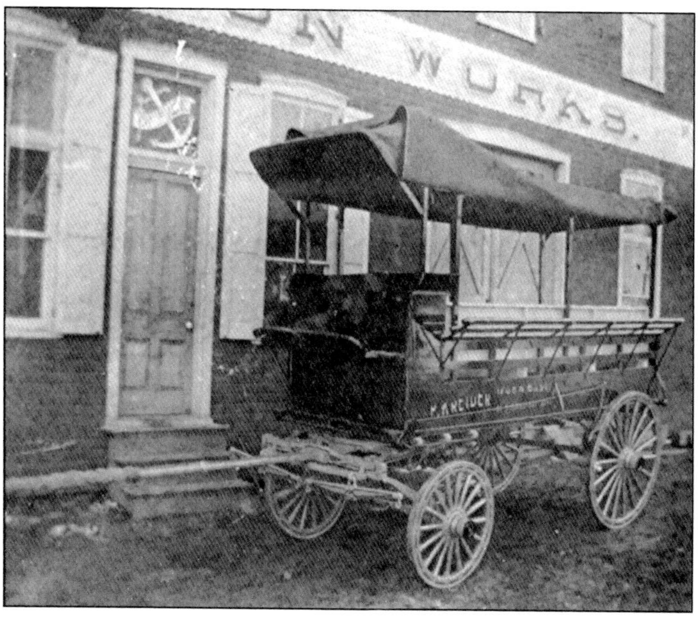

In 1896, Hiram Nissley opened Anchor Spring Wagon Works at West High and Brown Streets. He moved to the corner of South Market and Park Streets in 1909. His wife was Laura Buch, daughter of J.B. Buch, with whom he apprenticed in making wagons. Nissley's factory was on the former site of Fifth Wheel Manufacturing Company. From 1888 to 1896, Jacob Miller produced fifth wheels for the shaft assembly on wagons.

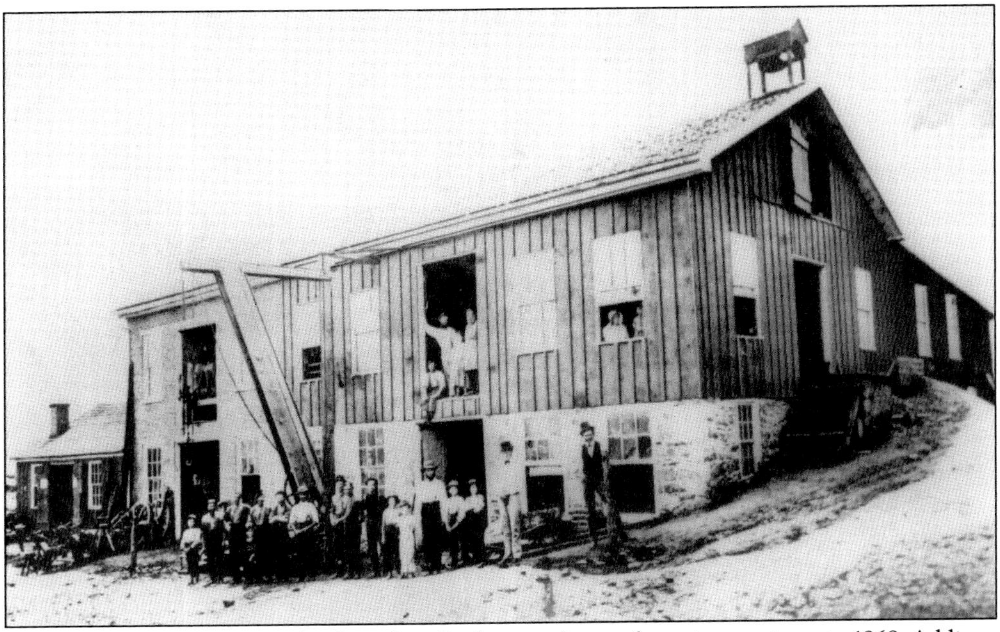

Church of the Brethren member Jonathan Buch started manufacturing carriages in 1868. Addison Buch, Benjamin Groff, and Mennonite T.W. Nissley partnered in a machine shop and foundry on the west side of South Market and Union Streets (College Avenue). An 1876 fire destroyed the factory, which was powered by a steam engine. A new factory, constructed in 1890, became A. Buch & Sons when J. Harvey and Royer S. joined their father.

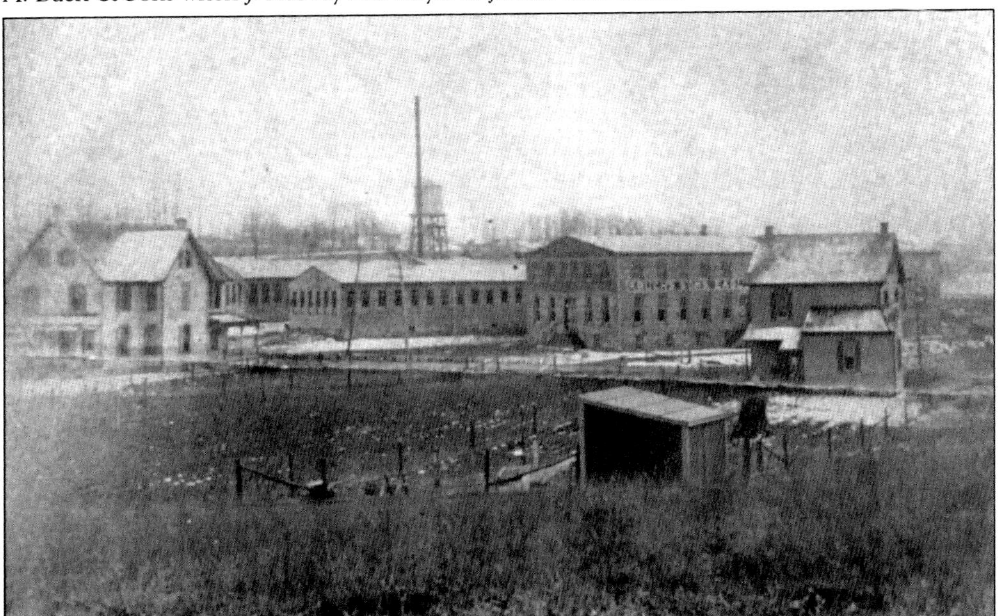

Beginning in 1900, Buch specialized in manufacturing wheelbarrows and steel lawn swings. The Buch Eagle lawn swing won bronze awards at the St. Louis World's Fair in 1904 and the Tercentennial Exposition at Jamestown, Virginia, in 1907. In 1960, Buch became a subsidiary of Moto-Mower, and the plant closed that year. R&R Electronics, subcontractors for AMP, moved to the Buch plant in 1968. In 1971, the firm became R&R Metal Finishing.

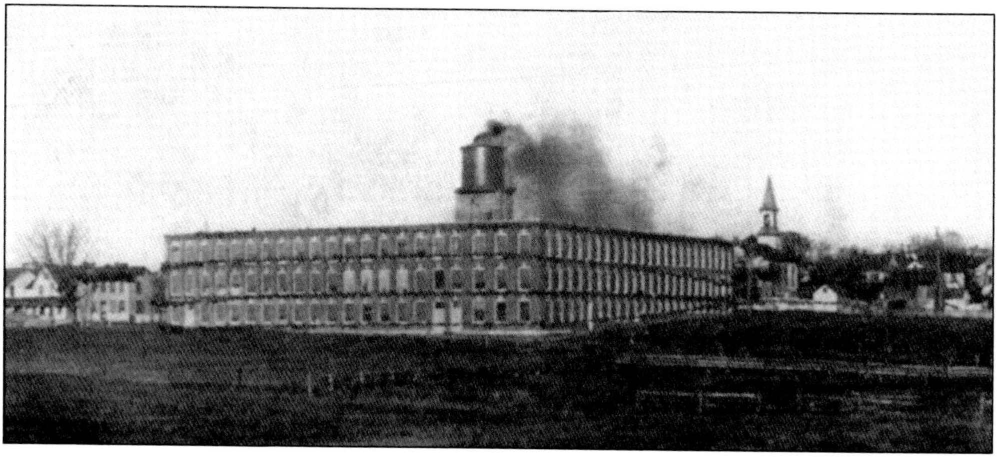

Aaron Shenk Kreider attended Lebanon Valley College. He was a member of Annville Church of the Brethren and served on the board of trustees of Elizabethtown College. He was president of the National Association of Shoe Manufacturing and served as a Republican in Congress from 1913 to 1929. He owned a grain business in Palmyra. With his wife, Elizabeth Horst, he founded the town of Lawn five miles from Elizabethtown. In 1893, he purchased Palmyra Boot & Shoe Company, opening new factories in Annville, Middletown, and Lebanon. He opened Kreider Shoe Manufacturing in the former Buch factory at South Market and College Avenue in 1901. Kreider built a new factory (shown in the photographs) in 1904 at Washington and South Poplar Streets. By 1915, the factory was daily producing 5,000 pairs of shoes. In the 1930s, the company depended on contracts with the Pennsylvania State Police.

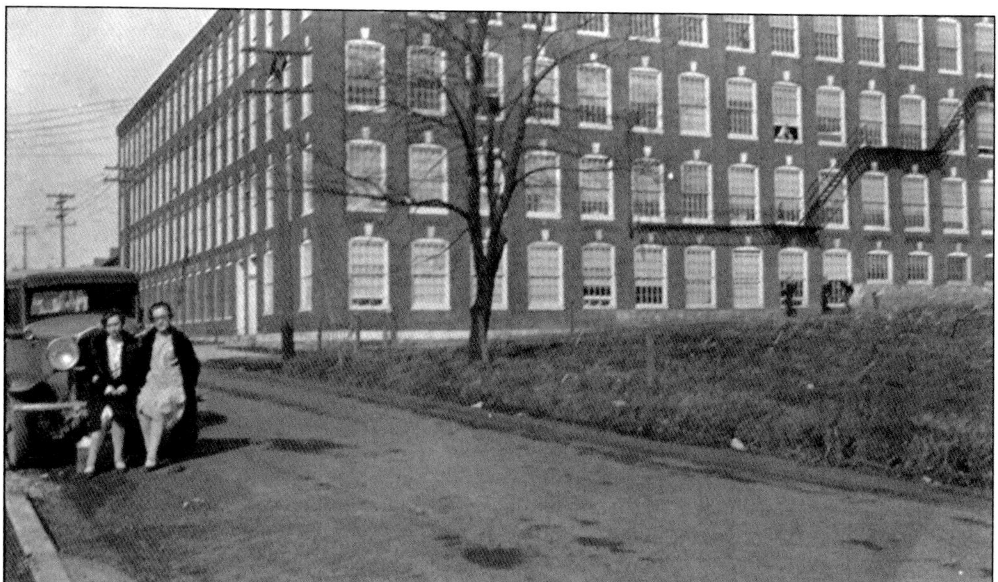

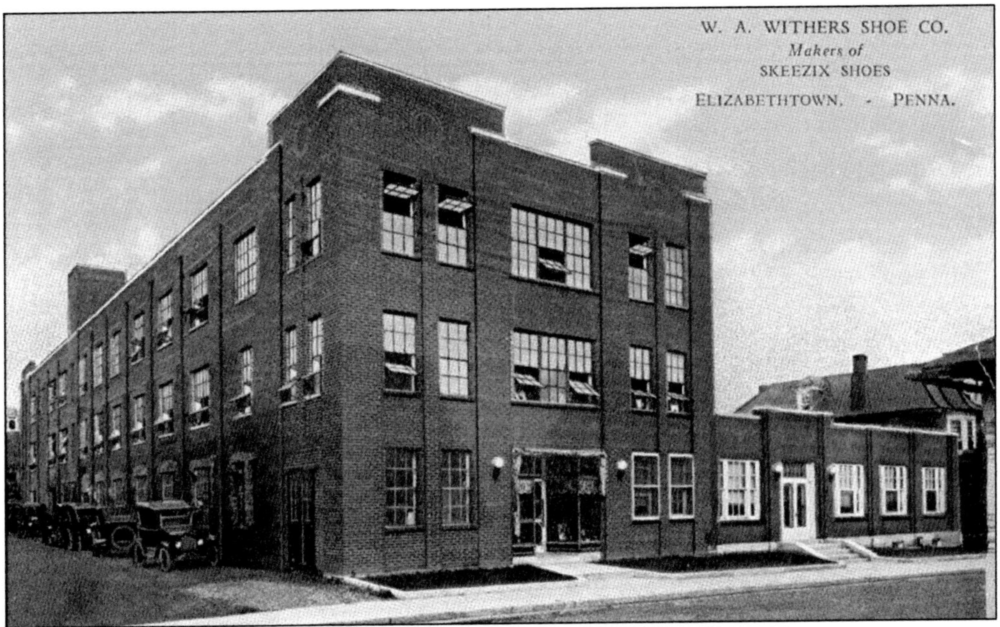

In 1918, William A. Withers, superintendent of the Kreider shoe factories, established a subsidiary company, W.A. Withers, as a mail-order and retail outlet for Kreider. Withers purchased the Elizabethtown Market House on South Poplar Street in 1920 to manufacture children's shoes. The firm produced 1,000 pairs a day. In 1928, this firm became the Lancaster Shoe Company before merging with Gerberich-Payne Shoe Company.

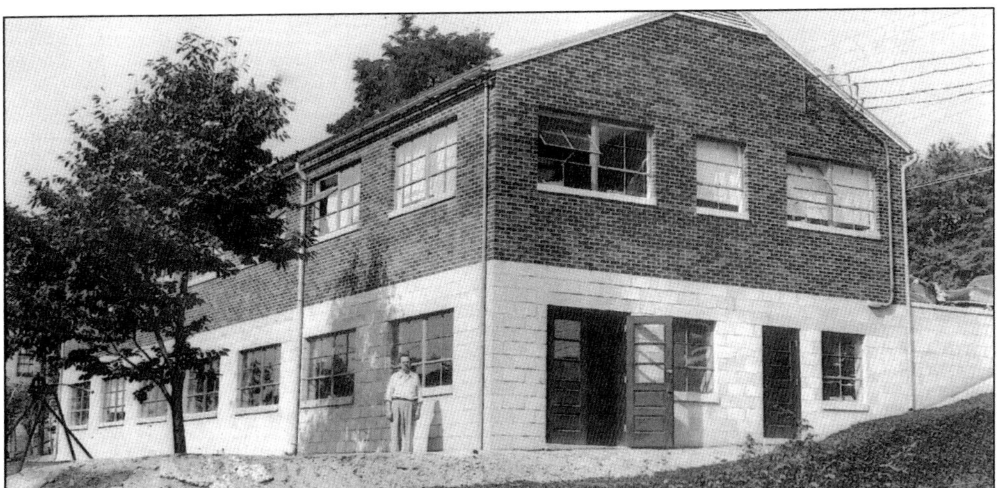

In 1927, the Elizabethtown Garment Factory was built on Poplar Street. Elizabethtown Shirt Company started on Bainbridge Street in 1909. Lewis Brothers began manufacturing pajamas at the same location in 1925; ten years later, this was Greenberg Garment Factory. In the 1920s, Harvey and Jacob Stern opened the first dress factory on East High Street. In 1935, this became Classic Hosiery. Jacob Risser opened Tiny Tots and Celeste manufacturing (pictured) in 1949.

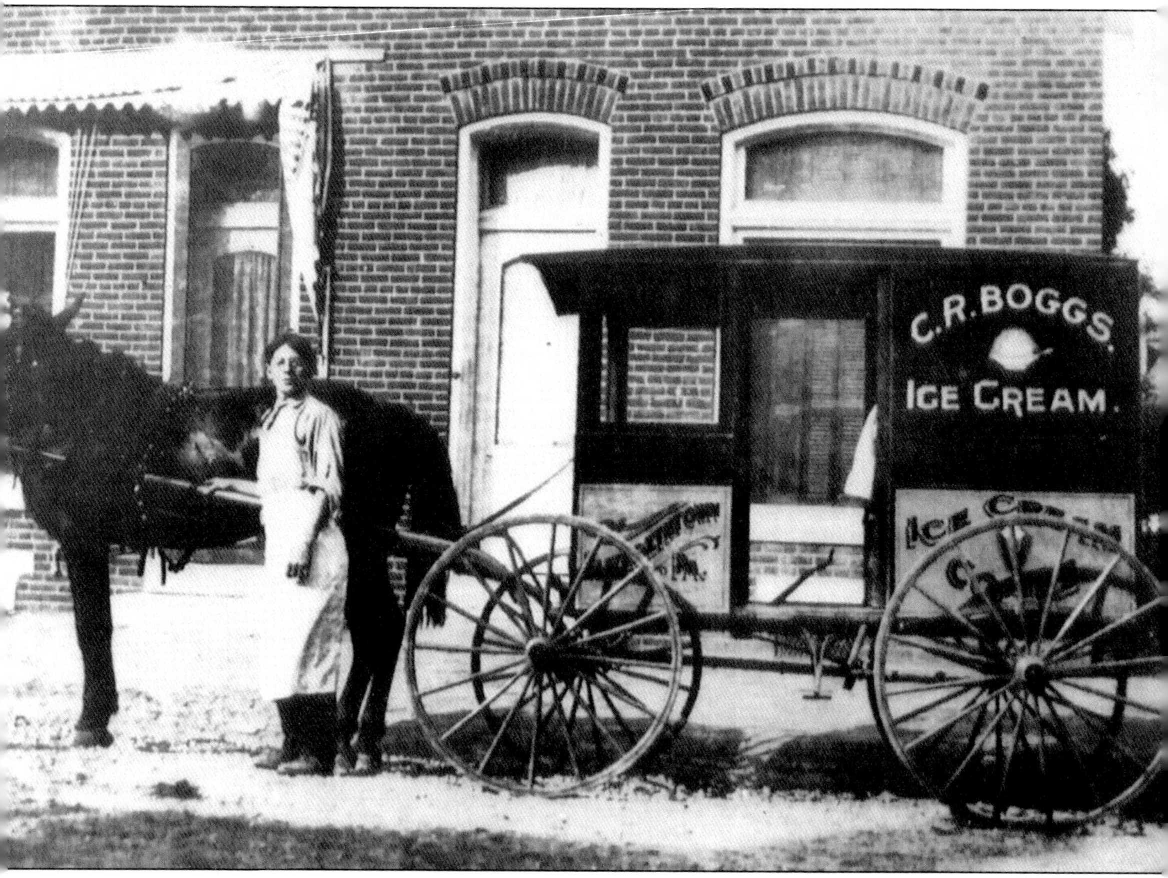

The Boggs family has a long history with Elizabethtown. In the 1720s, Andrew Boggs settled on Conoy Creek. In 1762, he advocated for building the road from Lancaster to Harrisburg, to be directed through Elizabethtown. As a sergeant, he fought at the Battle of Long Island in 1776; wounded, he was sent home as a captain and commanded the Donegal Township militia. His brother Alexander Boggs was a butcher and owner of the Sign of the Bear Tavern in 1789. Descendent George Boggs had a hardware store at 12 South Market Street. Samuel Boggs was a member of the Crescent Club; in 1917, he made the club's meeting rooms in Horst Hall available to the local Red Cross. In 1925, Charles R. Boggs bought the Kennewood Hotel (formerly the Phoenix Hotel and later the Garret Hotel) at 28 South Market Street. He owned a restaurant at 5 South Market Street and moved it next door to the Kennewood. The Boggs' Restaurant was famous for turtle soup. In 1940, Robert Boggs represented the chamber of commerce supporting the borough's installation of traffic lights and parking meters.

In 1919, J.K. Freymeyer built a bakery at 33 East Park Street. Food historians have noted that, prior to the 1940s, most meals in central Pennsylvania were frugal, one-pot recipes centered on homemade bread or from local Pennsylvania Dutch bakeries like Freymeyer's. Many of these dishes were "bread soups," such as *kaffesupp* (a coffee soup) and *brodsupp* (almost a soufflé), both particularly common at Mennonite and Brethren tables.

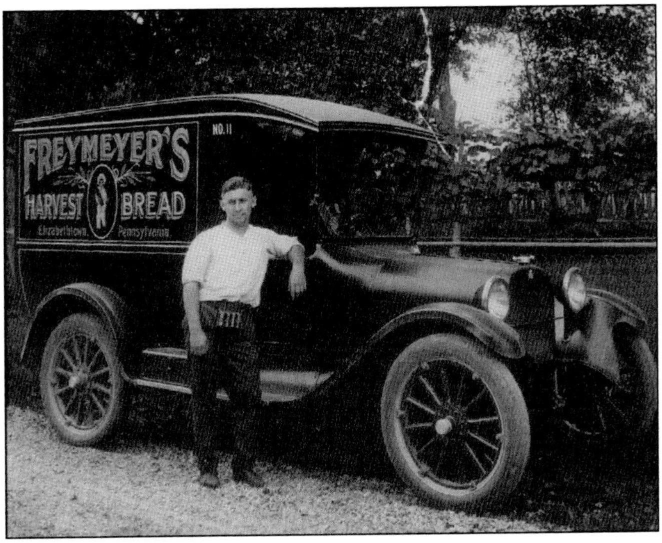

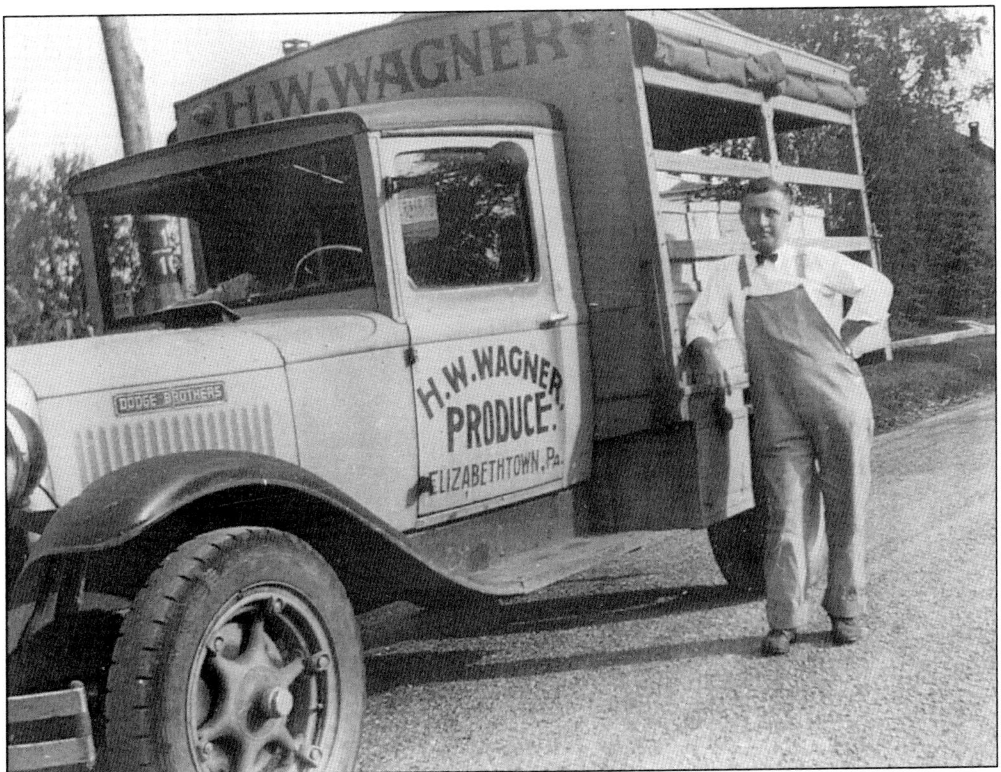

In 1926, Harry Wagner and Morris Hinkle operated a bottling company at 45 West High Street, formerly Boll's Hall. It purchased Orange Crush syrup from California and distributed the soft drink from Elizabethtown throughout southeastern Pennsylvania and Maryland. One of Elizabethtown's early public schools was located at 45 West High Street. The building was purchased by brewery owner Henry Boll, of St. Peter's, who created a public meeting venue, Boll's Hall.

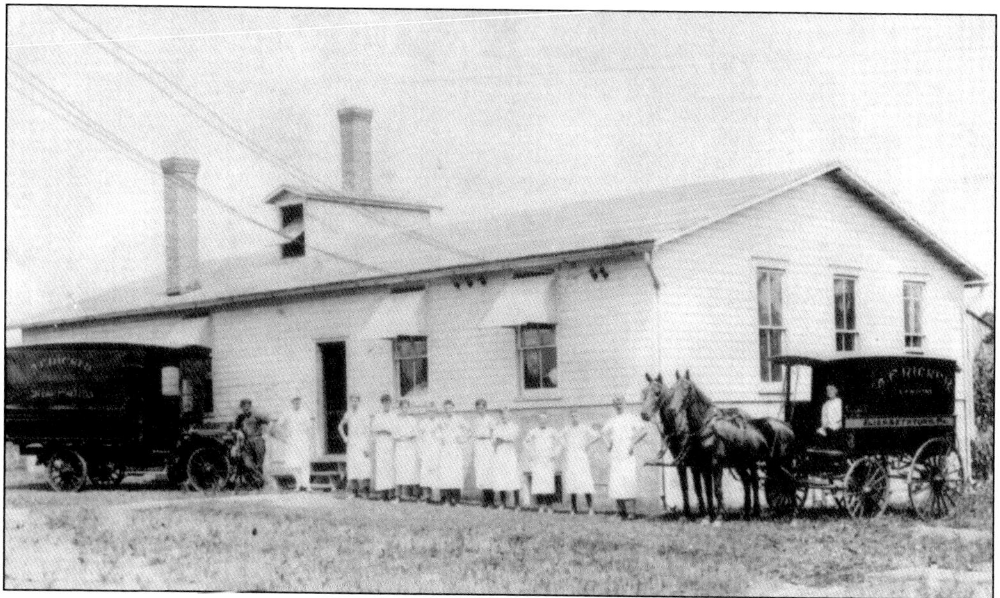

Shown here is Ricker Pretzels. All Pennsylvania Dutch bakers made pretzels. In 1745, Lancaster baker Andreas Beyerle had his case clock carved with dinner rolls and a pretzel. Pretzels were a symbol of the baker's trade. The mills established along Conoy Creek provided raw materials for distilling grain, brewing beer, and baking pretzels; all of these items were served in the numerous taverns at the transportation hub of Elizabethtown and became synonymous with Pennsylvania Dutch cookery.

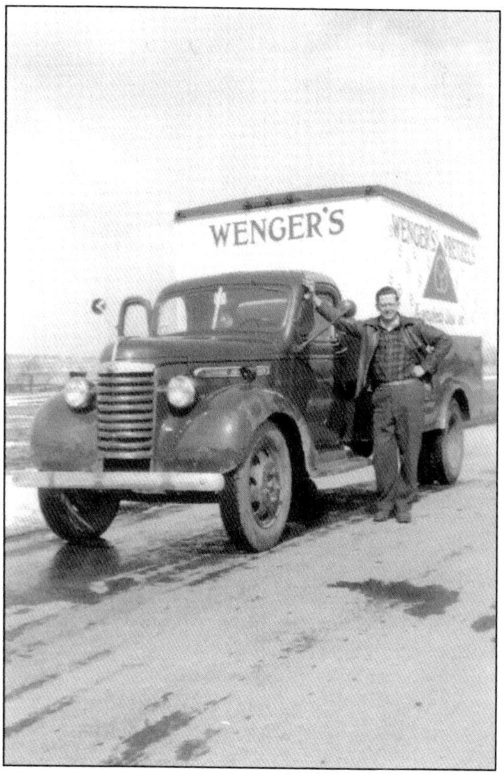

In 1935, Wenger Brothers opened a self-service grocery store in the Horst Building at 15 Diamond Square. The concept for the store came from Melvin Wenger's wife, Helen, and her experience shopping at a Piggly Wiggly grocery in Virginia. The Wenger brothers diversified the business, but they remained in grocery retail. Some brothers purchased feed mills, including today's Wenger Feeds (formerly J.W. Wolgemuth Mills in Elizabethtown), and some bought small local companies, such as Ricker Pretzels.

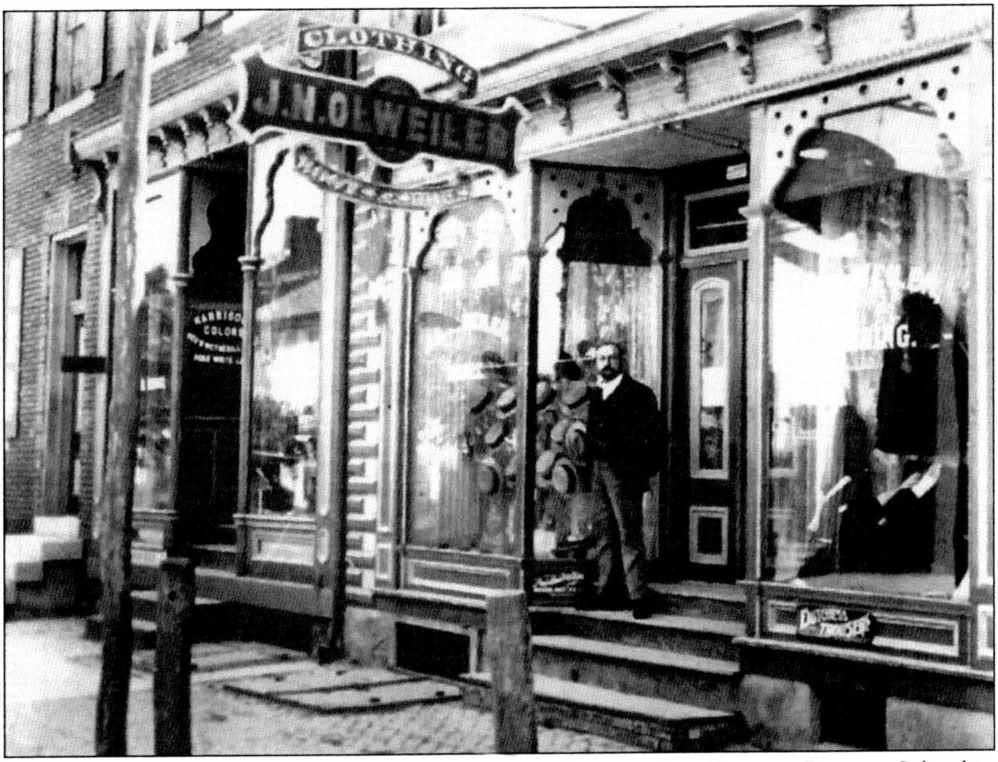

Jacob N. Olweiler returned to Elizabethtown in 1891 after attending Eastman Business School in Rochester, New York. He worked for the Brethren firm Hertzler Brothers department store, which opened in 1884 on Diamond Square. In 1893, he opened a men's clothing store at 10 South Market Street, introducing "ready mades or made to measure suits and overcoats." Olweiler was a member of the Elizabethtown Business Men's Association and president of the chamber of commerce in the 1930s. He served on the Welcome Home Celebration Committee, which honored World War I veterans with festivities on September 8–9, 1919. In 1920, Olweiler purchased the Peach Alley Schoolhouse and leased it to the school board in 1923. It was used by seventh and eighth graders and served as a meeting place for the Boy Scouts. He served on the Community Relief Association, founded in 1927.

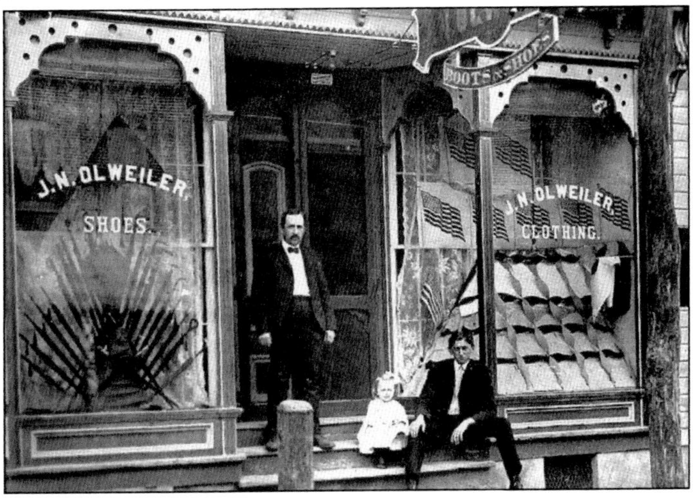

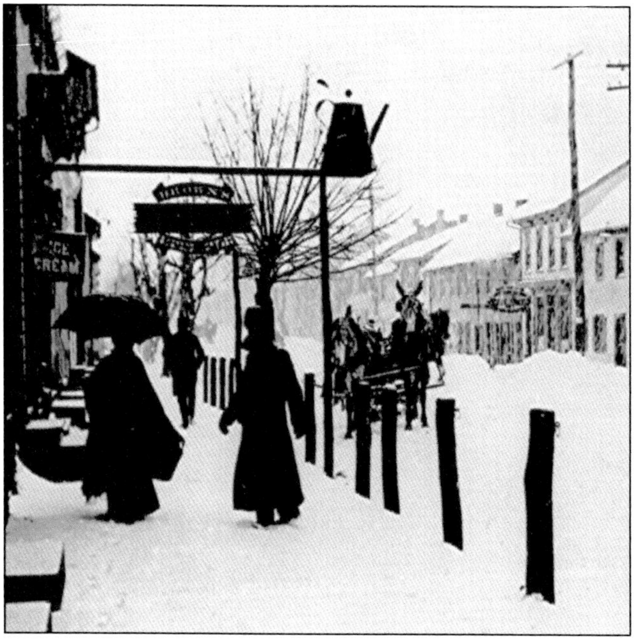

The silhouettes of "plain" women are seen on Market Street in winter. The traditional garb of Pennsylvania Dutch women included cape dresses and bonnets. They are still worn today, but are not representative of German heritage. When Germans immigrated to Pennsylvania, the Quakers dominated politics, economics, and fashion. Members of Historic Peace Churches assimilated into Quaker culture and traditions. Jesuit Father William Wappeler dressed "disguised as a Quaker gentlemen" when traveling between Elizabethtown and Lancaster.

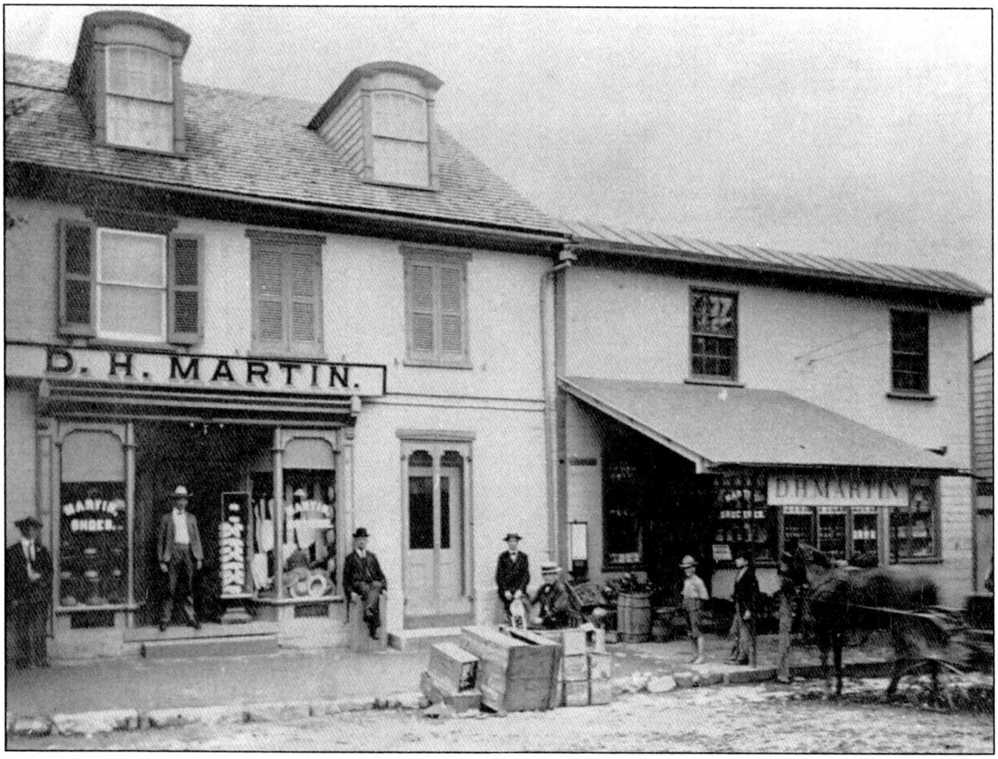

In 1895, David H. Martin opened his clothing store in the 1792 Samuel Grimes residence at 21–23 and 25 Diamond Square. In 1911, Martin relocated across Diamond Square, on the corner of South Market Street. At the store, advertised as "The Store for Plain Folks," Mennonite, Brethren, and Brethren in Christ customers had their suit coats tailored into "plain suits." The store carried a complete line of prayer veils, coverings, and bonnets.

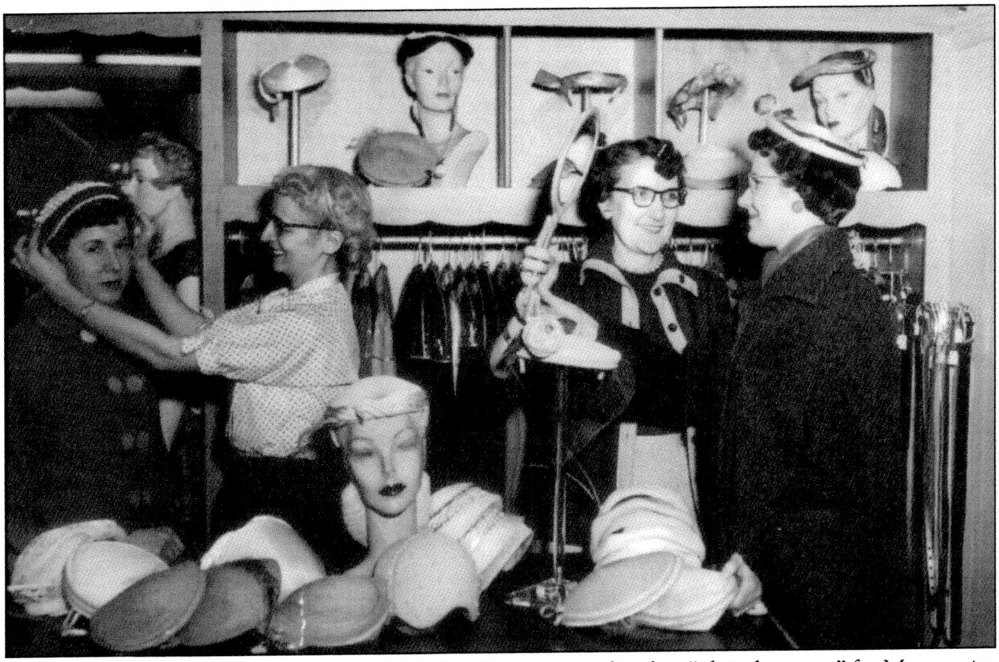

Grace Blough Dress Shop at 116 South Market Street specialized in "plain bonnets" for Mennonite and Brethren women. In 1913, the sisters Mollie and Fiana Leicht started a millinery store at this location. In 1929, Grace Blough began working there; she bought the store in 1938. Blough retired in 1976 and sold the store to Edith Metzler, who co-owned it with her husband, Charles. (Courtesy Elizabethtown Historical Society.)

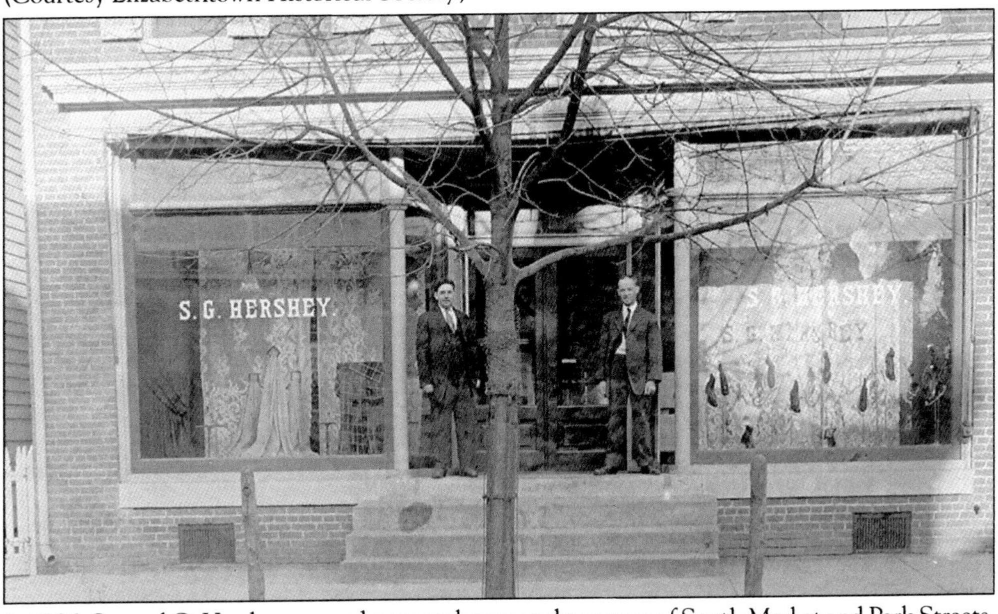

In 1906, Samuel G. Hershey opened a general store at the corner of South Market and Park Streets. He advertised dry goods, notions, groceries, and a full line of men's, women's, and children's shoes. His wife, Margaret, was president of the Elizabethtown Business Professional Women's Club, established in 1926. Hershey was extensively involved with the chamber of commerce, Rotary, and, particularly, the creation of the community park.

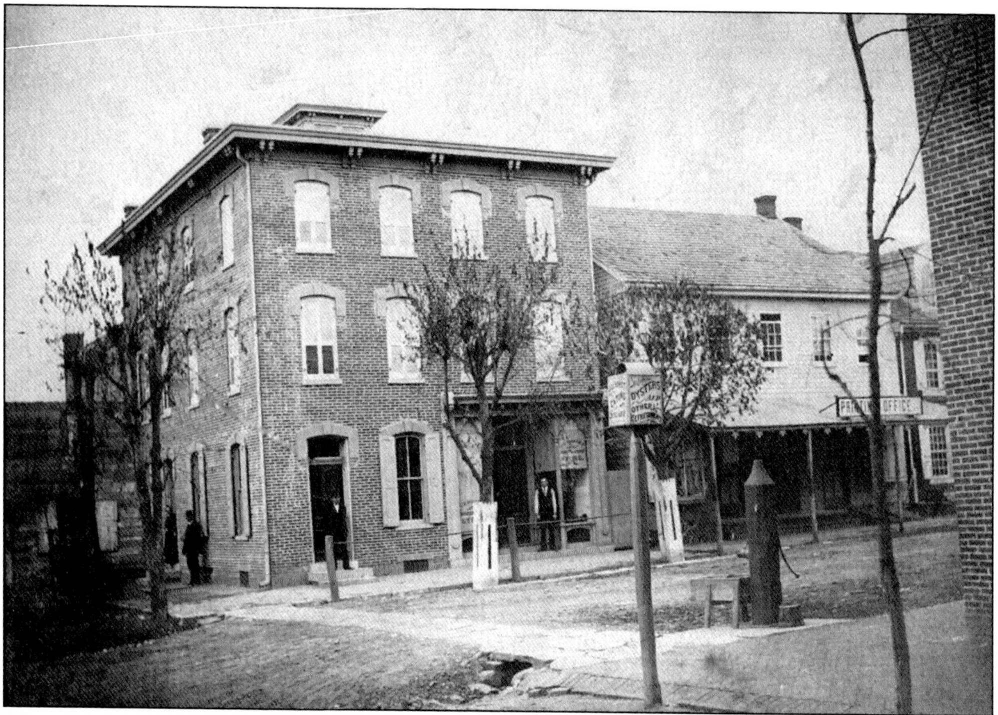

This is the printing office near Diamond Square. William Baxter of Elizabethtown published the weekly newspaper the *Hero of Tippecanoe*. In December 1839, the Whig National Convention assembled in Harrisburg. Elizabethtown held a rally for Benjamin Harrison and John Tyler in August 1840, displaying banners reading "The People's Candidate." Col. Abraham Greenawalt attended the national convention nominating Harrison and Tyler in Baltimore, entering the hall with banners reading "Whig Triumph 1840" and "We Resist Oppression."

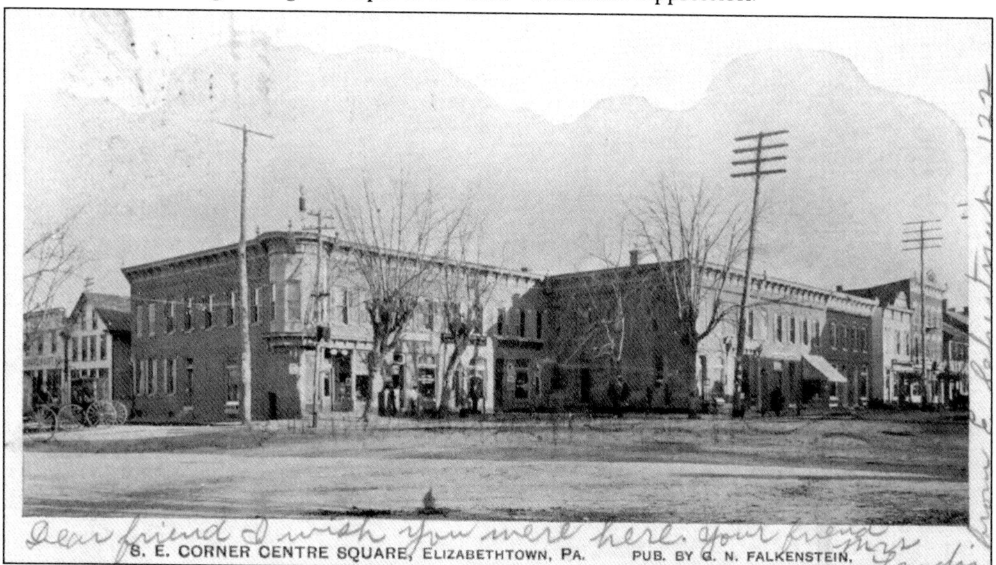

This George Ness Falkenstein postcard illustrates the southeast corner of Diamond Square. The John A. Fisher Shaving Parlor was located here, where tobacco and cigars were purchased next to the post office. On the second floor was the Young Men's Club of America.

The Young Men's Club of America was another name for the Young Men's Christian Association. At Elizabethtown College in 1920–1921, the Young Men's Welfare Association was established to "foster the spirit of brotherliness and helpfulness, to support such projects as will contribute to the common good and to stimulate interest in maintaining a distinctly Christian atmosphere in Elizabethtown College." The Young Men's Christian Association was created on campus in 1926–1927.

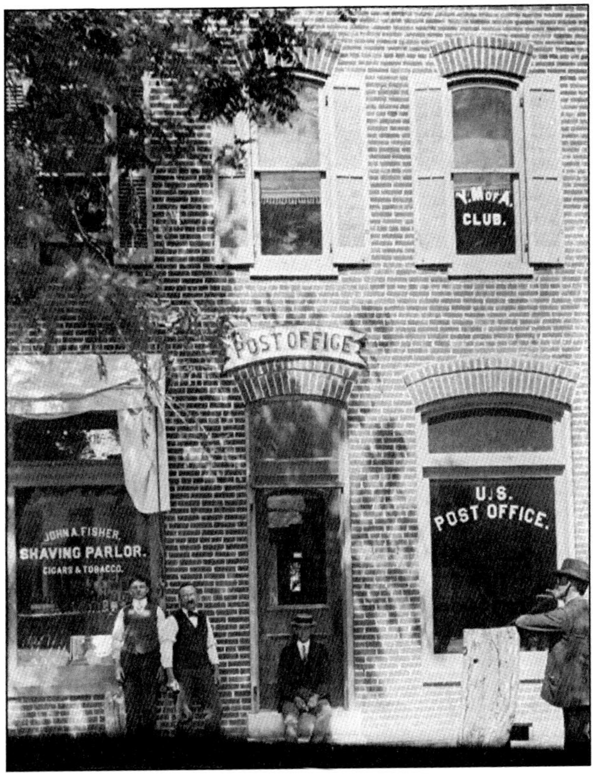

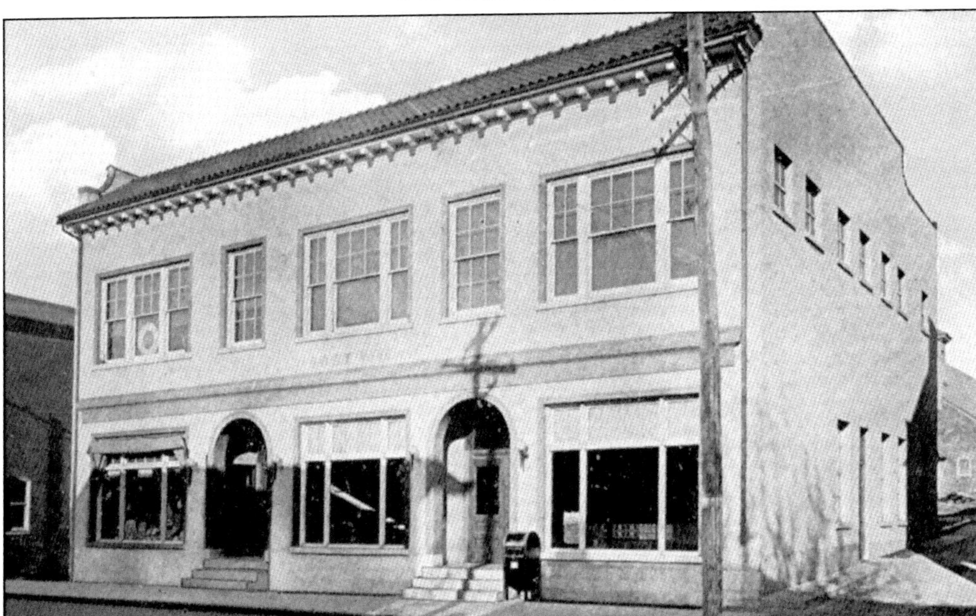

This is the Elizabethtown Post Office in the Odd Fellows Building in 1926. The Washington Hotel was joined to the IOOF Building with a unifying facade. In 1979, St. Peter's Catholic Church razed the IOOF and Washington Hotel Building. The parish obtained permission to close an adjacent alley, creating a green space with a car park. This gave the church access and exposure to South Market Street.

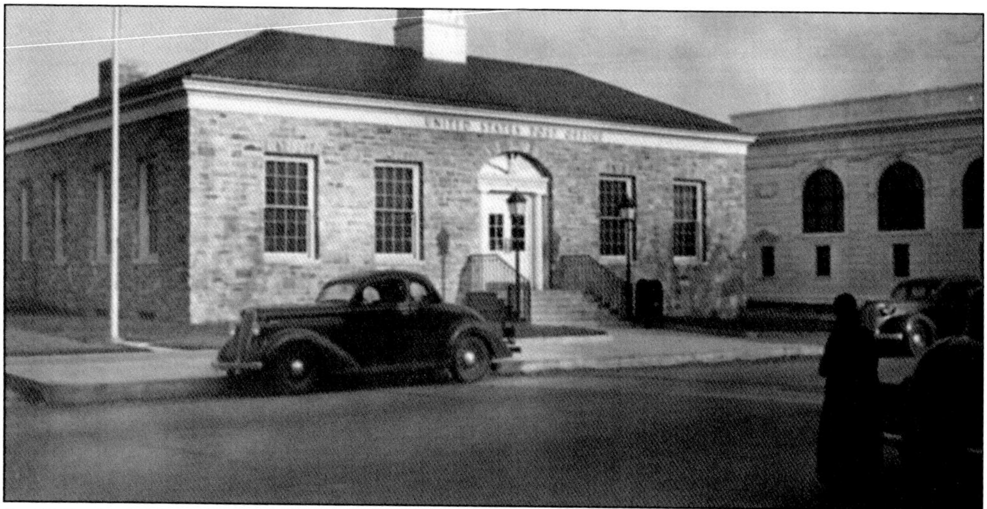

In 1931, Congress appropriated $90,000 to construct a new post office in Elizabethtown. The former J.H. Rider Hardware store and two houses on either side on South Market Street between Park and Washington Streets were selected as the site of the new post office, built in 1939 by the Works Progress Administration.

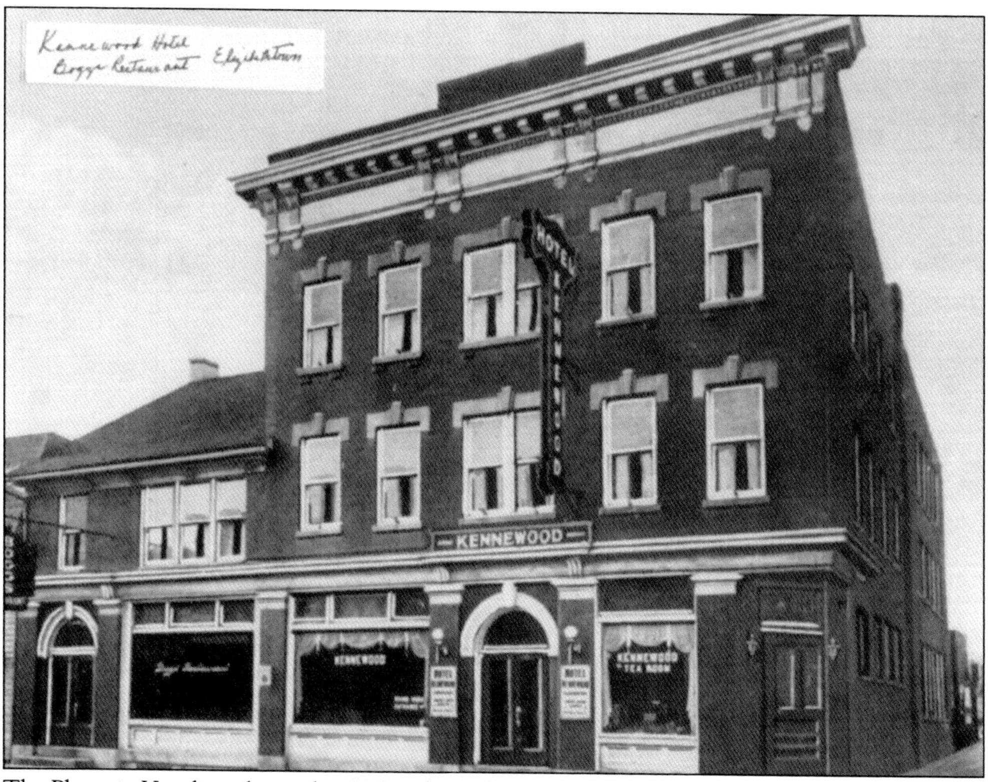

The Phoenix Hotel was located at 28 South Market Street. In 1910, A.L. Garrett bought the hotel, then demolished it in 1915 and erected the three-story brick Hotel Garrett, later the Kennewood. In 1925, Charles Boggs purchased the hotel, moving his restaurant next door. The Union Army Veterans of John Good Post No. 502, Grand Army of the Republic, and its auxiliary Women's Relief Corps No. 91 held meetings there.

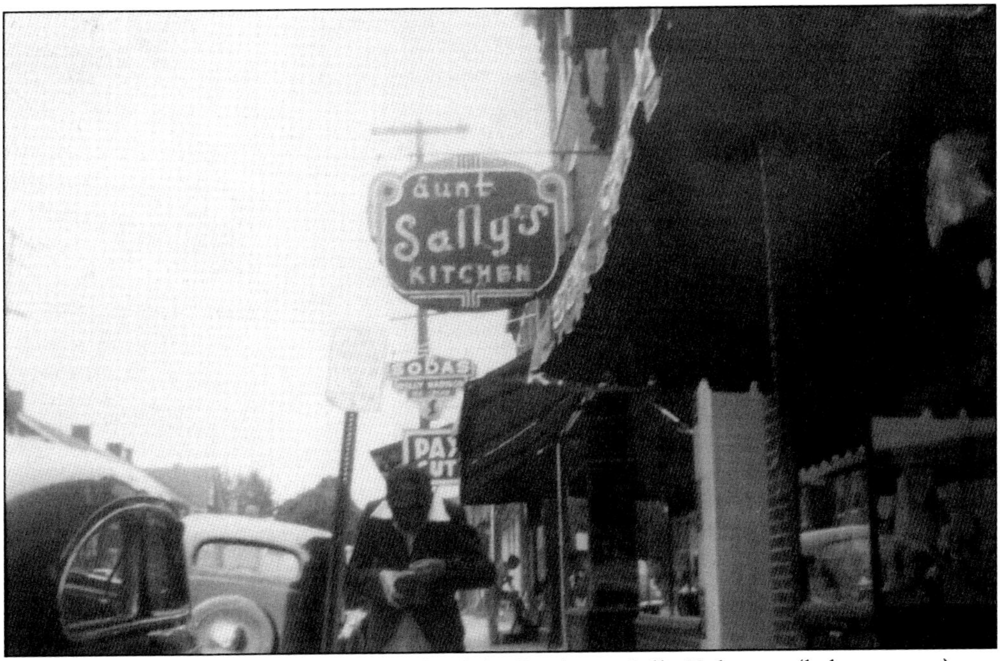

A member of the Elizabethtown Church of the Brethren, Sally Holsinger (below, center) was proprietress of Aunt Sally's Kitchen on 17 West High Street. Today, this property is the French butcher shop Rooster Street Provisions, owned and operated by Tony (from York) and Kristina (from Washington Boro) Page. They have modeled their specialty charcuterie on a butcher shop on the Île Saint-Louis in the Seine River in Paris. Tony explains: "We work with local farmers, we bring in happily and humanely raised pigs and we buy the whole animal because we feel it is right. We utilize [the pig] from head to tail." Kristina commented, "The community in Elizabethtown has been great. We wanted to be back close to family." The Pages looked at 40 potential locations in Lancaster County, finding Elizabethtown a strategic home for their market.

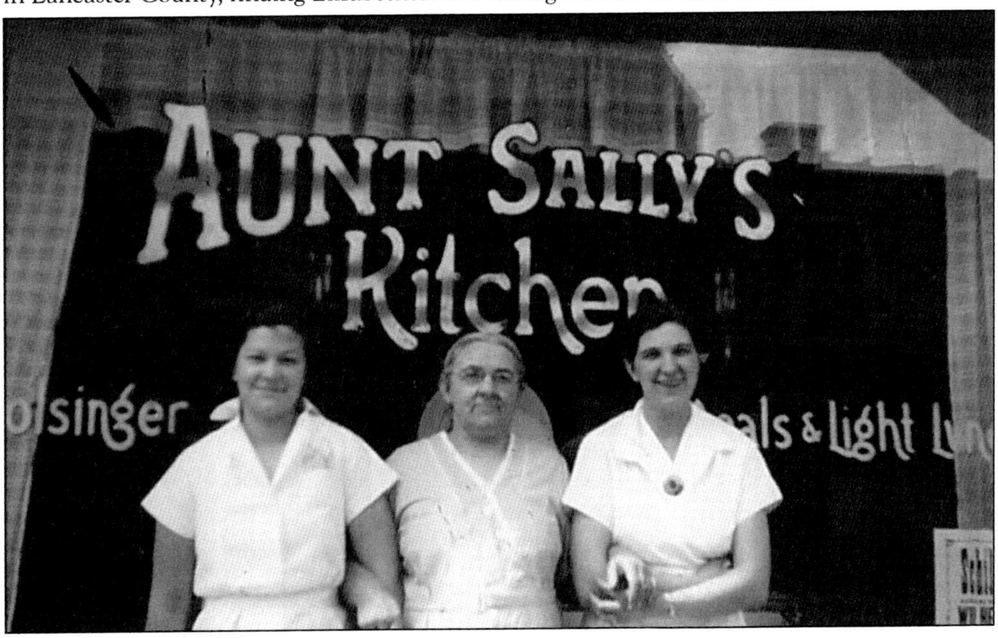

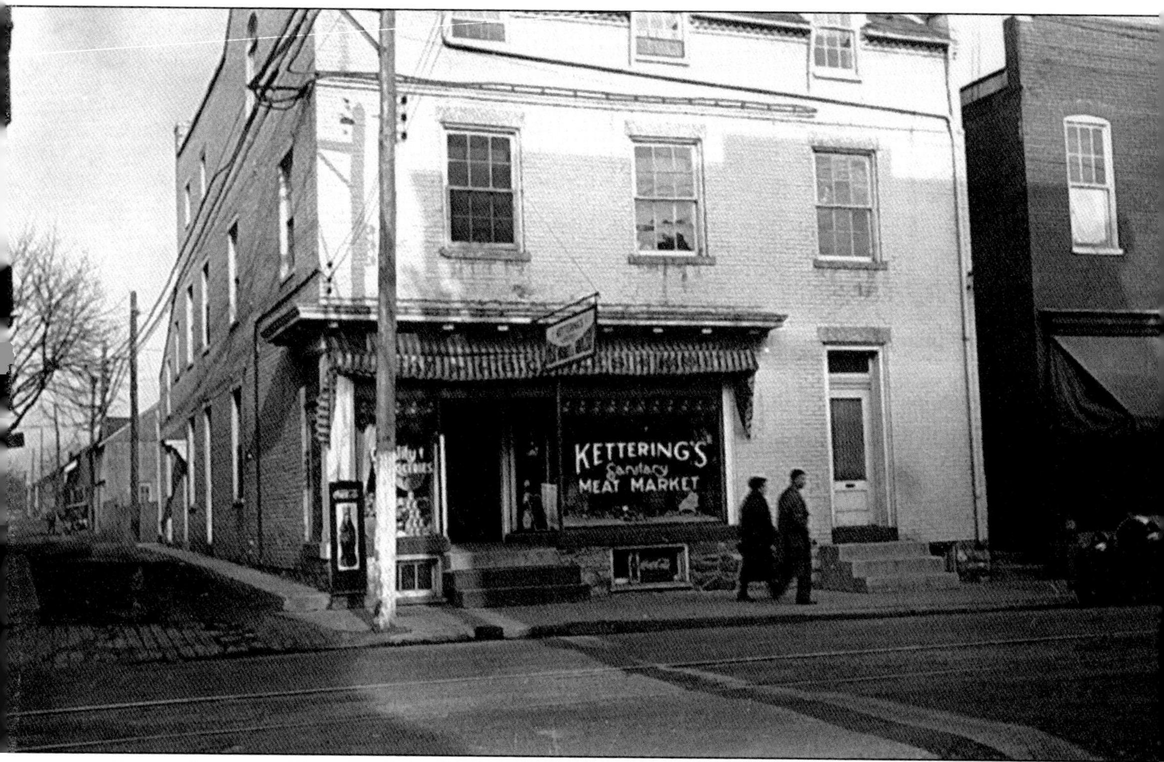

Shown here is a Church of the Brethren family business. J.W. Kettering served on the building committee for the new Elizabethtown Church of the Brethren, built in 1954 on South Mount Joy Street, adjacent to the campus of Elizabethtown College.

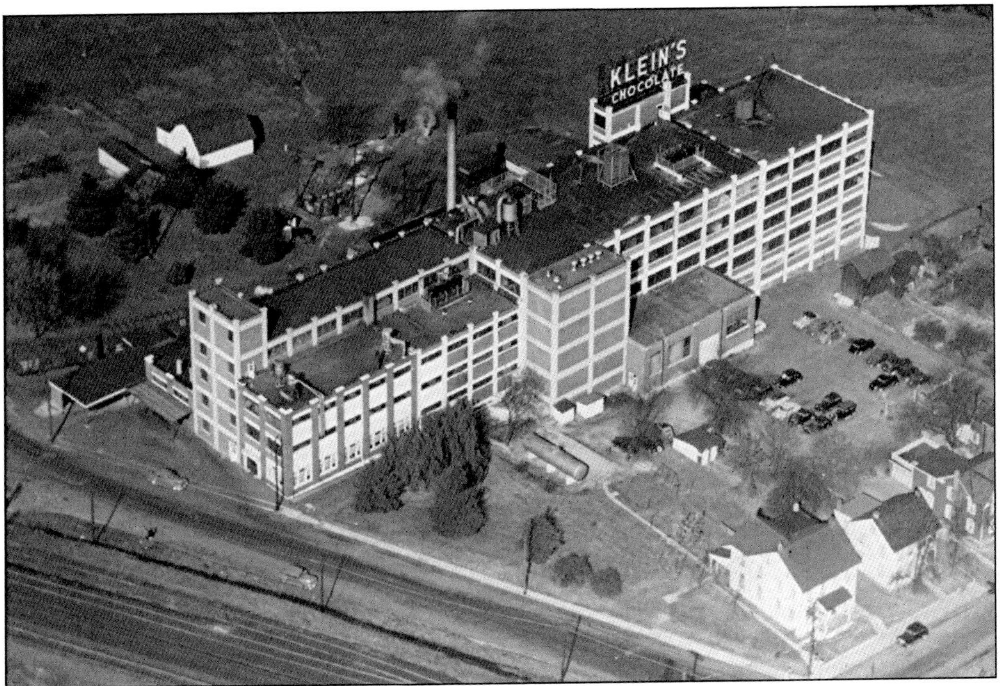

Natives of Elizabethtown, brothers William and Frederick Klein went to work in Milton S. Hershey's chocolate factory in 1898 and 1900, respectively. In 1912, the Klein brothers, joined by their brother Paul, founded the Klein Chocolate Company. The factory required six million quarts of milk a year. By 1922, Klein's was the largest milk chocolate factory in the nation, producing 250,000 bars a day. It had warehouses in Philadelphia, Chicago, and St. Louis. During World War I, Klein's shipped 20 million milk chocolate almond bars to American servicemen and servicewomen. In 1970, Klein's sold to Mars Inc. The plant specializes in producing chocolate "liquor" (pure liquid cocoa), shipping nationally to eight other plants. Virtually every chocolate product made by Mars begins in Elizabethtown. The company's research and development facility is located at the Elizabethtown plant.

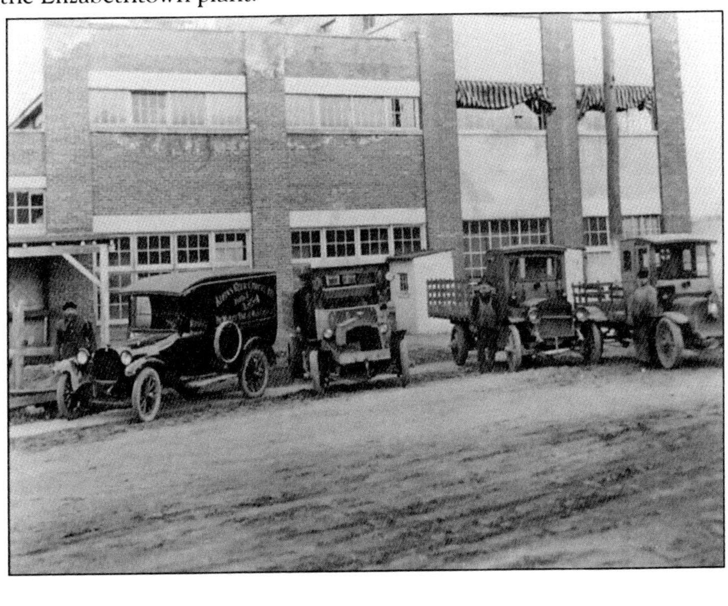

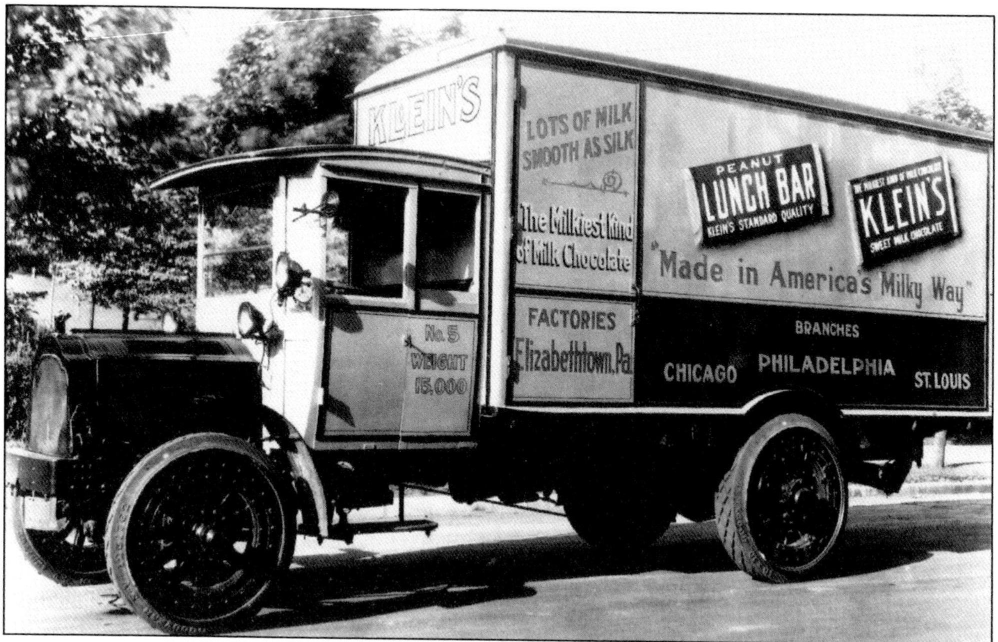

The Klein's factory had a hospital with a registered nurse on duty every day. The Klein Chocolate Company Relief Association, begun in 1923, provided unemployment insurance to workers. In 1924, Klein's provided life insurance for its employees. William Klein constructed a small six-hole golf course at the chocolate factory when his plans for building the Elizabethtown Country Club failed in 1929 as a result of the stock market crash.

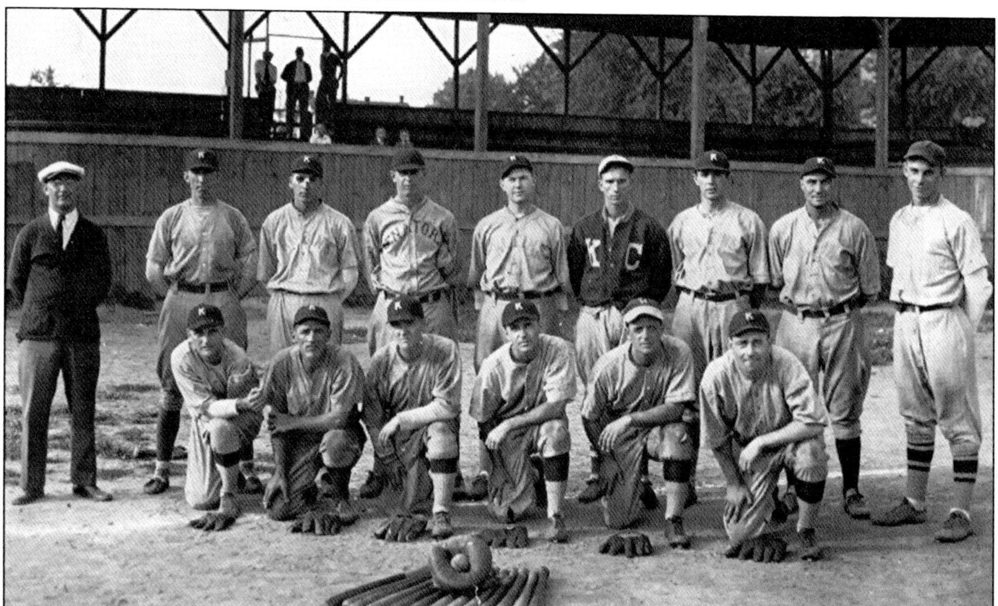

In the 1920s, the Klein Chocolate Company Athletic Field was built, with the factory sponsoring a semiprofessional baseball team. In one week, it defeated the Brooklyn Dodgers, Washington Senators, and Boston Red Sox. It played local teams, such as the African American Harrisburg Marvels. In 1931, the Klein team played the Israelite House of David team, featuring the star of the 1926 World Series, Grover Cleveland Alexander.

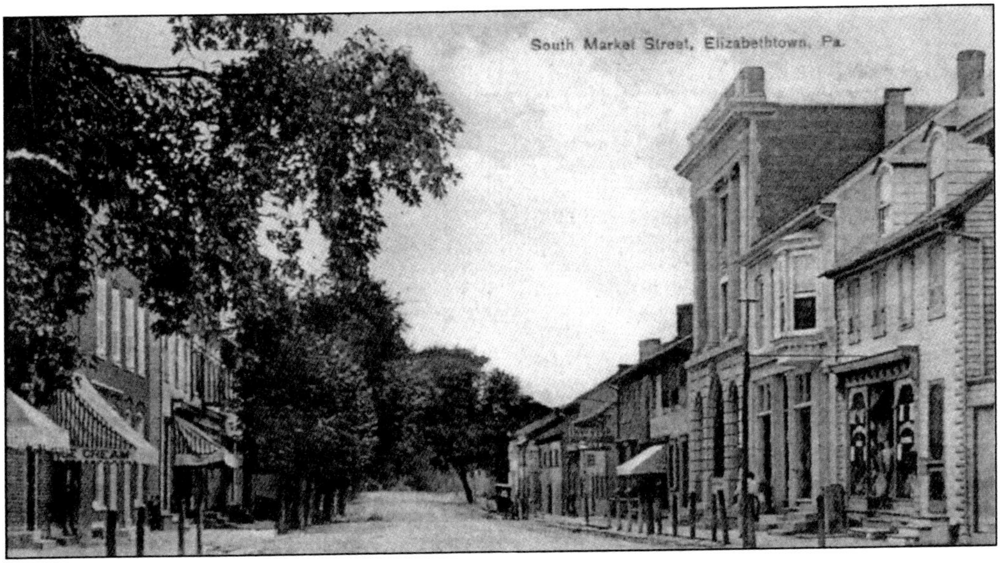

The first bank serving Elizabethtown was the Marietta and Susquehanna Trading Company, established by Jacob Gish at George Shocker's tavern. Jacob Gish created the Bank of Swatara. The Union Bank of Lancaster offered stock to investors in Elizabethtown at Michael Coble's Inn. Abram Collins established the Farmer's Bank of Elizabethtown at 244 South Market Street in 1869. Collins's daughter married Mennonite Samuel Eby, who managed the bank. In the 1870s, the bank went public, becoming First National Bank before reverting back to a private bank and failing in January 1885. Collins withdrew his interest in the bank when Eby lost his investments in the Reading, Marietta & Hanover Railroad. Under the National Bank Act of 1864, the Elizabethtown National Bank shown in the photographs was organized in 1885.

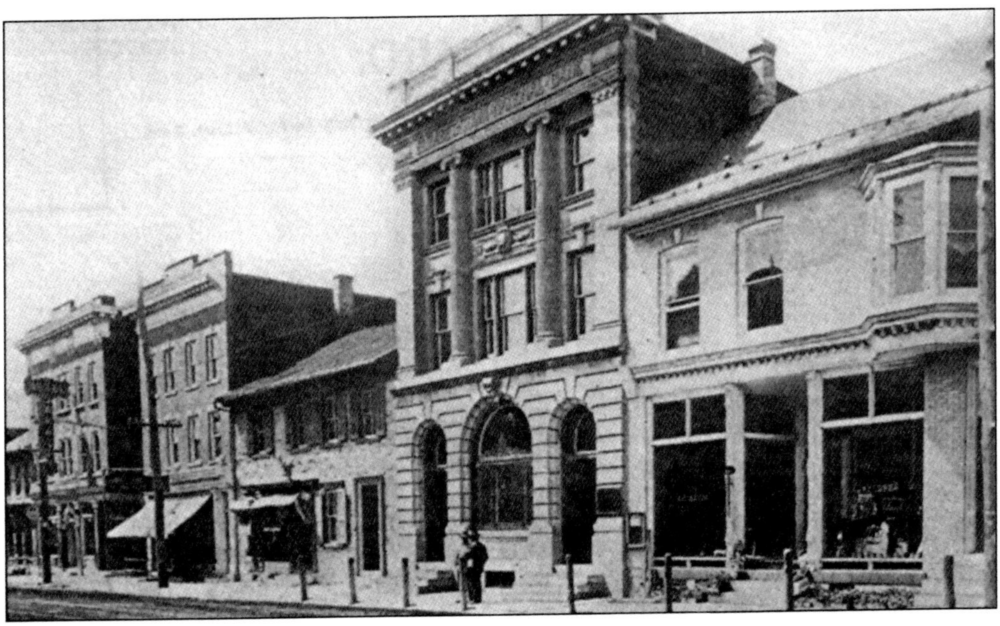

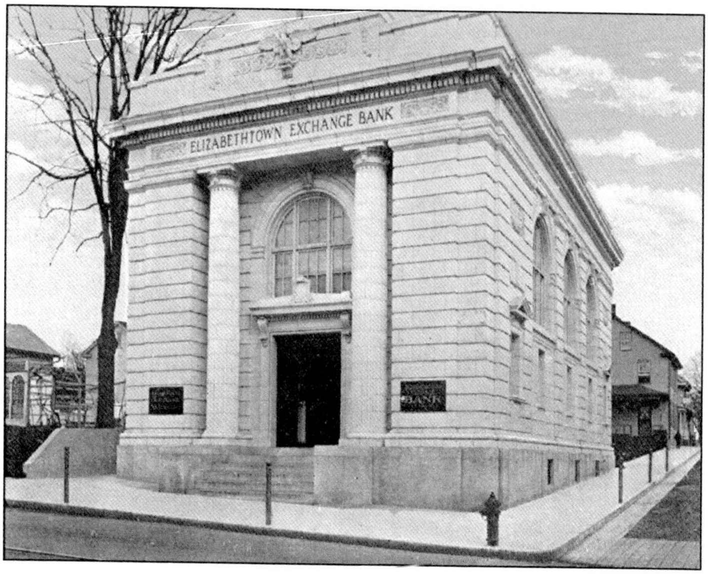

The Elizabethtown Exchange Bank opened on March 8, 1887, in the Brethren A.G. Heisey Building at 244 South Market Street. In 1917, the bank moved to a new building on the corner of South Market and East Washington Streets. Located in the same building today, the bank became the Elizabethtown Trust Company in 1927 before merging with Farmers First Bank in 1981.

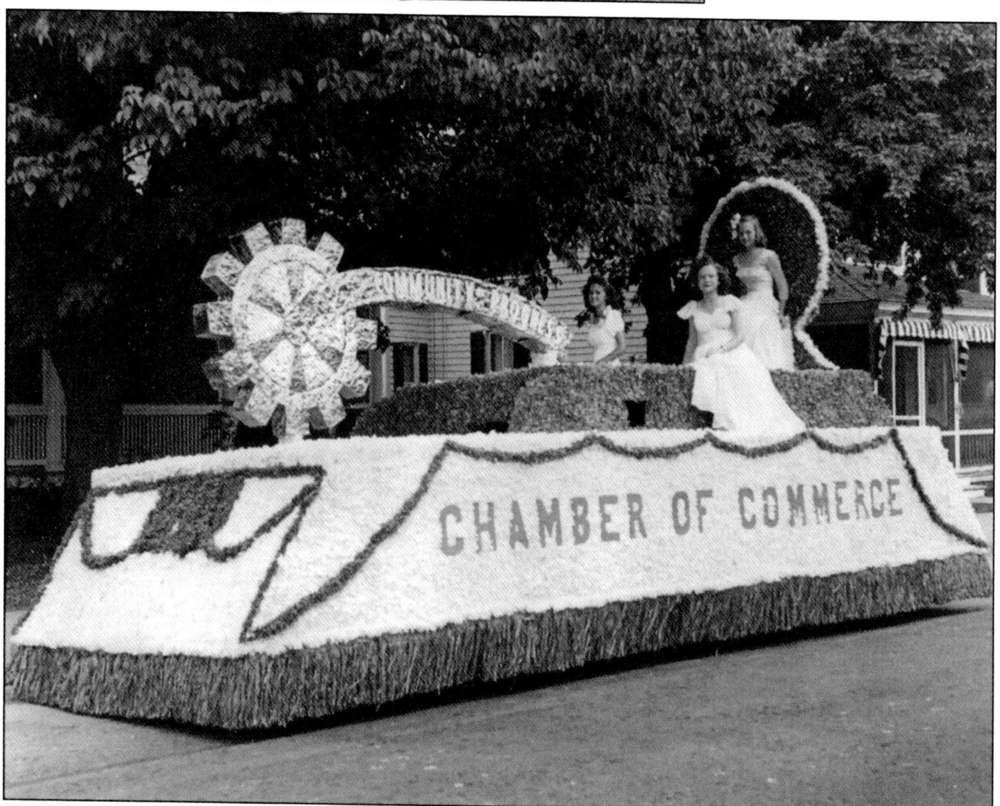

The Elizabethtown Chamber of Commerce was organized in 1928. Today, it is located in the train station at 50 South Wilson Avenue. In 2011, the station underwent a $9.4 million renovation, mindful of principles of historic preservation. The work resulted in more than doubling the length of the elevated platforms reached by new elevators, a bus shelter, expanded car park, and improved waiting area with an automated ticket machine. The station serves over 100,000 riders annually.

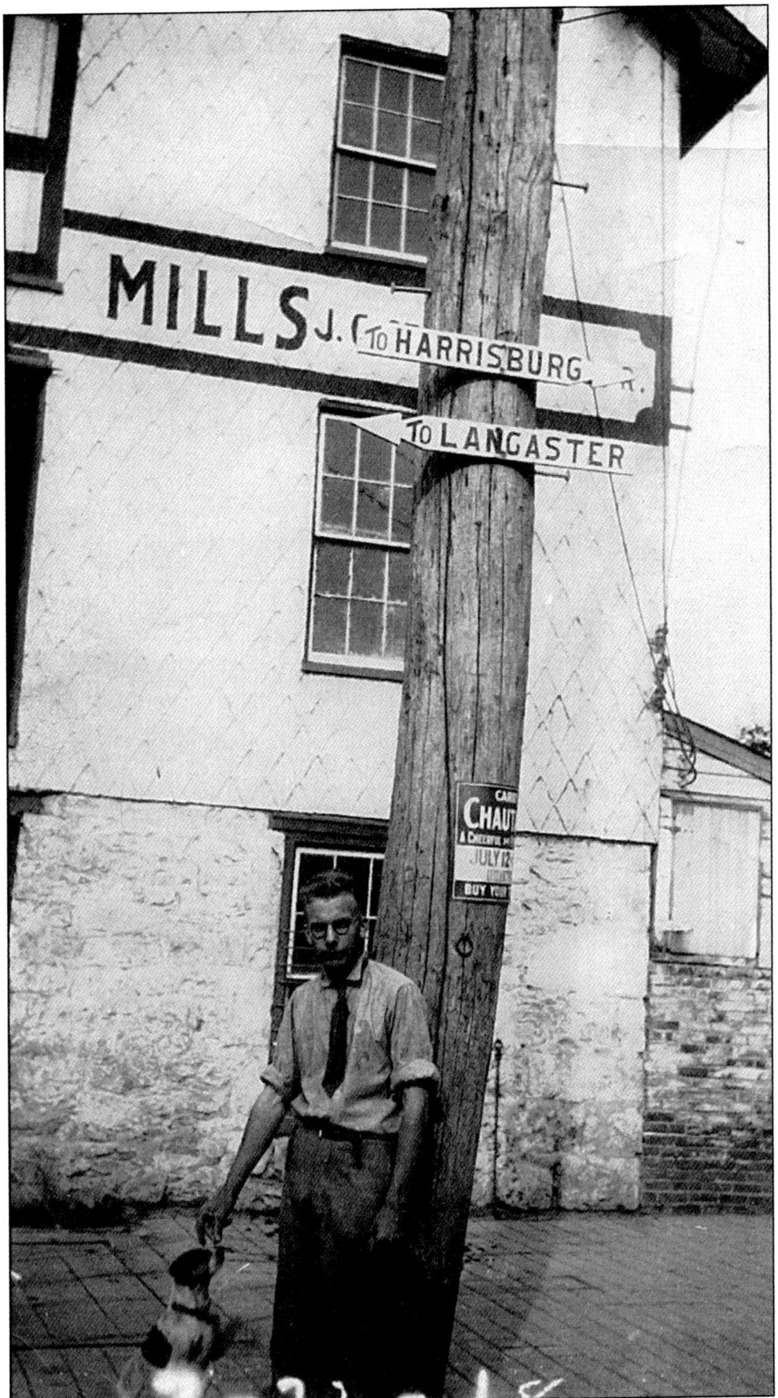

Elizabethtown councilman J. Harvey Buch convinced founders of Elizabethtown College and the Masonic Village to locate in Elizabethtown, arguing that the location was strategic, as the town was "eighteen miles from Harrisburg, eighteen miles from Lancaster, eighteen miles from Lebanon, eighteen miles from York, six miles from the Susquehanna River and on the Pennsylvania Railroad." The man in the photograph is not identified.

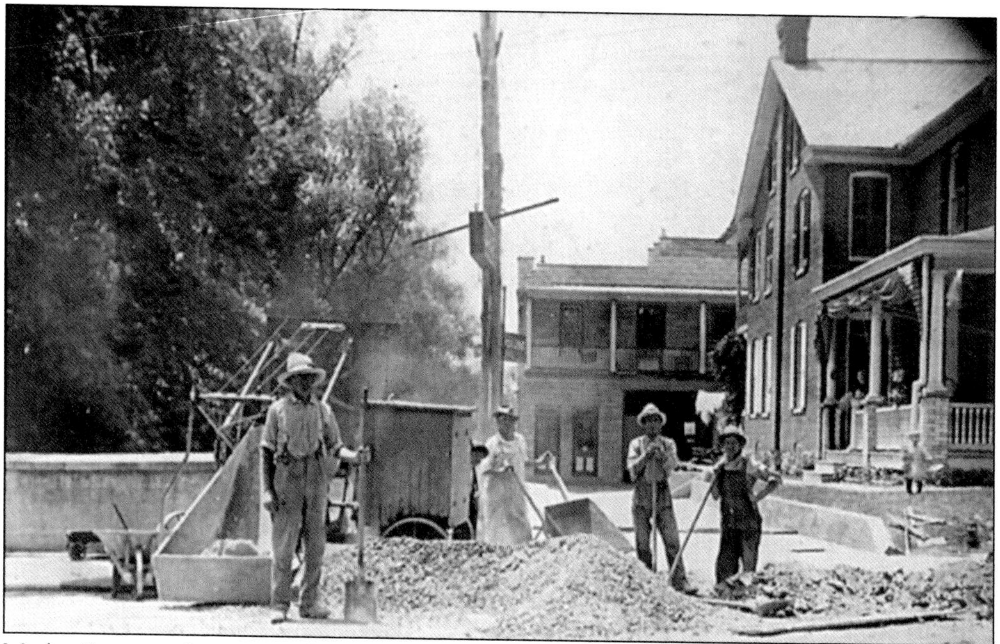

Market Street in downtown Elizabethtown is the original Harrisburg Turnpike or PA Route 230. Prior to the completion of the Pennsylvania Turnpike in 1940, the path of US Route 230, US Route 30 (the Lincoln Highway), Market Street, and the Harrisburg Pike was the most direct route from Philadelphia to the state capital. In 1794, the Philadelphia & Lancaster Turnpike Road Company completed the first turnpike in North America. It facilitated agricultural commerce between Lancaster and Philadelphia. In 1805, the Lancaster and Susquehanna Turnpike was built, linking Lancaster to Columbia along the Susquehanna River. In 1804, the Lancaster, Elizabethtown & Middletown Turnpike Company was chartered. The Falmouth & Elizabethtown Turnpike Company was incorporated in 1810.

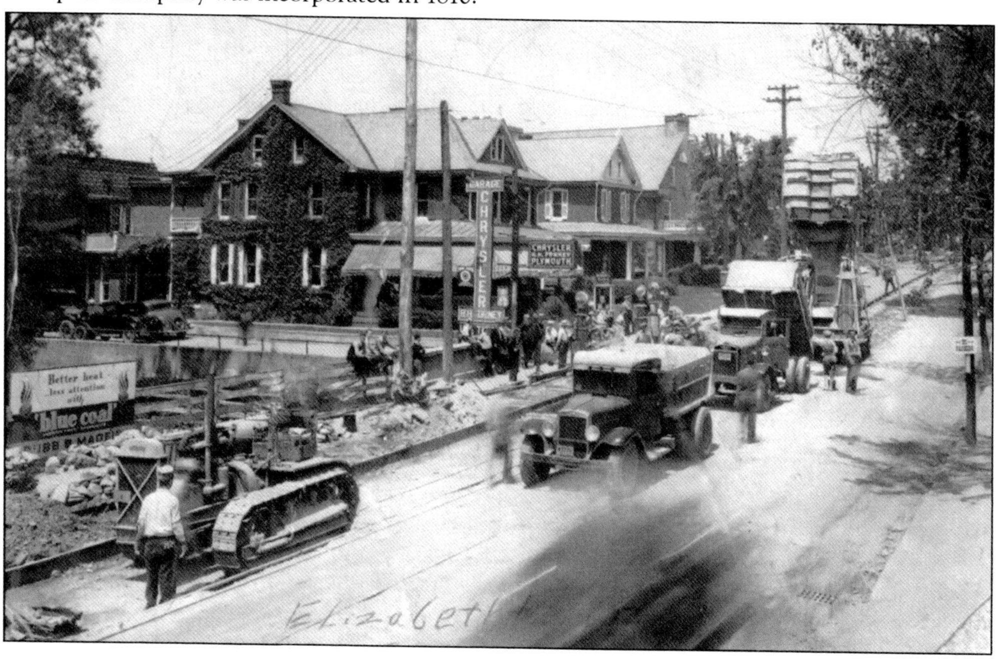

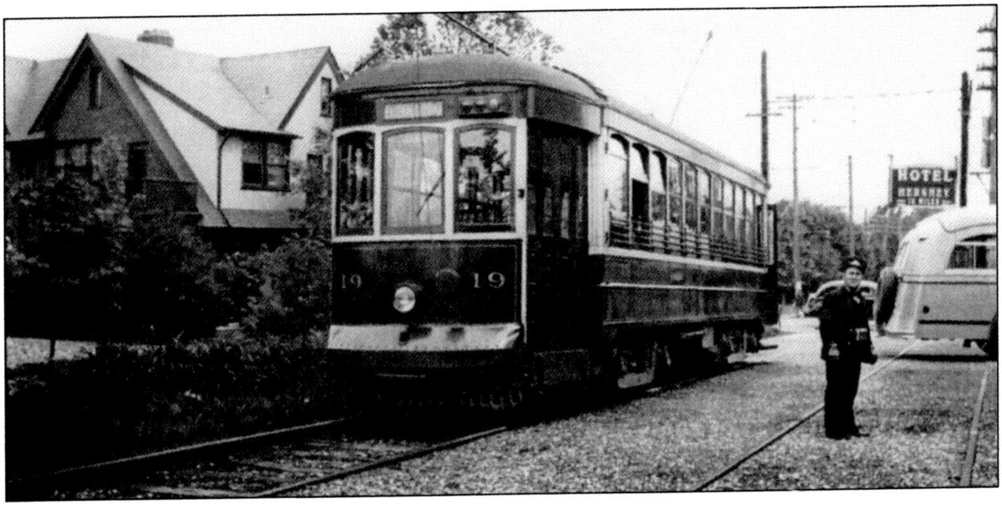

In 1906, Elizabethtown & Florin Street Railway Company laid tracks linking Elizabethtown to Lancaster. The Conestoga Traction Line operated the electric trolley cars. The first trolley car entered Elizabethtown from Lancaster on August 30, 1908. In 1915, the Hershey Transit Company opened, connecting Hershey to Elizabethtown. The Hershey Chocolate Company built milk stations along the line. Farmers brought cans of milk to the stations, such as the one located at the intersection of North Market Street and Linden Avenue. The Hershey Transit Company transported milk and workers to the Hershey and Klein chocolate factories.

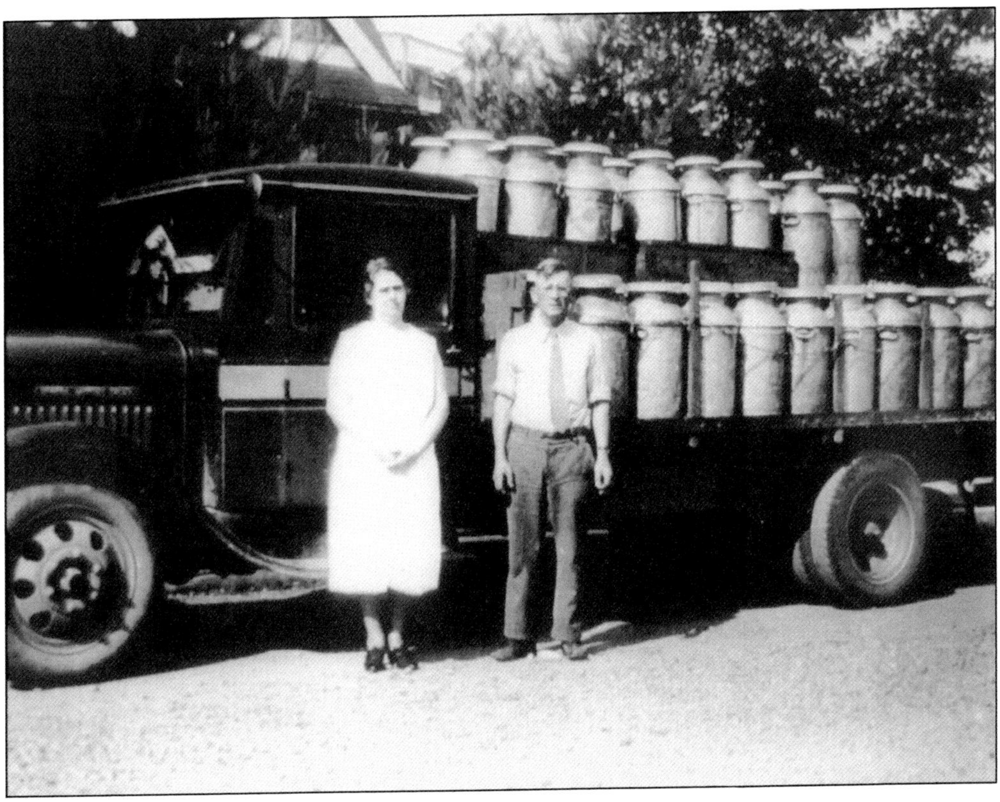

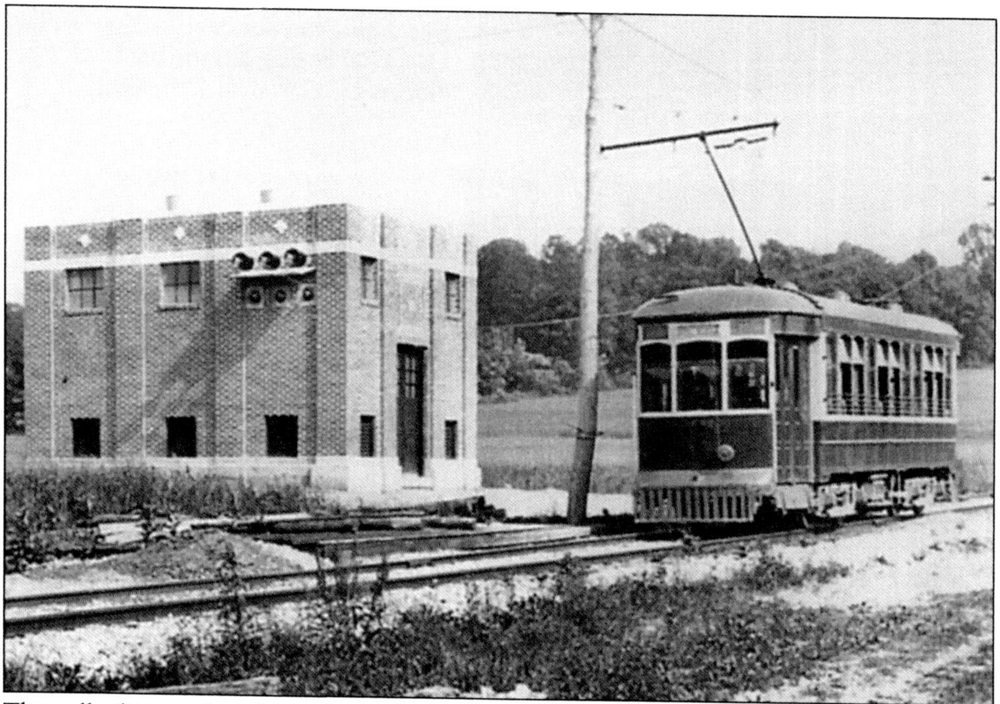

The trolley line ran from Lancaster to the center of Elizabethtown, where passengers could transfer to the Hershey trolley line running down East High Street. In Hershey, transfers were available to trolley lines to Harrisburg and Hummelstown. In these photographs, passengers are reaching the final destination in front of the Greenawalt Inn on Diamond Square (below) and passing the substation on the way to Hershey (above).

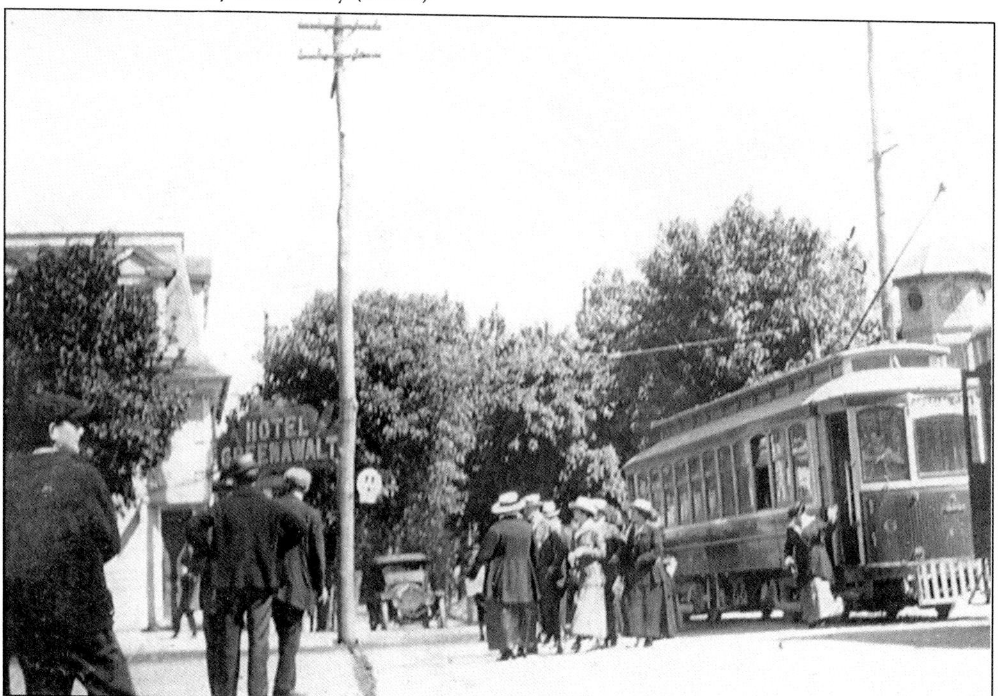

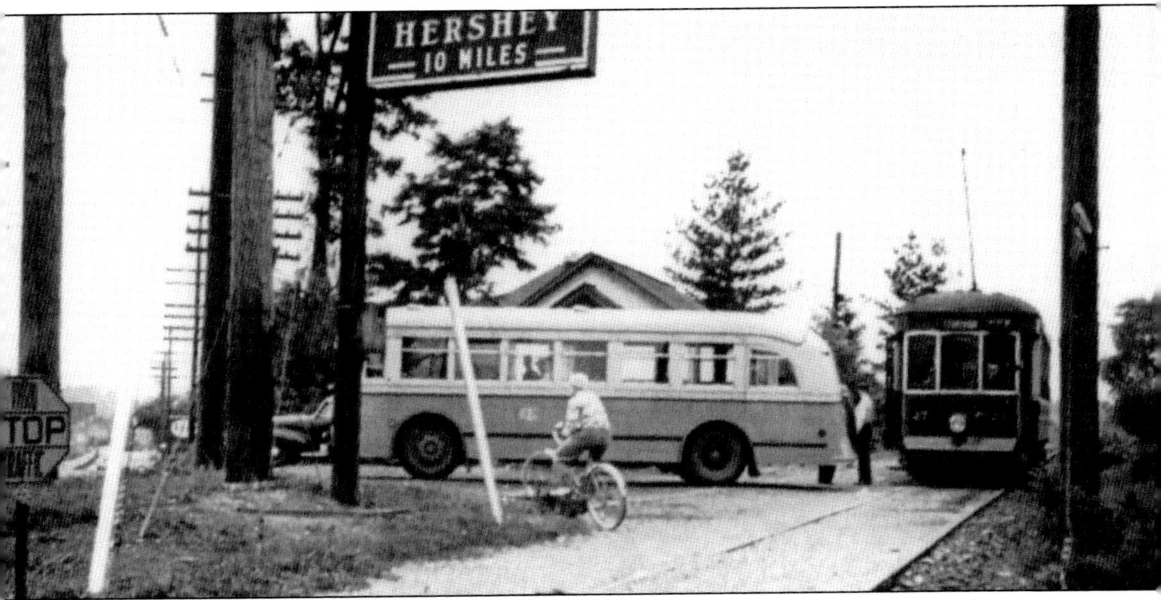

Market Street was unpaved when the trolley lines were installed. In 1909, both North and South Market Streets were macadamized with stone from the Heisey Quarry. In 1931, the Conestoga Transportation Company took over the franchise of the Conestoga Traction Company, replacing the existing network of trolley lines with motor buses. The last trolley car from Lancaster entered Elizabethtown on June 13, 1932; dismantling of the line began the same day.

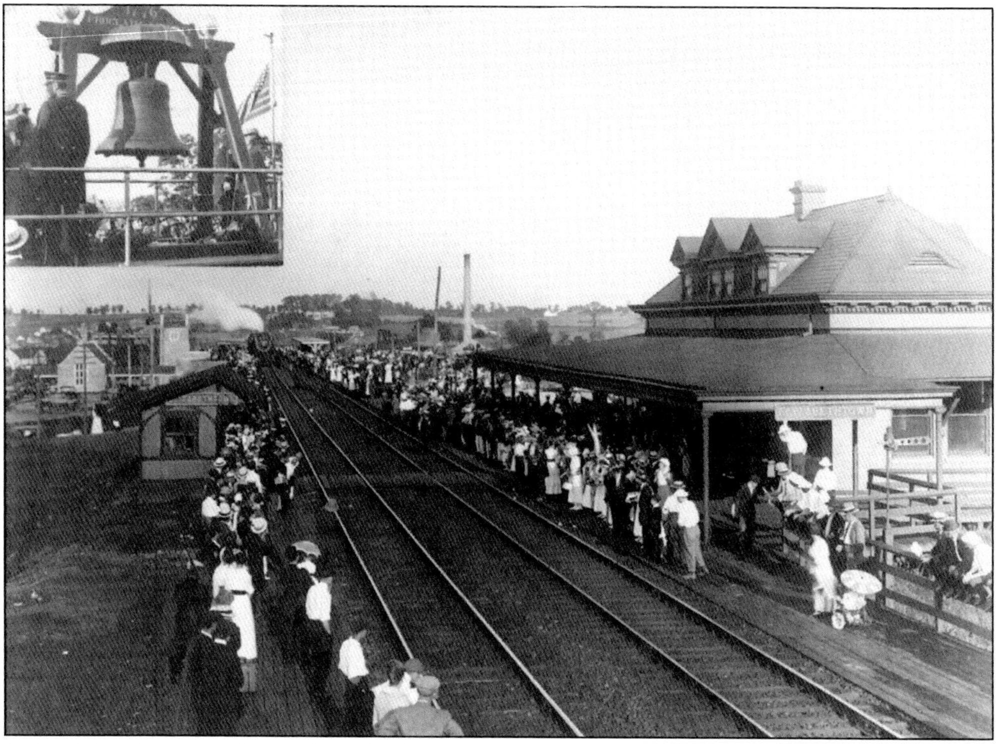

In 1797, the Conewago Canal along the Susquehanna River opened, improving navigation between Columbia and Middletown. The Union Canal connecting Reading to Middletown opened in 1828. By 1834, the Main Line of Public Works, a system of interlocking canals and railways, transported passengers and freight between Philadelphia and Pittsburgh. The Pennsylvania General Assembly granted a charter to the Portsmouth, Mount Joy & Lancaster Railroad Company for construction of a single-track line between Lancaster and Harrisburg. Elizabethtown's Andrew Wade was one of the contractors. The first station was erected on West High Street. In 1839, Zenos Wells built the Railroad Hotel on West Bainbridge Street. By 1858, postmaster James Lynch, ticket and freight agent, owned the Railroad House. In May 1874, a spark from a locomotive started a fire that burned down the railroad station and Railroad Hotel.

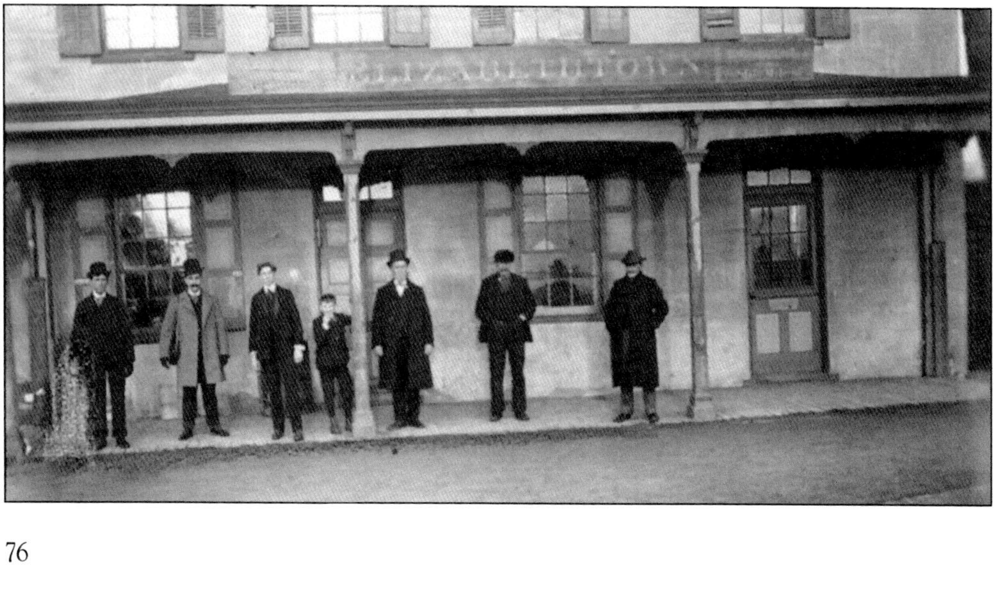

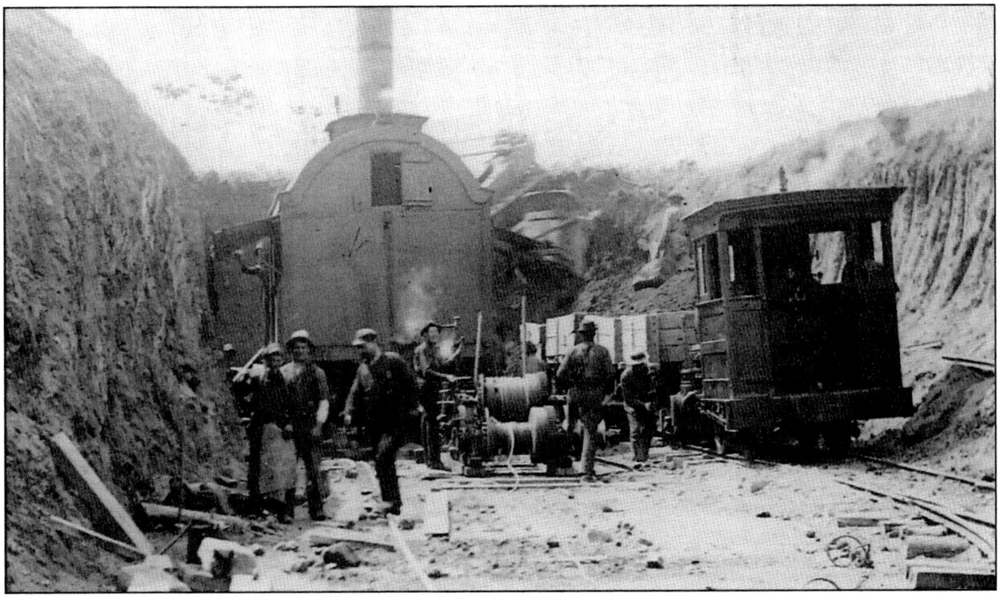

The most formidable task in building the railroad was cutting a tunnel through the solid rock of Red Hill in Elizabethtown. As with the canals, most of the work for building the railroad was completed by Irish immigrants. In building the tunnel through Red Hill, later known as Tunnel Hill and today as Mount Tunnel, two Irish workers, George Redmond and Michael Daly, died. They are buried in the cemetery of St. Peter's Catholic Church. In 1898–1899, the Pennsylvania Railroad constructed the present two-track line. The old tunnel through Red Hill was removed, creating an open passage. On July 4, 1915, the Liberty Bell stopped at the Elizabethtown station while being transported to the Panama-Pacific International Exposition in San Francisco. Jacob N. Olweiler arranged for the Liberty Bell's train to visit Elizabethtown, where 7,000 people gathered at the station.

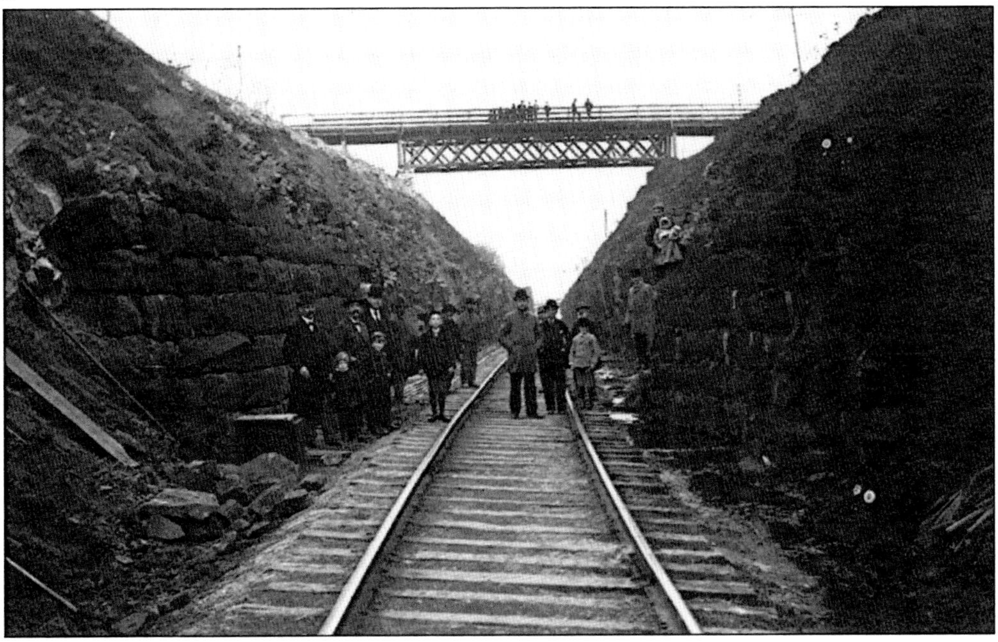

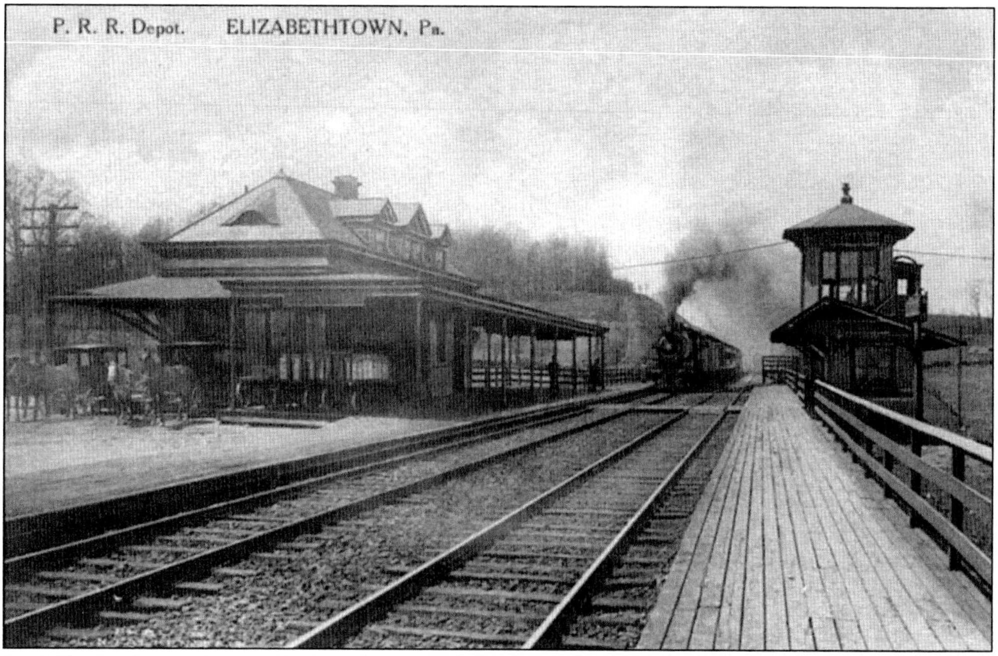

In 1857, the Pennsylvania Railroad acquired the line of public works between Philadelphia and Pittsburgh from the Commonwealth of Pennsylvania. This included the state-owned railroad between Philadelphia and Columbia. In 1861, the Pennsylvania Railroad leased the privately owned Harrisburg, Portsmouth, Mount Joy & Lancaster Railroad for 999 years. Elizabethtown was now a stop on the Pennsylvania Railroad main line. In 1900, the Pennsylvania Railroad employees constructed a new railroad station 100 feet west of the railroad bridge over West High Street. A large buff-colored brick structure stood on the eastbound track (above, left), and a frame waiting room stood on the opposite side (above, right) for passengers waiting for westbound trains. With the building of the Masonic Village, the Pennsylvania Railroad in 1915 constructed a new station (below) out of the same Indiana limestone as that used for the buildings on the Masonic campus.

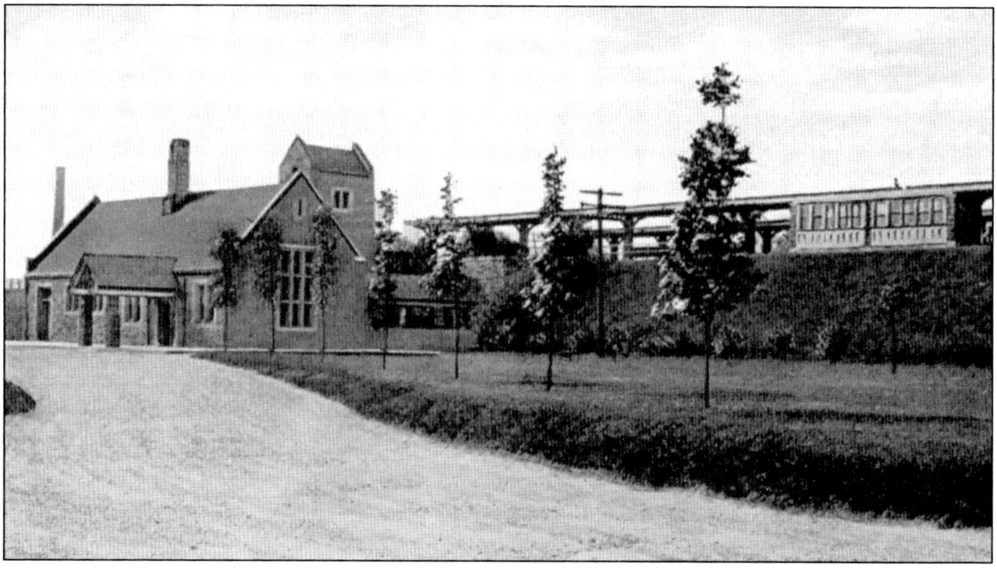

Three

CAMPUSES

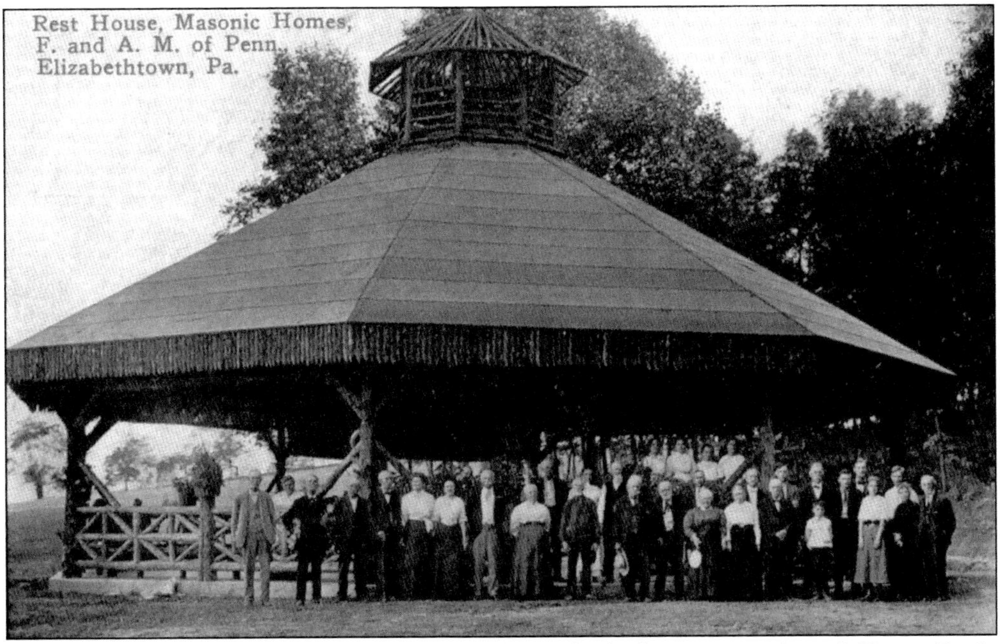

Residents pose on the campus of the Masonic Village. Elizabethtown councilman J. Harvey Buch, of Buch Manufacturing, chaired a citizens committee appealing to the German Baptist Brethren to locate its college in Elizabethtown. Buch served on a committee of Masons encouraging the Pennsylvania Grand Lodge to locate its home for children, widows, and elderly Masons in Elizabethtown. Gov. Gifford Pinchot chose Elizabethtown as the location for a state hospital for children.

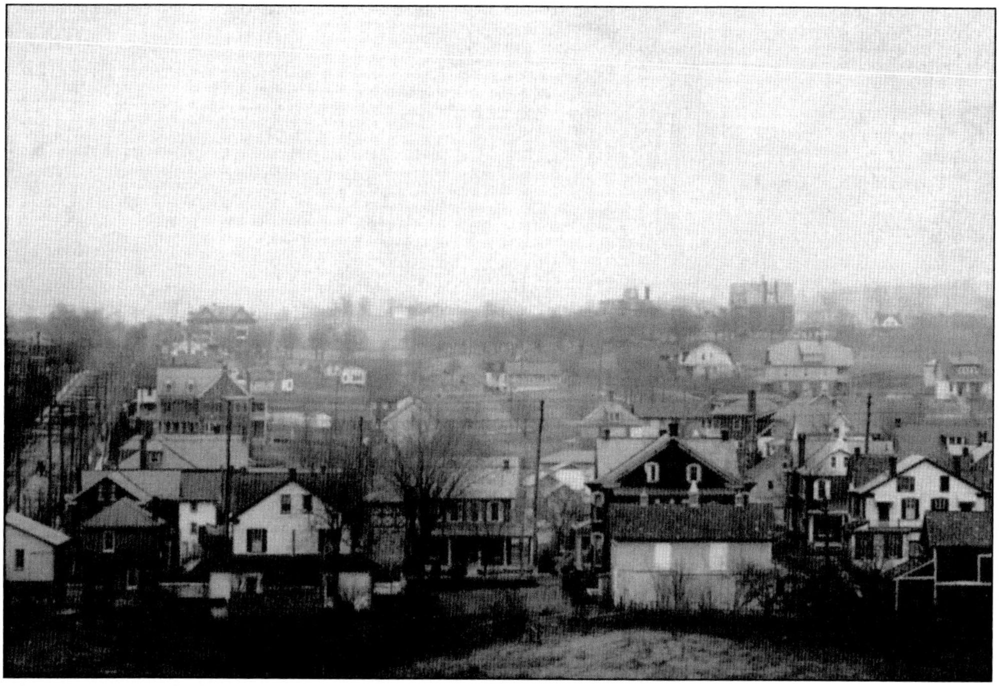

This is a view of Elizabethtown College from the railroad station. The campus was established on 10 acres owned by Brethren Benjamin G. Groff of Groff Mills. The brothers Royer S. and J. Harvey Buch of the Brethren firm Buch Manufacturing paid one third; their father, Adison Buch, trustee of the Elizabethtown Church of the Brethren, paid one third; and Groff donated the remaining third of the tract to the college.

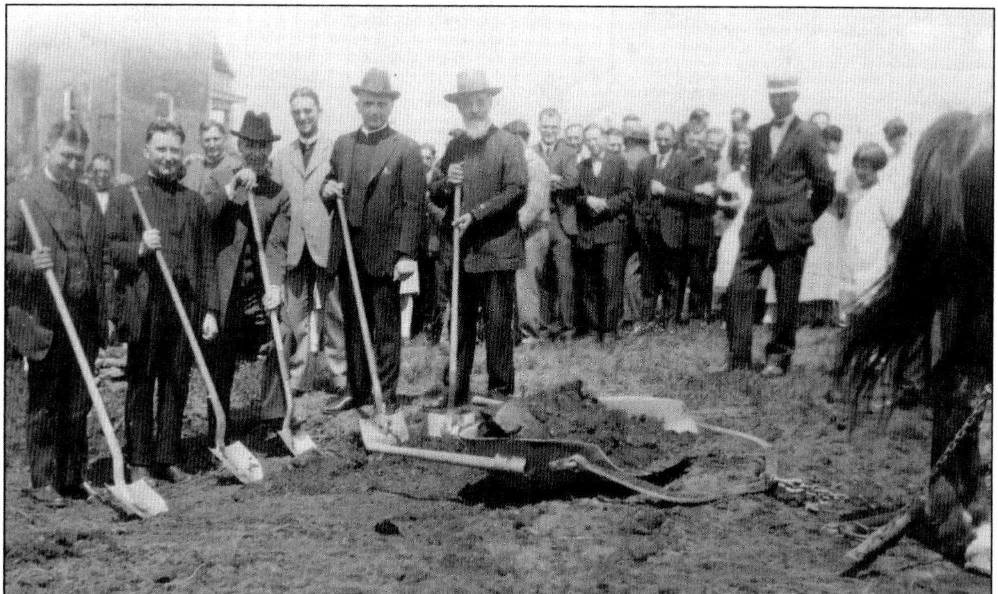

Ground breaking takes place at the Groff farm for Alpha Hall in 1899. George Falkenstein (sixth from left with shovel) designed Alpha Hall with plans drafted by architect A.A. Richter of Lebanon. Benjamin Groff was the contractor. Alpha Hall was dedicated on March 4, 1901.

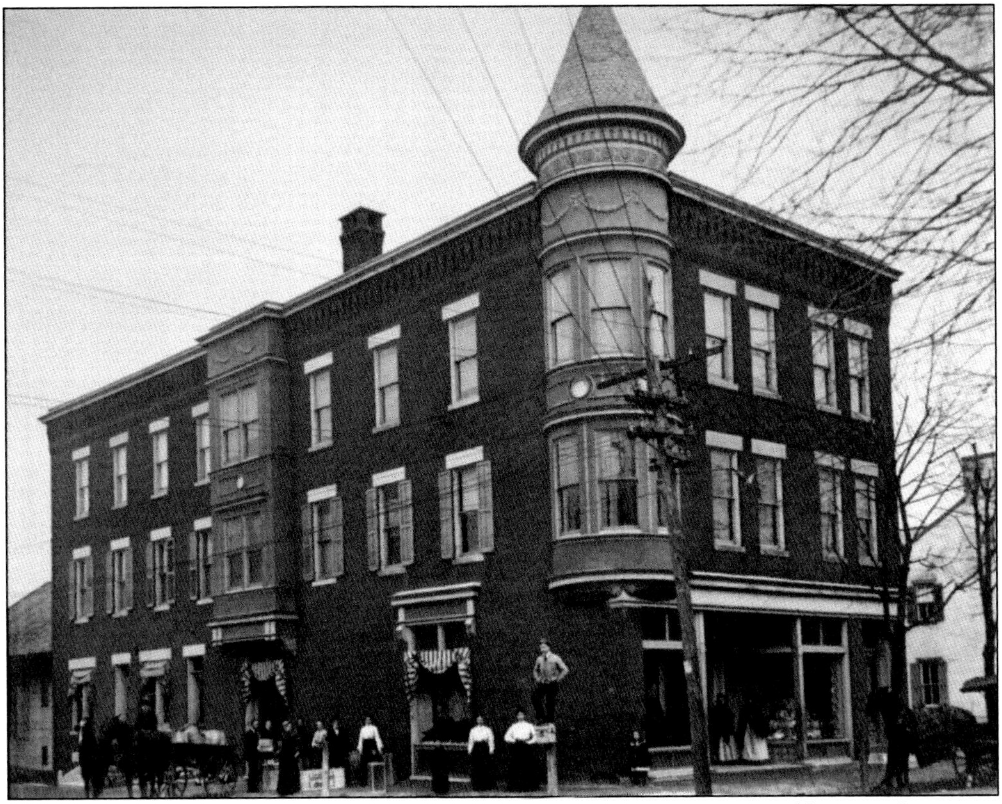

Alpha Hall was not completed on time, so the third floor of the Heisey Building, on the corner of South Market and Bainbridge Streets, was rented. Falkenstein held opening exercises on November 13, 1900. The first students, the "Faithful Six," were all men; among them were John Boll and Willis Heisey of Elizabethtown.

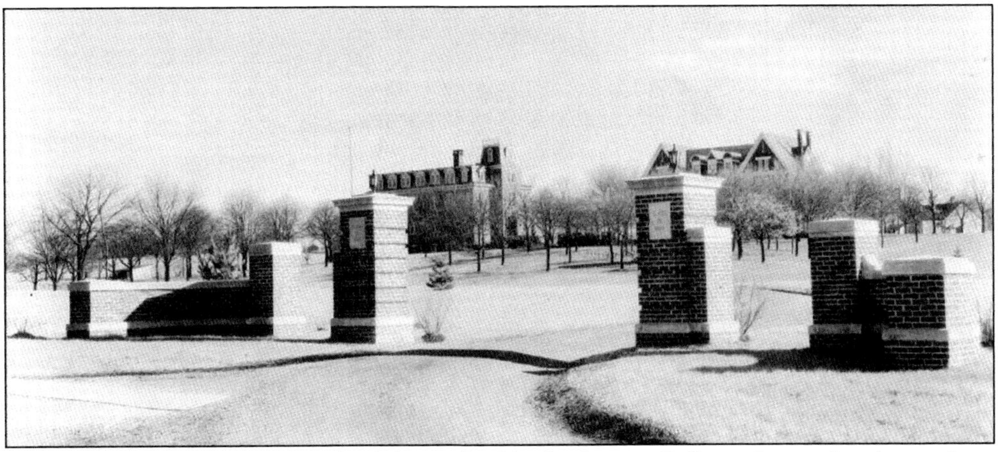

Shown here are Rider (left) and Alpha Halls. Elizabethtown College obtained a charter from the Commonwealth of Pennsylvania in September 1899. The incorporators were Brethren grocer Simon P. Engle; Brethren banker J.H. Eshleman of the Elizabethtown Exchange Bank; Brethren Joseph G. Heisey, member of the board of directors of the Elizabethtown Exchange Bank; Brethren storekeeper Rev. Samuel H. Hertzler; and Brethren hardware dealer Joseph H. Rider, first president of the Elizabethtown Exchange Bank.

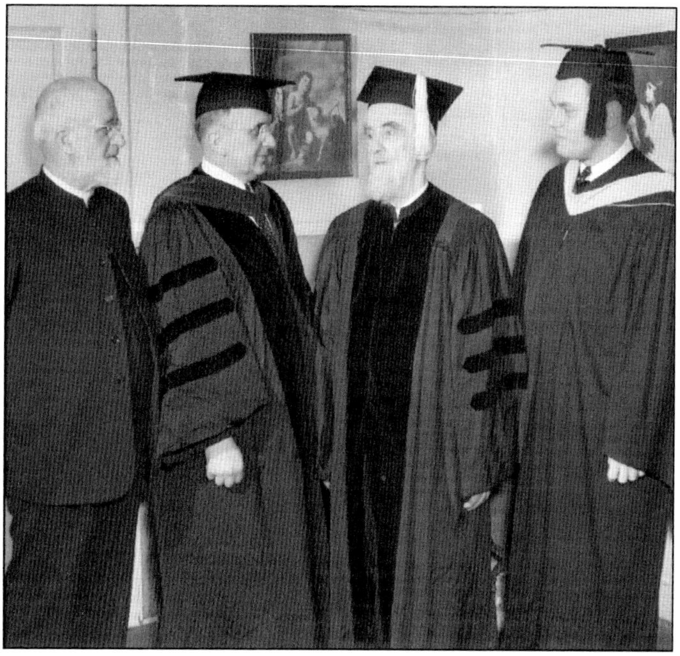

On November 20, 1948, the Elizabethtown College board of trustees conferred on George Falkenstein (second from right) an honorary doctor of divinity degree. He pastored the first Brethren church in America, Germantown Church of the Brethren. In addition, Falkenstein authored the history of the Brethren church, the first history of the college, the college constitution, and the college catalog. He was secretary of the board (1899–1903), acting principal (1900), and president (1901–1902). He taught history, government, and the classics.

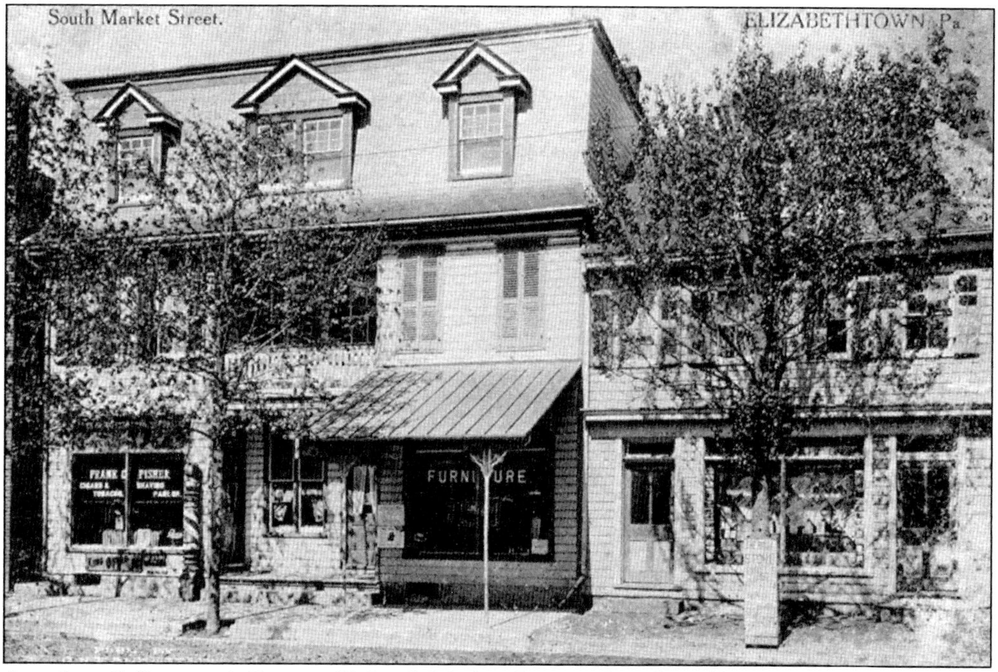

At right is Falkenstein's Store at 39 South Market Street, where he sold college textbooks, school supplies, and stationery. In addition, Falkenstein established a lending library, operated a printing press, and sold his postcards of Elizabethtown.

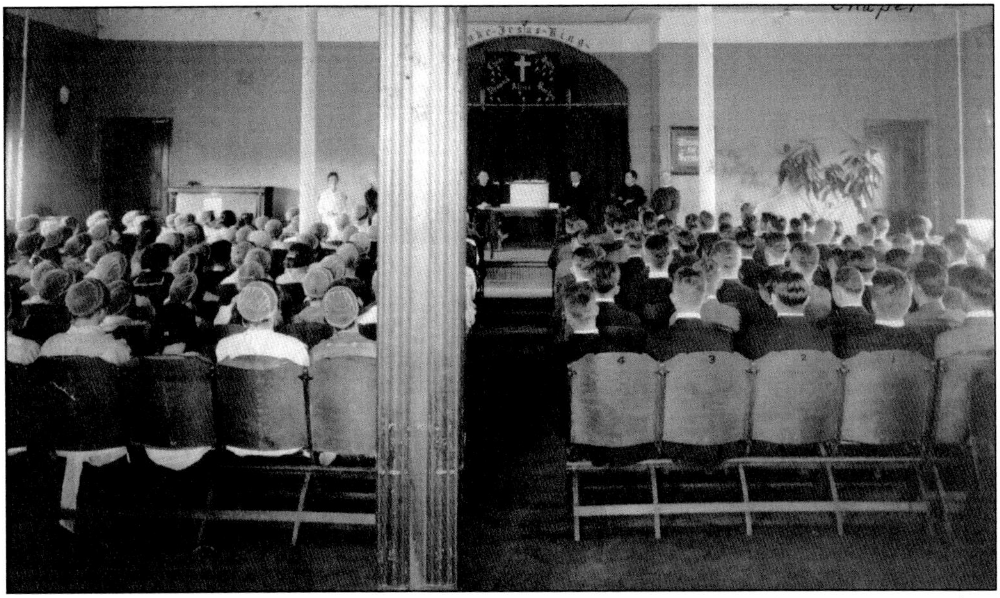

An important motivation for establishing a Brethren college was facilitating a curriculum based on the values of the Historic Peace Churches. In 1931, students Leroy Rosenberger and Ray Kurtz organized a "Peace Caravan," speaking at local churches about peacemaking. In 1951, college president Rev. Dr. A.C. Baugher was part of a delegation, the National Council Against Conscription, testifying before Congress against universal military training. (Courtesy Elizabethtown College.)

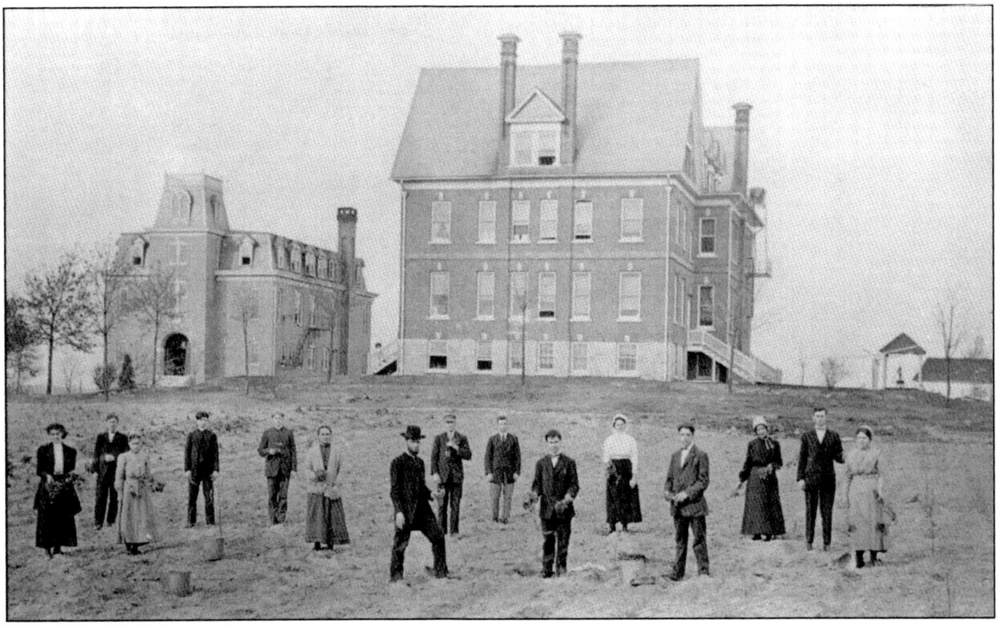

Despite its liberal arts curriculum, the school experimented with an agricultural education department, planting vegetable gardens and orchards. In July 1911, chickens were purchased and a poultry house was erected. Part of the coursework involved students helping President Ober survey the land developed into College Heights. By 1917, the experiment ended when only three students completed the program. (Courtesy Elizabethtown College.)

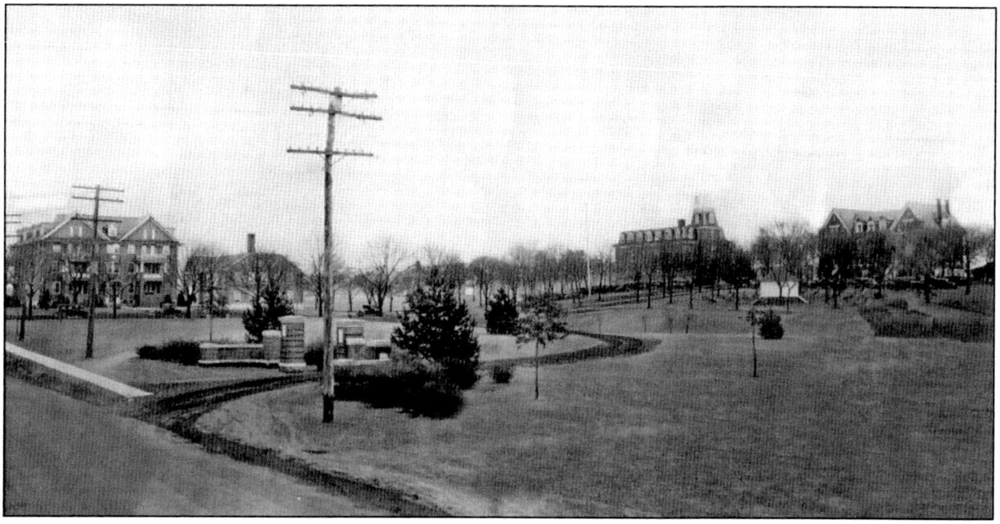

Elizabethtown native Isaiah Oberholtzer was the only student enrolled in the college preparatory course in 1902–1903. Oberholtzer transferred to Juniata College to graduate. Elizabethtown could not grant degrees until 1921; it was accredited in 1948. Lewis Rose (librarian/archivist for the Brethren Heritage Room in the college library) and Ralph Schlosser (Evangelist, English professor, and college president) had already graduated from college when they enrolled in 1907 for the classical courses curriculum.

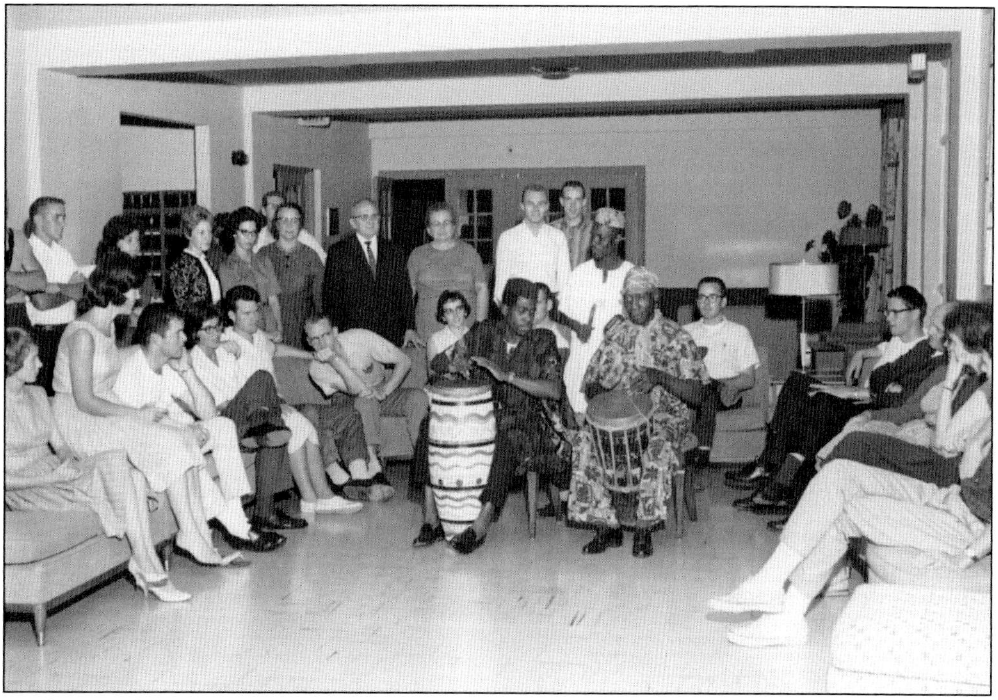

Students and faculty host educators from the Teachers for West Africa Program. In 1961, the college received a $250,000 grant from Hershey Foods to select, prepare, and support American teachers staffing high schools in Ghana and Nigeria. Teachers worked for two years, with a renewed contract by mutual agreement. In 1968, the college offered courses at the University of Ghana. (Courtesy Elizabethtown College.)

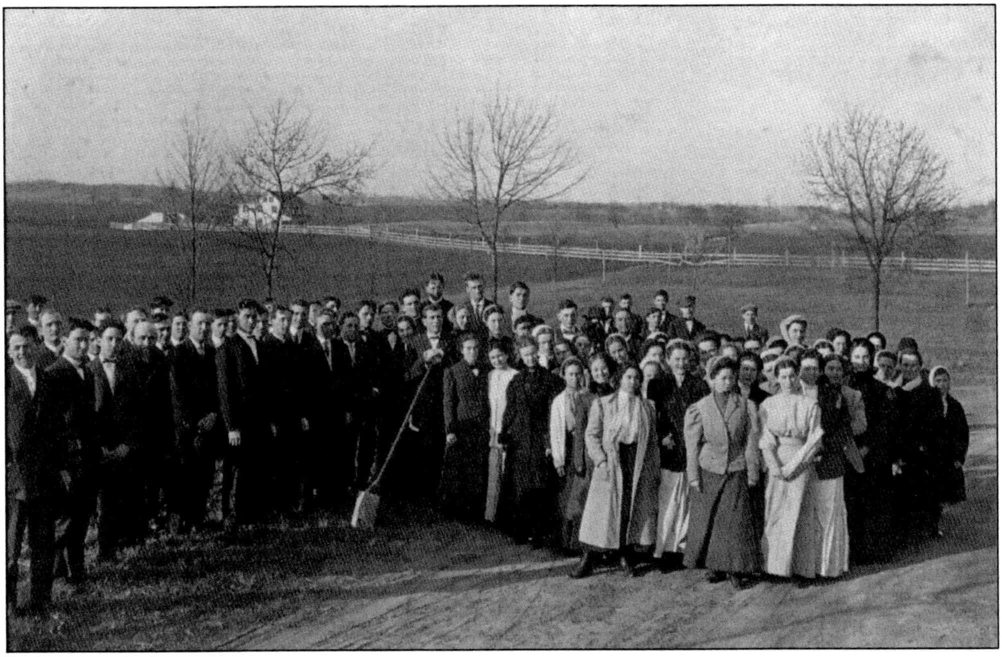

Shown here is Campus Improvement Day, April 6, 1901. Students and faculty planted 200 donated maple trees north of Alpha Hall. The first female student, Anna Brenneman of New Danville, a descendent of Elizabethtown founder Melchoir Brenneman, planted the first tree. (Courtesy Elizabethtown College.)

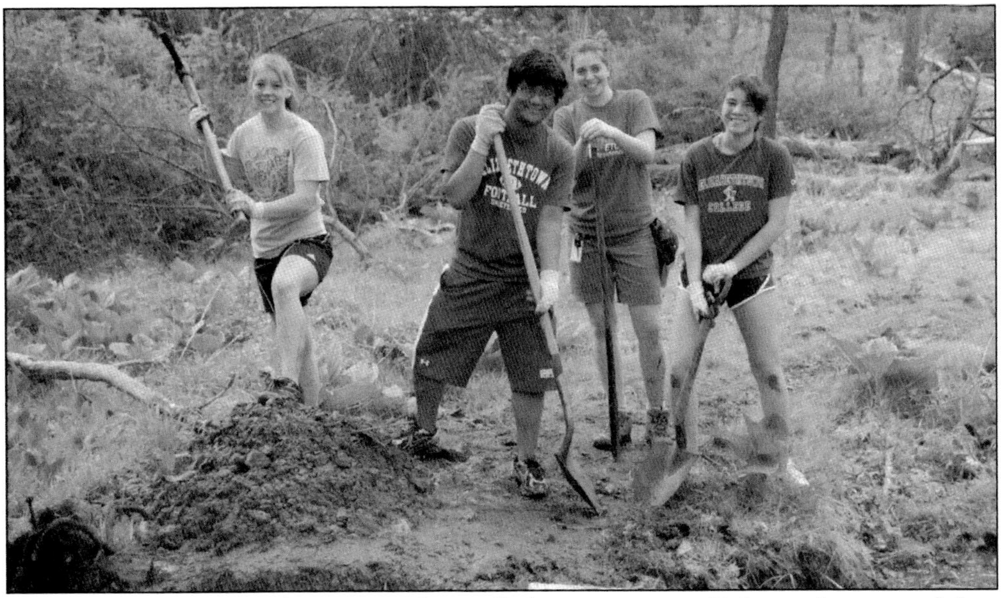

Campus Improvement Day has continued annually for over a century. Today, students expand their service beyond the campus. These students volunteered with the Appalachian Trail Conservancy in Michaux State Forest, 50 miles west of Elizabethtown. The college's Center for Community and Civic Engagement hosts "Into the Streets." This annual event engages over 650 students, faculty, staff, administrators, alumni, and community members in more than 55 community-service projects in Elizabethtown.

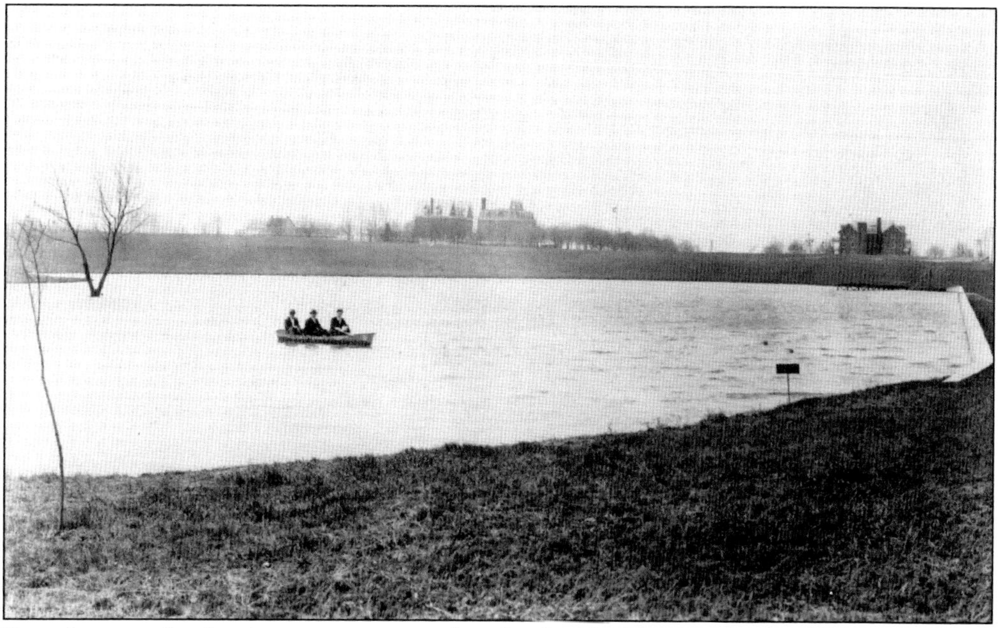

East of campus, land with a stream was purchased to build a lake. On April 1, 1925, Lake Placida was completed. Eli Engle (class of 1927) won the competition to name it. The lake's name, Placida ("peace"), is consistent with the values of the Historic Peace Churches that founded Elizabethtown College. Today, the college hosts the Center for Global Understanding and Peacemaking and offers a peace and conflict studies minor. (Courtesy Elizabethtown College.)

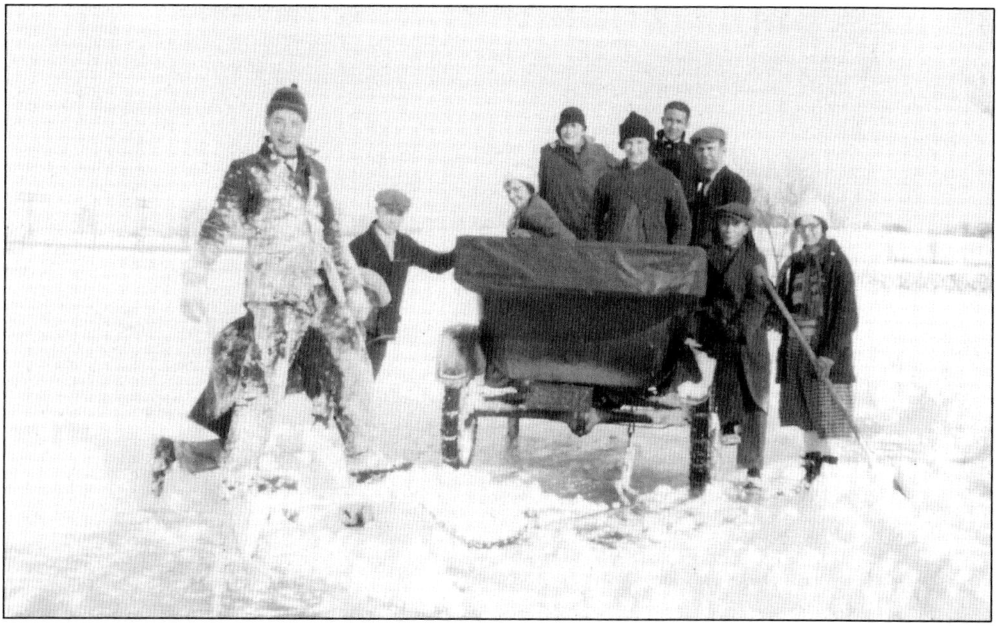

Students drive and skate on Lake Placida in 1925. In keeping with the values of the Church of the Brethren and Historic Peace Churches concerning peacemaking, nonviolence, and conscientious objection to war, the Elizabethtown College Alumni Peace Fellowship hosts two- and three-day residency programs on campus featuring prominent peace writers, scholars, and activists. This group sponsors the Paul M. Grubb Jr. Student Peace Award. (Courtesy Elizabethtown College.)

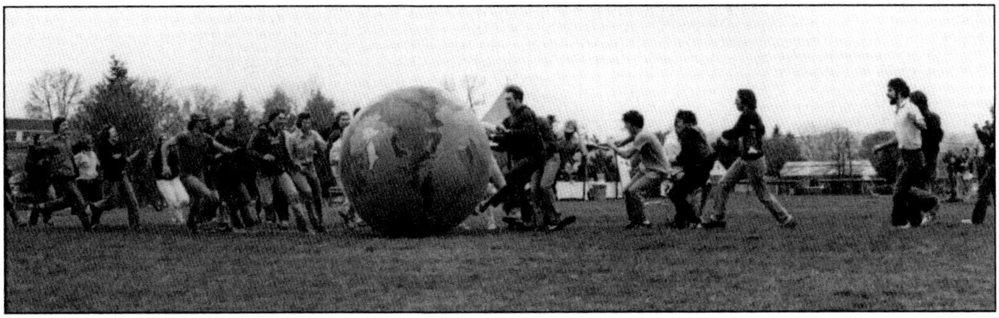

Students celebrate Earth Day in 1970. On March 28, 1979, at Three Mile Island nuclear power plant, six miles from Elizabethtown, the cooling system of reactor No. 2 failed. College president Mark Ebersole sent a resolution, adopted by the college, to Walter Creitz, president of Metropolitan Edison, urging permanent closure of TMI and a moratorium on all future nuclear plants. (Courtesy Elizabethtown College.)

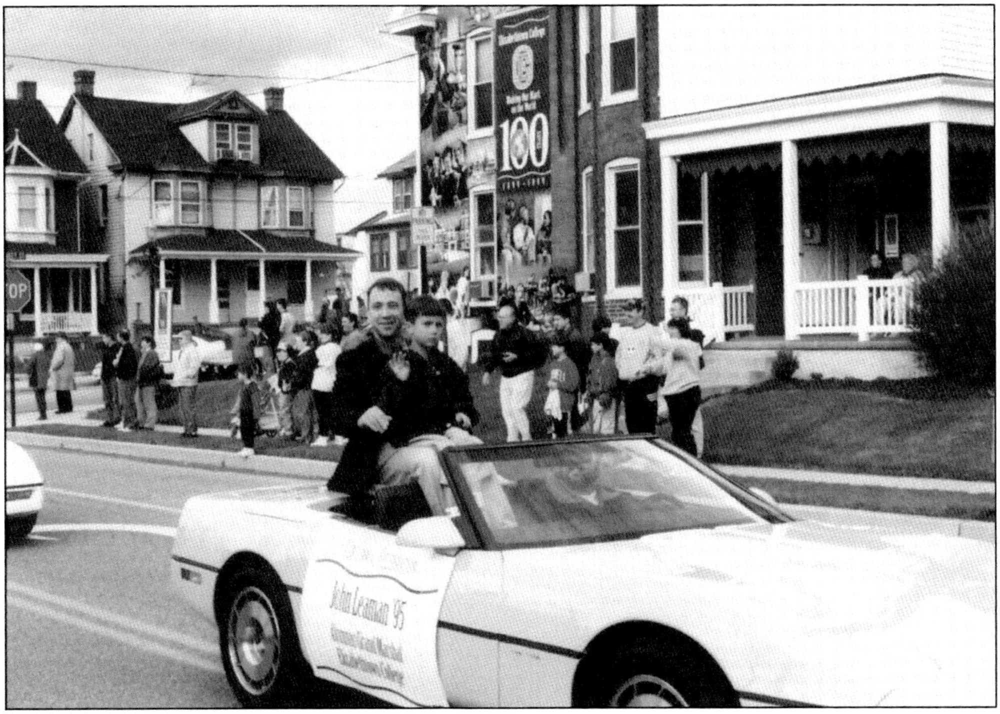

John H. Leaman (class of 1995) was the alumnus grand marshal for the College Centennial Parade in 1999. Leaman was the college's first Rhodes Scholar, in 1995. A biology major with a GPA of 3.94, he conducted independent research at Hershey Medical Center, captained the cross-country team, was a resident assistant, and participated in civic engagement. He studied two years at Oriel College of Oxford University, where he was president of the basketball team. (Courtesy Elizabethtown College.)

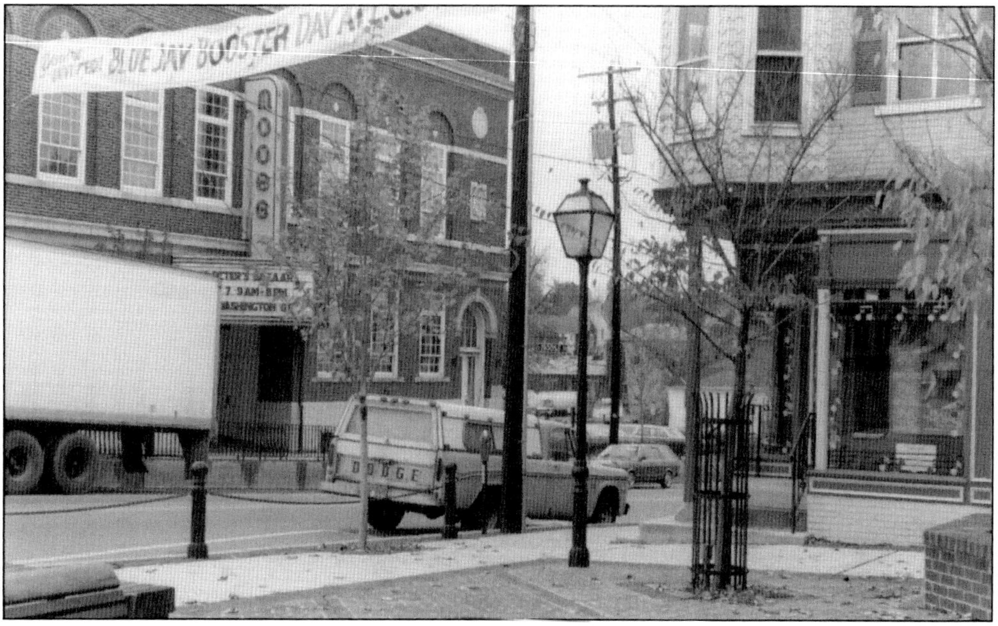

The community has offered strong support for college athletics. Initially, many Brethren church leaders associated intercollegiate athletics with student fraternities, class rushes, and hazing. When students requested permission to compete against teams from town, the board of trustees denied it, claiming "modern match games of baseball and football are not in accord with Christian virtue and true education." Today, there is a robust intercollegiate athletics program.

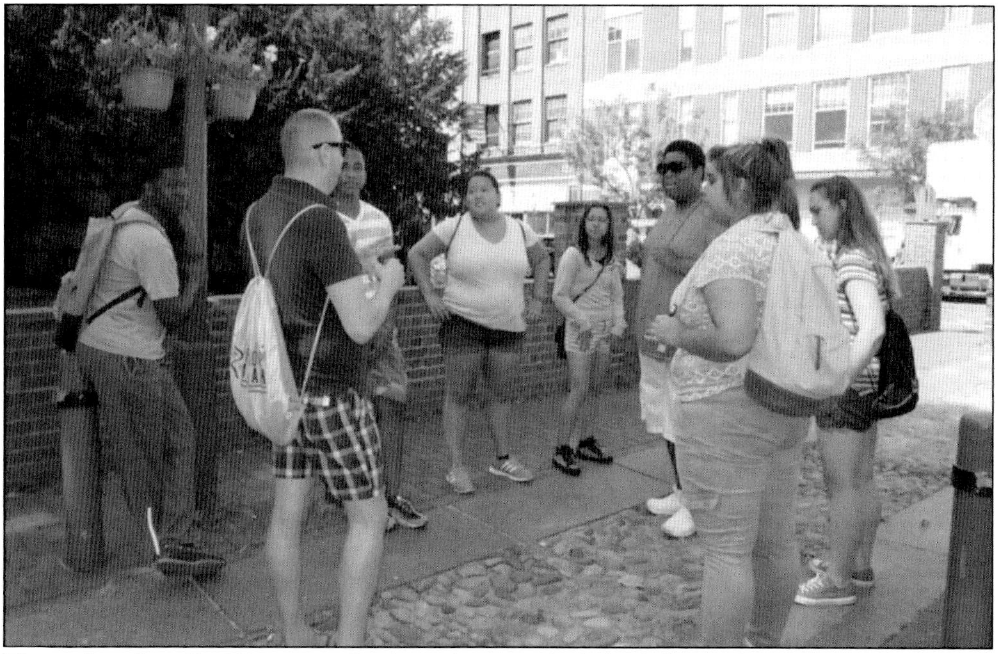

The author, Jean-Paul Benowitz (back to photographer), leads his students on a walking tour, exploring history, interpreting architecture and public art, and learning about historic preservation. Such field experiences compliment what students read and hear in the classroom. Experiential learning is emphasized in the college's curriculum.

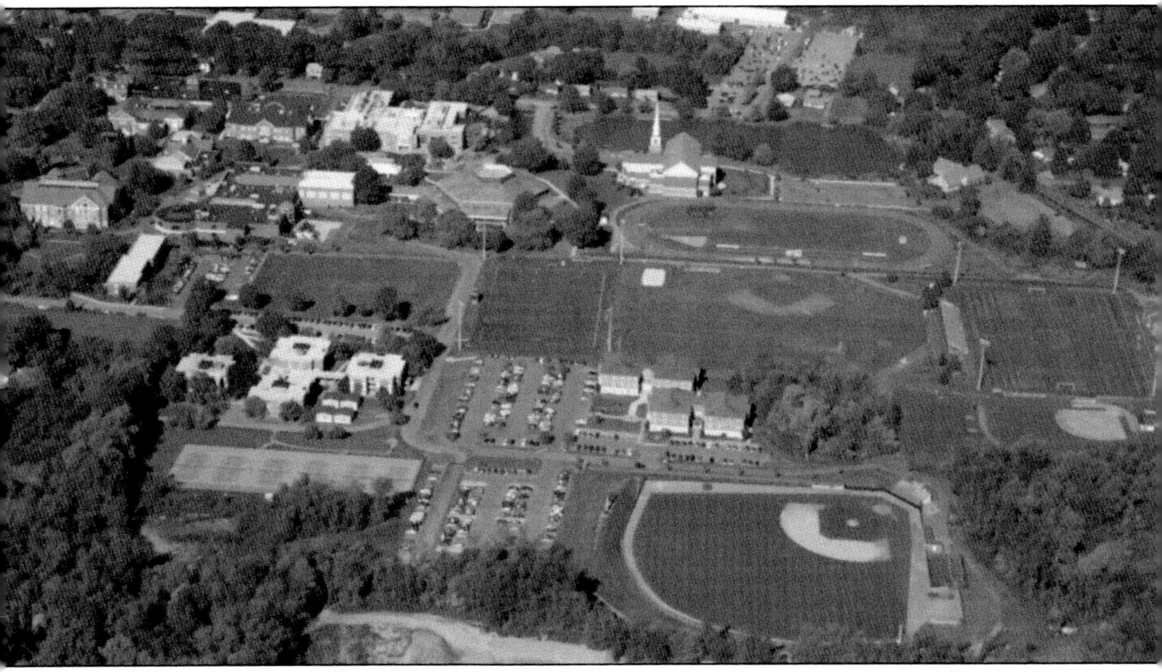

Today, Elizabethtown College has a 200-acre campus, 19 academic departments offering 53 majors and over 90 minors and concentrations, and students representing 30 states and 20 foreign countries, with a 12:1 student faculty ratio. The school has 20 NCAA Division III athletic teams, intramural and club sports, and over 80 student clubs, with an emphasis on academics and civic engagement. (Courtesy Elizabethtown College.)

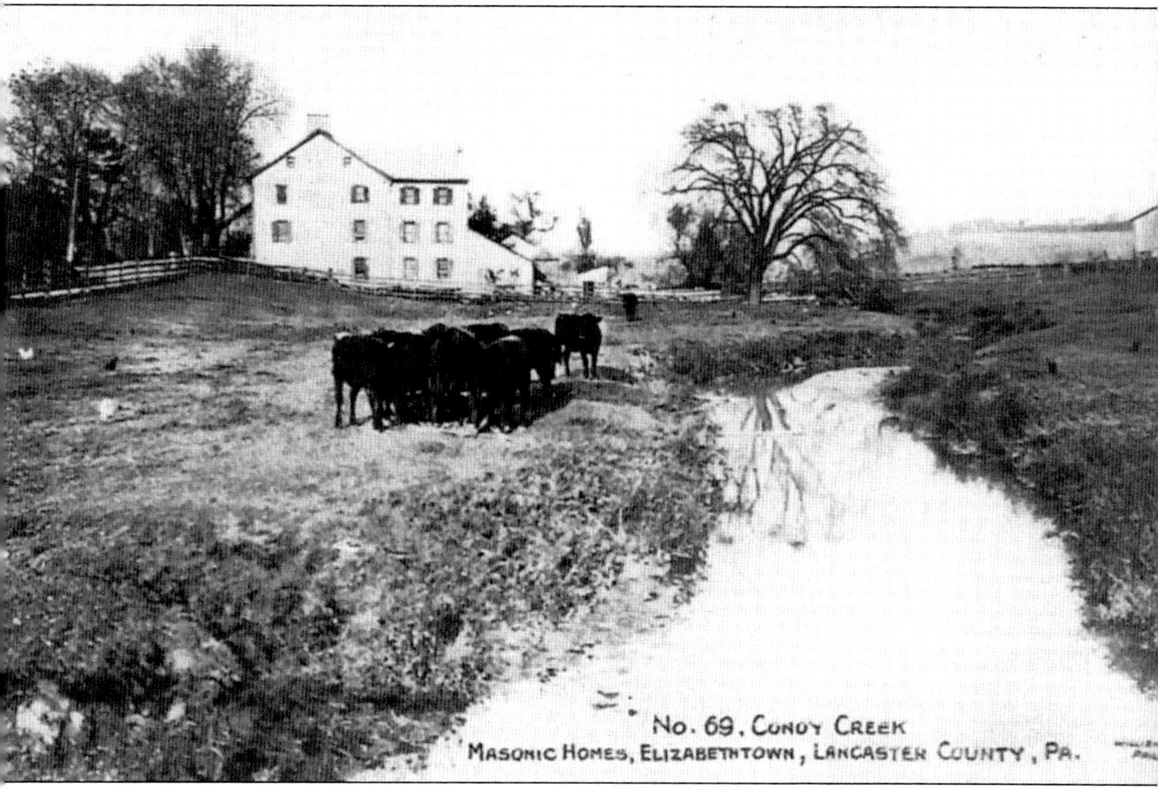

The site chosen for the Masonic Village was a series of farms on Conoy Creek with 18 springs. On April 1, 1910, the Grand Lodge of Pennsylvania took title to 957 acres in Elizabethtown for $134,296.54. The site is 87 miles from Philadelphia and 20 miles from Lancaster and Harrisburg.

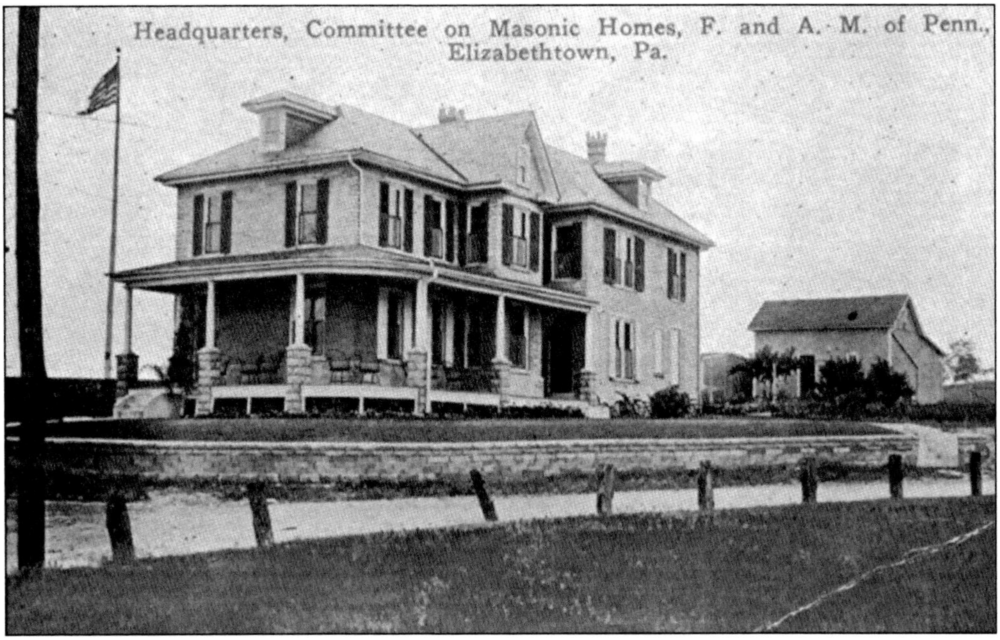

The Grand Lodge approved a proposal for the creation of a Masonic Home in December 1908, with the requirements that it be centrally located within the state and readily accessible on the main line of a railroad. The Grand Lodge appointed a committee of 11 with authority to "purchase real estate, employ architects, and erect the necessary buildings for a Masonic Home."

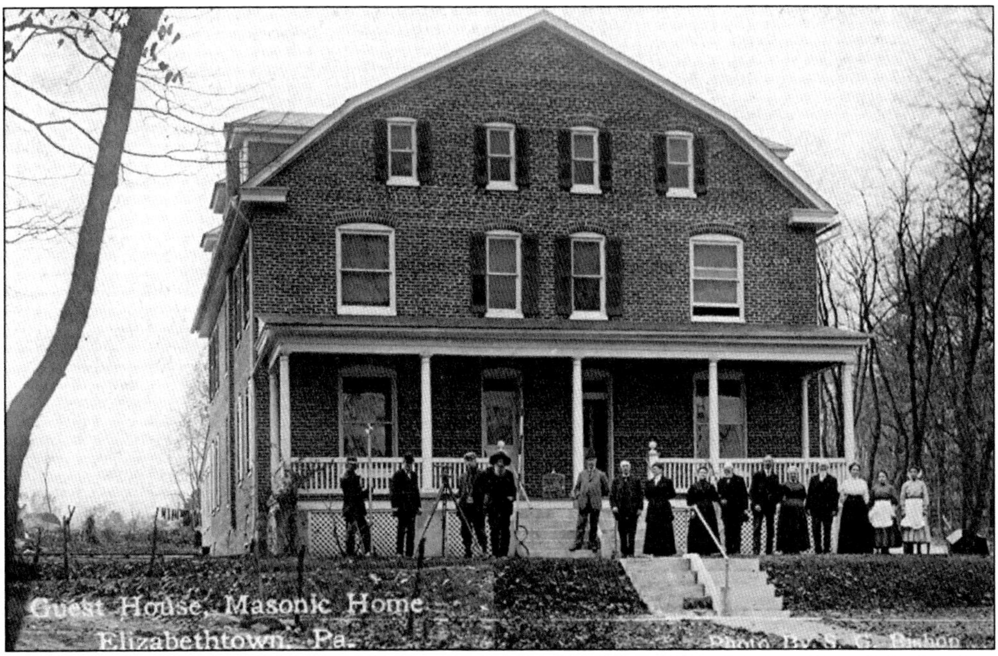

In 1903, at a meeting of the Grand Lodge of Pennsylvania in Philadelphia, David A. Sawdey, Perry-Keystone Lodge No. 392, Erie, proposed the idea of locating "homes for the care of our indigent Brethren, their aged wives, widows, and orphan children" at one convenient place in a country setting.

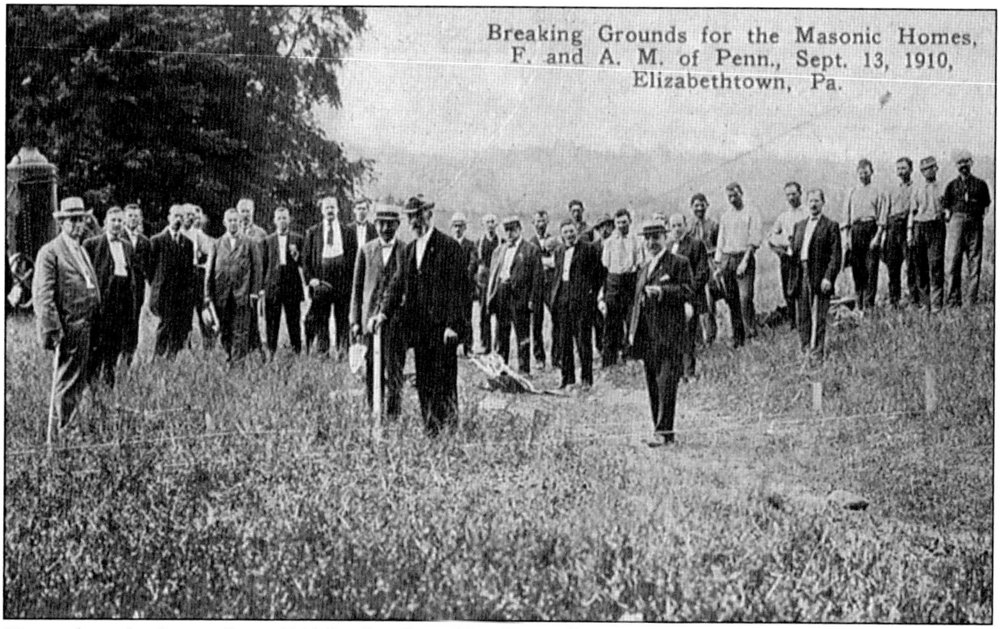

Ground was broken in June 1911 for the Grand Lodge Hall. Milton S. Hershey of Hershey Chocolate stands to the right, holding a cigar. The Elizabethtown Masonic Lodge was reinstated four years later. On September 3, 1810, Capt. John Wolfley organized Elizabethtown Amictia Lodge No. 116. In 1814, the Elizabethtown and Marietta Masonic lodges merged. The resulting lodge was dissolved in 1837, when the Anti-Masonic Party controlled Pennsylvania.

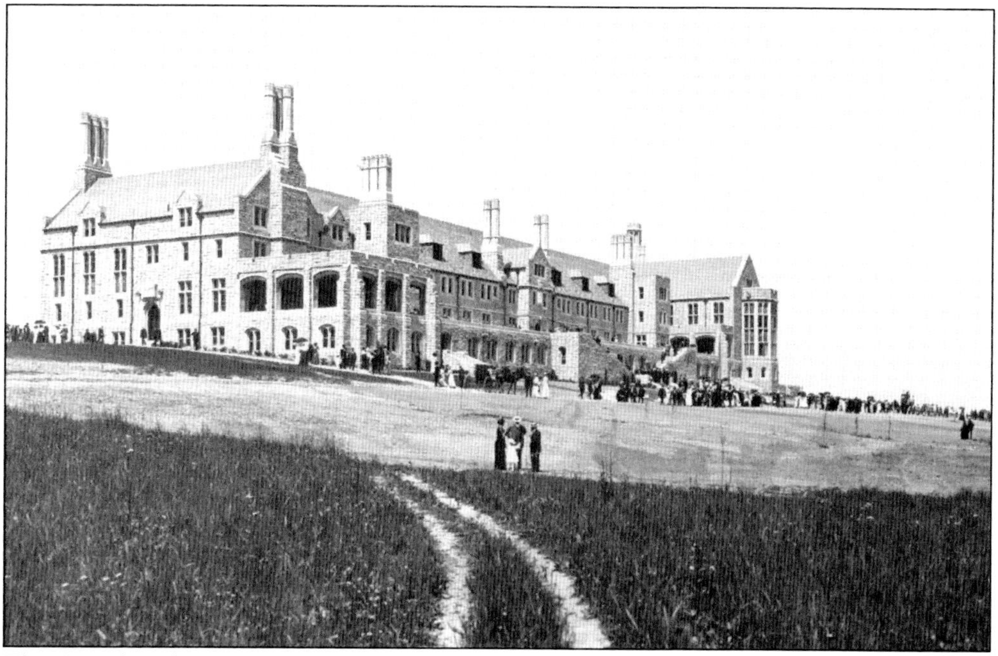

The Grand Lodge Hall was designed by architect Clarence C. Zantzinger from Lodge 610 Philadelphia in conjunction with expert Warren P. Laird, professor of architecture at the University of Pennsylvania. The contractor was John R. Wiggins of Philadelphia. The hall was constructed out of Holmesburg granite, Indiana limestone, and Wyoming bluestone.

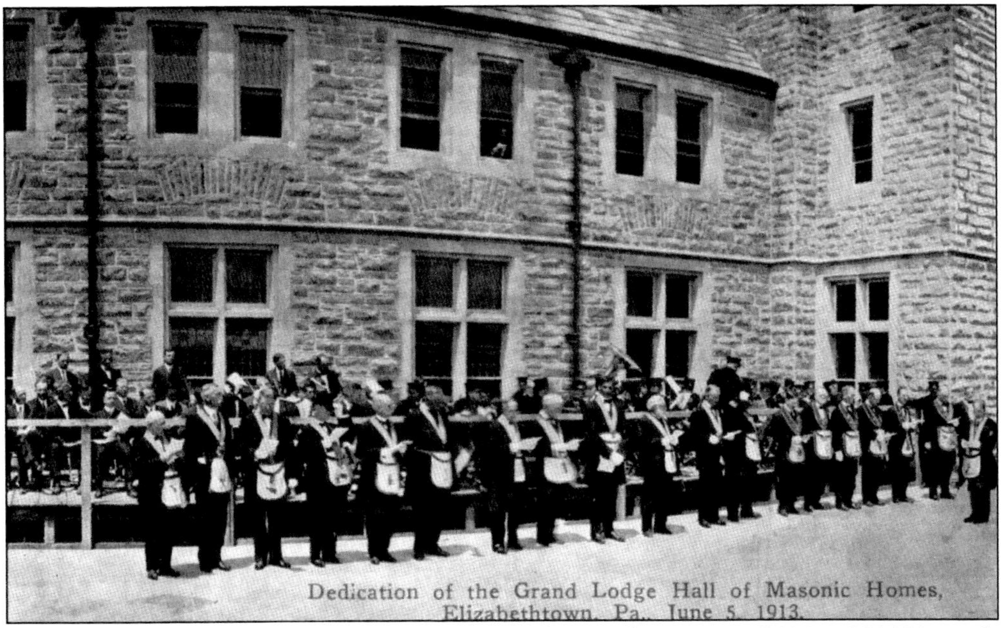

The Grand Lodge Hall was dedicated on June 5, 1913 (pictured). Between 25,000 and 30,000 people attended the dedication. More than 8,000 people attended the cornerstone-laying ceremonies two years earlier, at noon on September 26, 1911. The latter date was already significant, as it marked the 125th anniversary of the Grand Lodge of Pennsylvania's independence from the Grand Lodge of England.

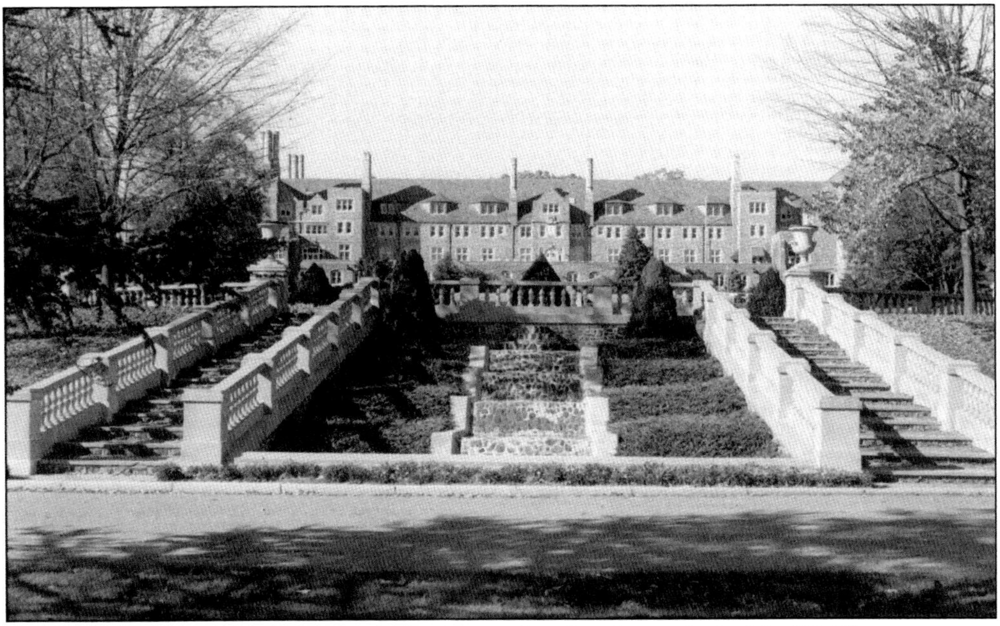

The Masonic Village was the vision of Edgar Tennis from Lamberton Lodge No. 371, Thompsontown; Davis Sawdey, from Perry-Keystone Lodge No. 392, Erie; and Thomas R. Patton, Union Lodge No. 121 (Pilgrim Lodge 712), Philadelphia. In 1910, the editors of *American Architect* noted that the Masonic Village had the "character of a place of comfort and protection for the members of a family" with aspects of "dignity and hospitality." (Courtesy LancasterHistory.org.)

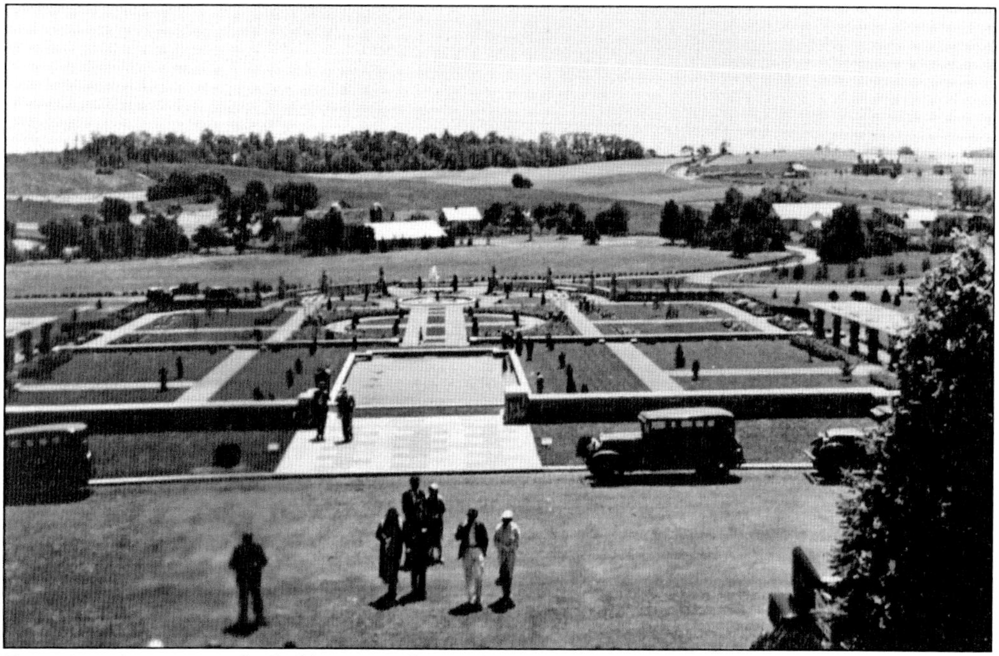

Formal gardens, six and a half acres in front of Grand Lodge Hall, were built from 1930 to 1932 by Gustaf E. Malmborg. The subcommittee on trees and planting was headed by George Orlady, Mount Moriah Lodge No. 300, Huntingdon. The committee on Masonic homes reported, "No single phase of our development at the Homes has made a larger contribution to the beauty of the place." (Courtesy Masonic Village.)

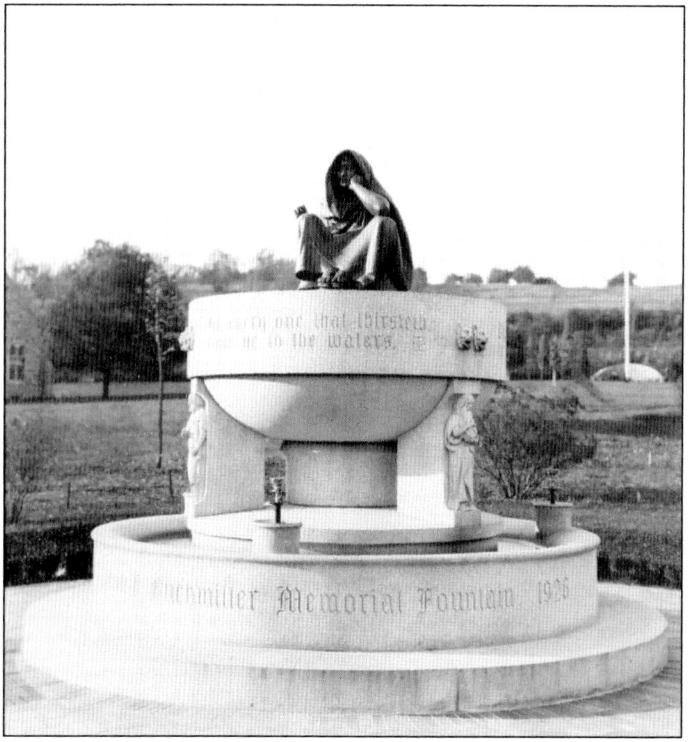

This is the Dulon F. Buchmiller Memorial drinking fountain, near the Sell Chapel on the Village Green. Buchmiller was a member of Lamberton Lodge No. 476, Lancaster. The fountain, designed by sculptor Henry Augustus Lukeman, was presented on October 15, 1927. Water was iced inside of the Grand Lodge Building and then piped into the fountain (outside), which provided iced drinking water. (Courtesy Masonic Village.)

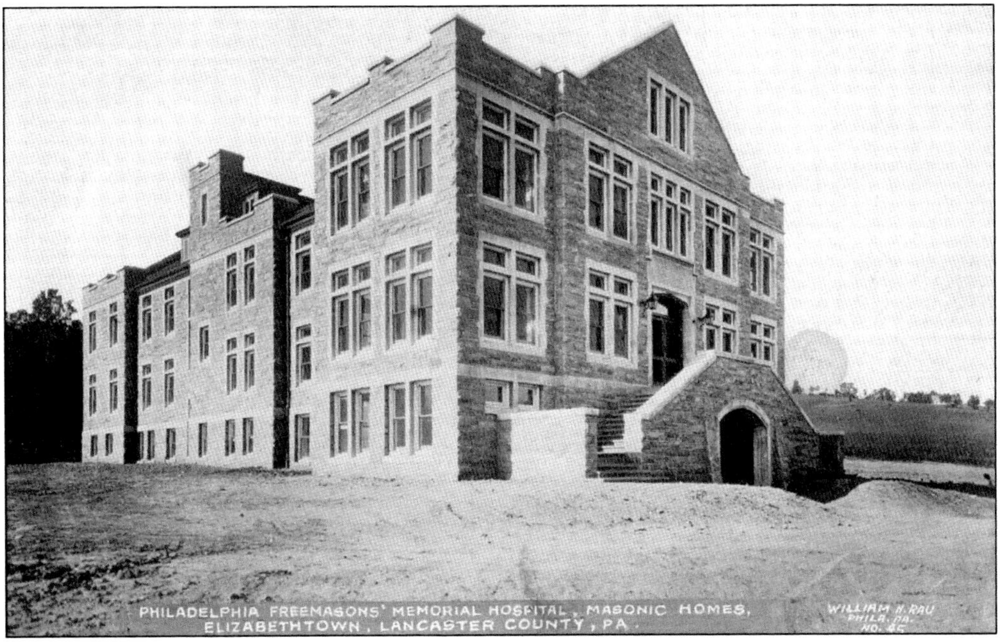

During the influenza epidemic of World War I, the Masonic Village admitted non-Masonic residents from the local Elizabethtown community for treatment at the Philadelphia Freemason's Memorial Hospital on campus. (Courtesy Masonic Village.)

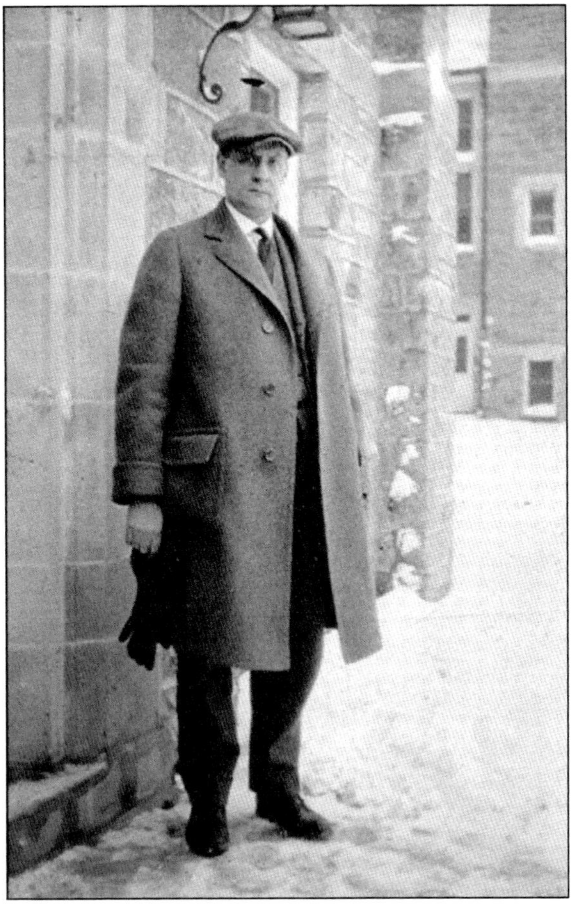

Dr. Vere Treichler was the resident doctor at the Masonic Village and son of Dr. Abraham C. Treichler. Both men were graduates of Jefferson Medical School, now the Sidney Kimmel Medical College at Thomas Jefferson University in Philadelphia. Descended from the Swiss Mennonite founding families of Elizabethtown, Treichler purchased the 1745 Thomas Harris Sign of the Bear Tavern in 1915, remodeling it as his residence.

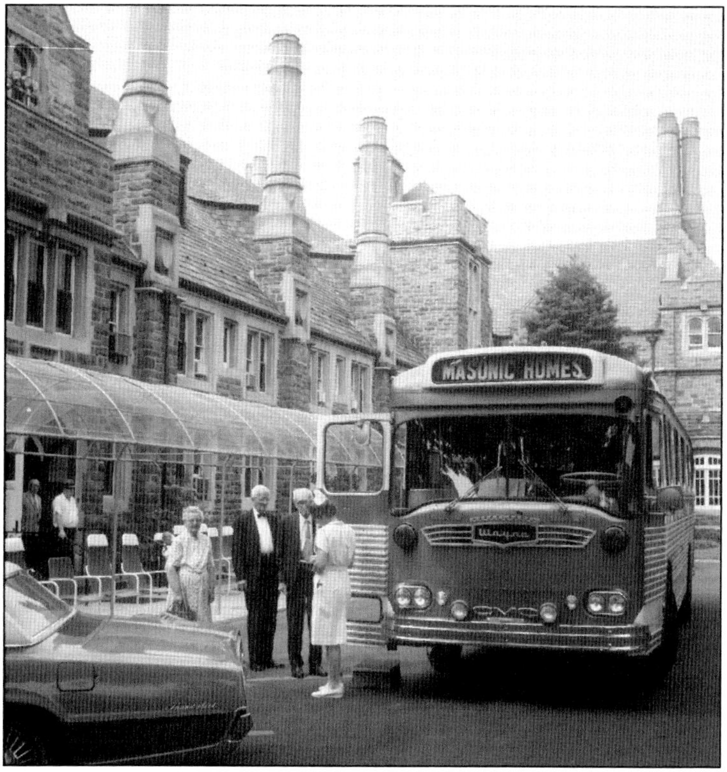

The Masonic Village has always incorporated modern approaches to the care of residents, both children and adults. Since 1999, Masonic Village has been part of the Eden Registry Alternative model for elder care. The philosophy stresses personal growth of the residents as well as the values of respect and collaboration between residents and caregivers. (Courtesy Masonic Village.)

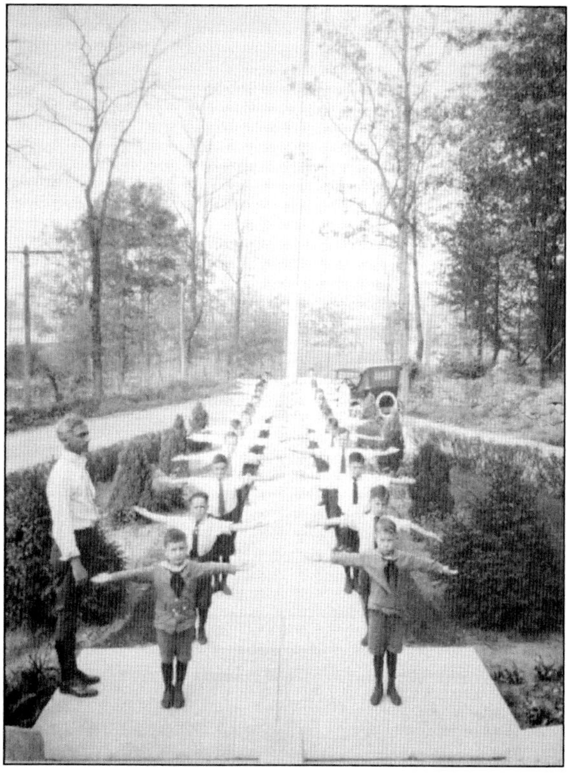

Boys Home at Masonic Village is seen here in the 1920s. In 1913, Louis Waters from Peter Williamson Lodge No. 323, Scranton, was chiefly responsible for the creation of the Masonic Children's Home "for the maintenance, development, and education of orphaned children of Masons." School-age boy and girl residents attended Elizabethtown public schools; younger children enrolled in the kindergarten on campus. After graduation, many Masonic Village student residents attended Elizabethtown College. (Courtesy Masonic Village.)

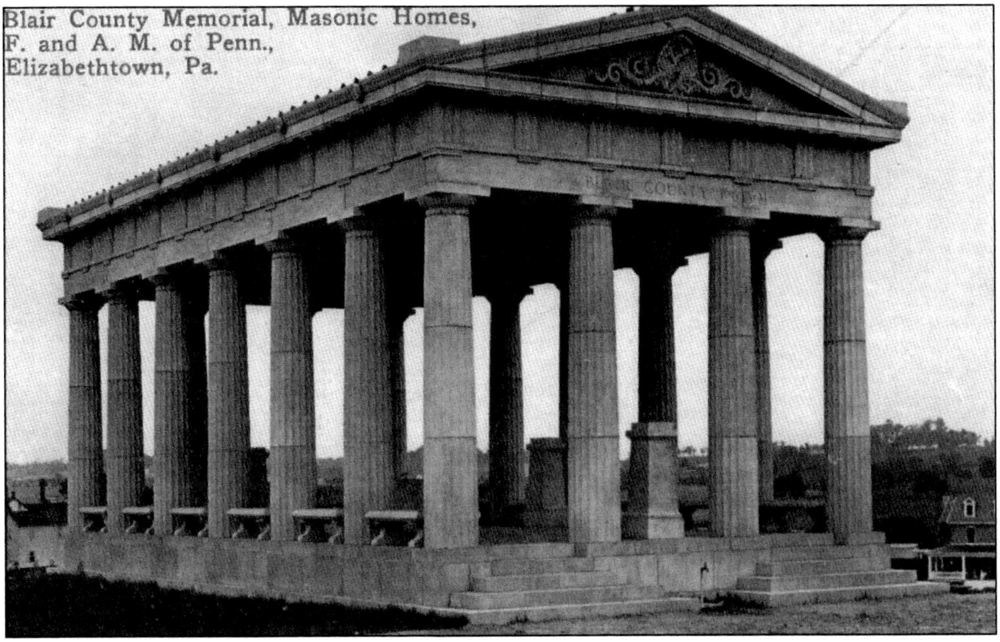

The Blair County Memorial Doric temple was built in 1911. The six acres surrounding it were dedicated in 1920 as a World War I veterans memorial grove of 268 oak trees. George B. Orlady of Mount Moriah Lodge No. 300, Huntingdon, advocated planting trees memorializing every Mason from Pennsylvania who died in World War I. In 1921, red poppies covered the memorial grove as a reminder of Flanders Fields in Belgium.

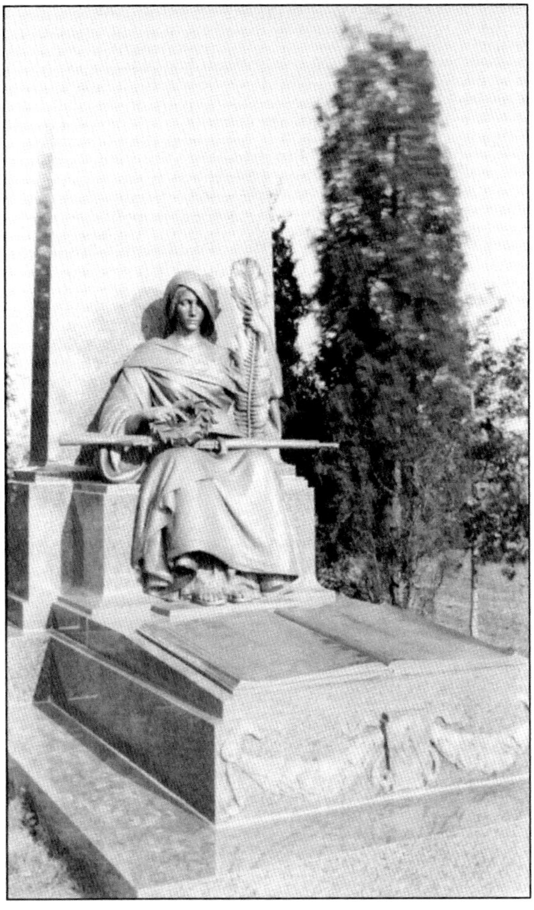

In 1927, sculptor Henry Augustus Lukeman was commissioned to create this armistice memorial monument. Lukeman was best known for his World War I monument in Prospect Park, Brooklyn; the Kit Carson Monument in Trinidad, Colorado; and the Stone Mountain Confederate Memorial in Georgia. (Courtesy Masonic Village.)

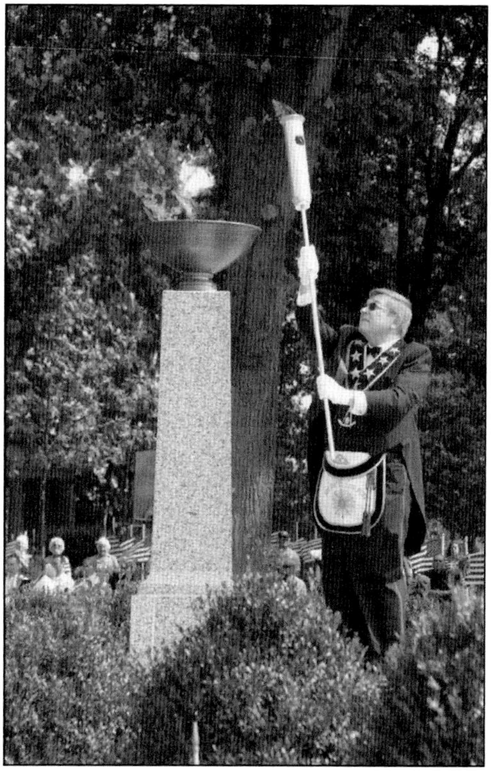

On September 20, 2014, at the annual Masonic Village Autumn Day, an eternal flame was dedicated in Veterans Grove, recognizing all veterans and active military persons. Robert J. Bateman, Springfield-Hanby Lodge No. 767, 120th Right Worshipful Grand Master of Masons in Pennsylvania, lights the eternal flame. (Courtesy Masonic Village.)

On September 15, 1915, the Grand Lodge of Pennsylvania constituted Elizabethtown Lodge No. 682. In 1926, the lodge was named in honor of Dr. Abraham C. Treichler, local attending physician of the Masonic Village. A new lodge was built in 1954, designed by Mitchell and Ritchey Architects, Pittsburgh. The Potteiger Company, Reading, was the contractor. On April 26, 1958, the Masonic lodge (left) and recreation building (right) were dedicated. (Courtesy Masonic Village.)

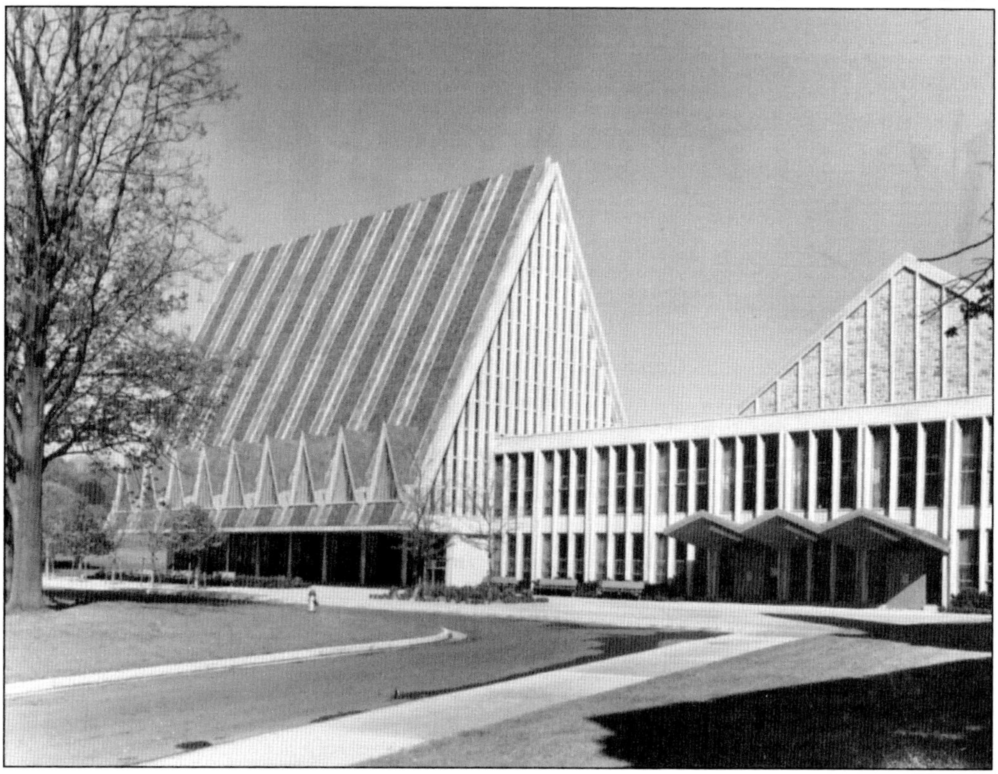

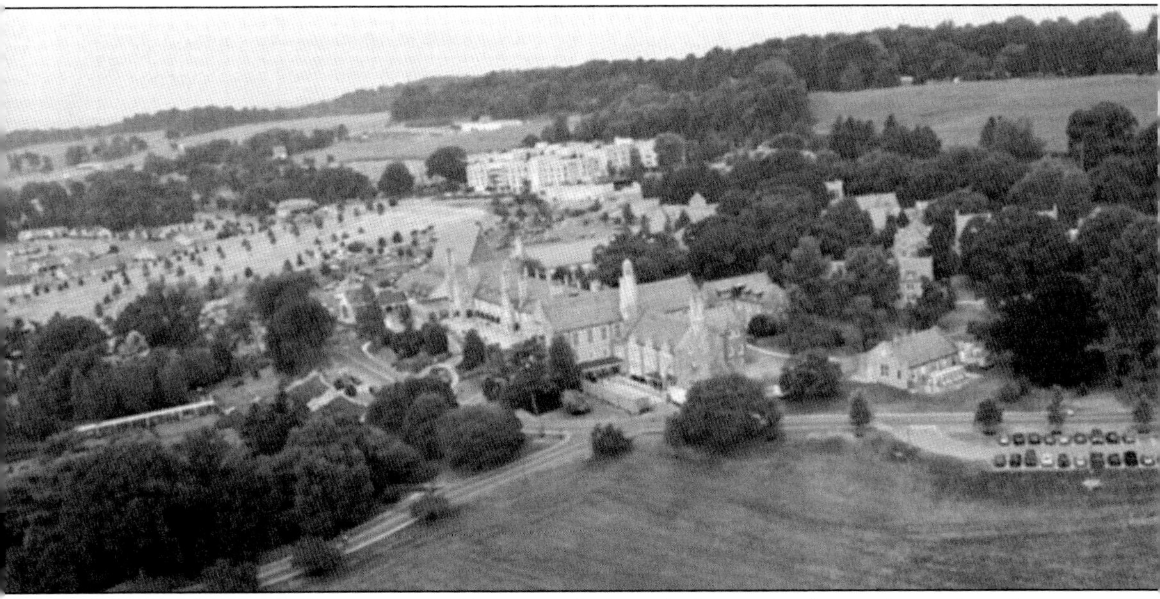

Today, the Masonic Village owns 1,400 acres, which includes on-site farms, farmers' market, children's home, childcare center, a home for adults with developmental disabilities, adult day care, short-term rehabilitation, and hospice. A full continuum of retirement living, personal care, and nursing services are offered to more than 1,800 residents. More than 971 residences are for retirement living in apartments and cottages. More than 1,500 people are employed on the campus. (Courtesy Masonic Village.)

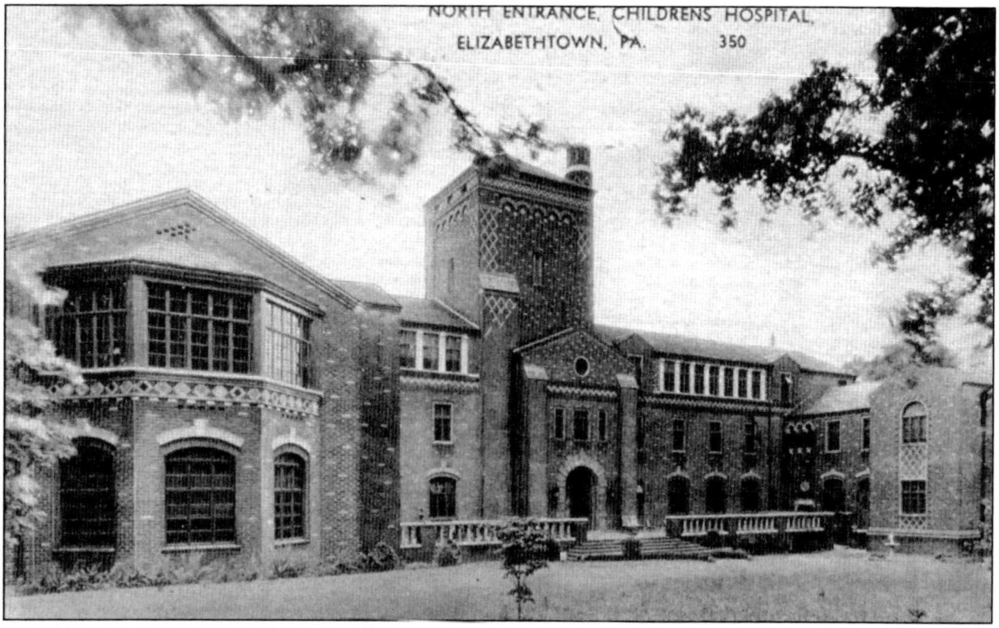

In 1925, Gov. Gifford Pinchot established the Pennsylvania State Hospital for Crippled Children in Elizabethtown. According to an article in the *Elizabethtown Chronicle*, it was for the "care, vocational training, and treatment of indigent children who are afflicted with surgical tuberculosis and allied conditions. It will be the second medical research center of its kind in the world. The other is in Copenhagen, Denmark."

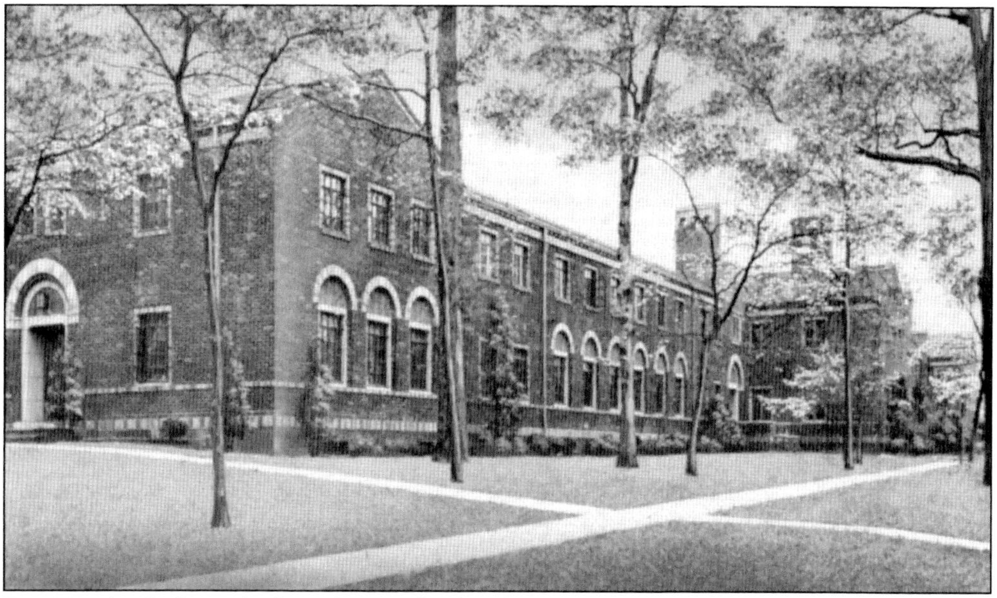

By 1962, the decline of tuberculosis and polio changed the surgical emphasis to correction of congenital deformities and spinal injuries. In 1974, the Penn State Orthopaedic Residency Program began with conferences for surgeons. Today, the annual Elizabethtown Pediatric Orthopaedic Lecture at Hershey Medical Center continues this educational mission. It was named to "honor the legacy of an institution that provided care for thousands of patients and training for hundreds of orthopaedic surgeons."

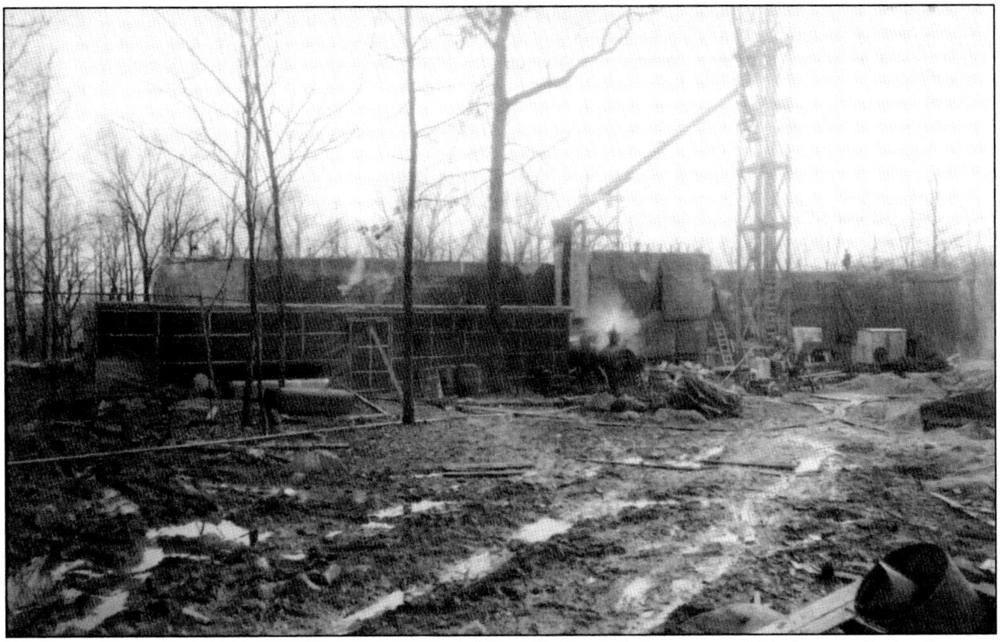

The Classical Revival complex was designed by Thomas, Martin, and Kirkpatrick Architects and built in 1929. In 1933, a nurses residence was added, as, by law, nurses could not marry and were required to live on campus. In 1941, two additional wings were built by the Work Projects Administration, and three buildings were constructed in 1949. The auditorium, classrooms, and library were constructed in 1965.

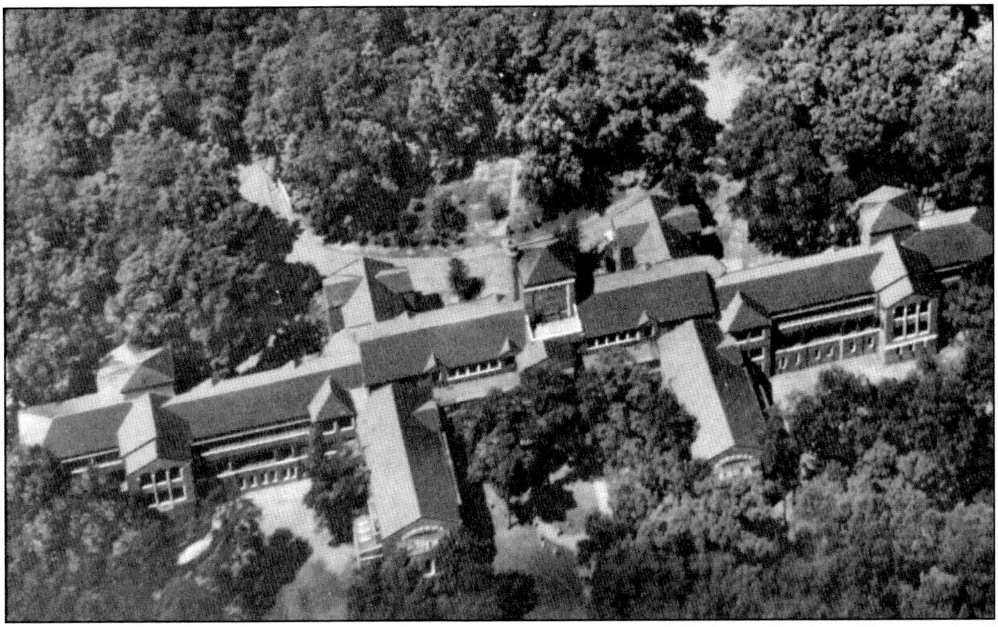

The first patients were admitted in 1930 to "get a longer lease on life through a $1 million medical research center with special emphasis on the fight to eradicate diabetes and infantile paralysis," according to a 1929 *Elizabethtown Chronicle* article.

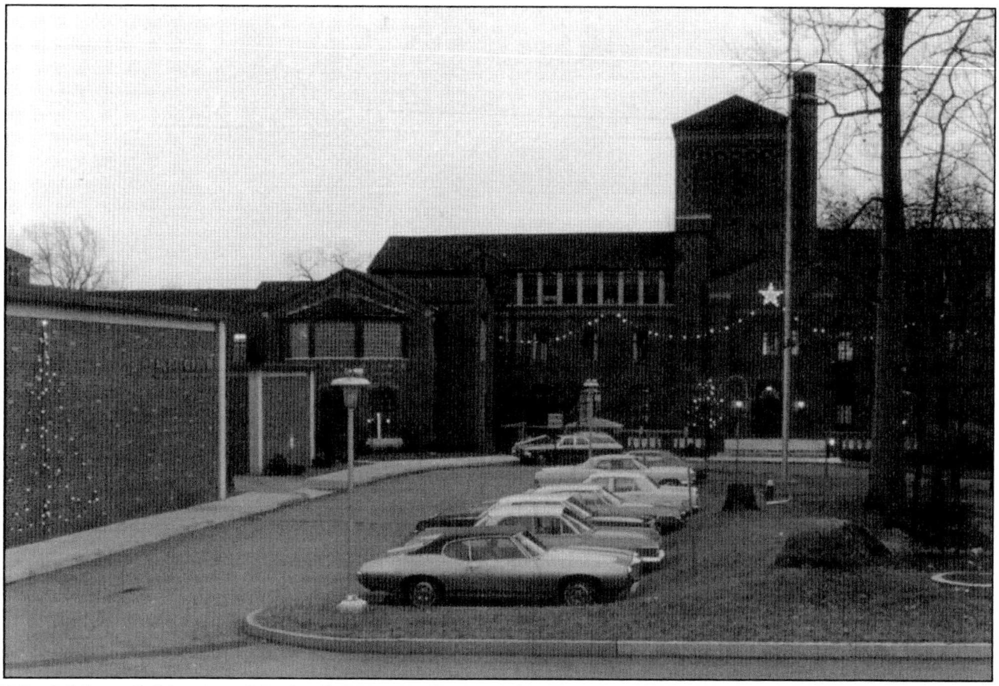

The Milton S. Hershey Medical Center of Pennsylvania State University took over the hospital in 1972. The facility, renamed Elizabethtown Hospital for Children and Youth, operated as a rehabilitation center with an emphasis on occupational therapy, determining the patient's physical, mental, and emotional needs and abilities.

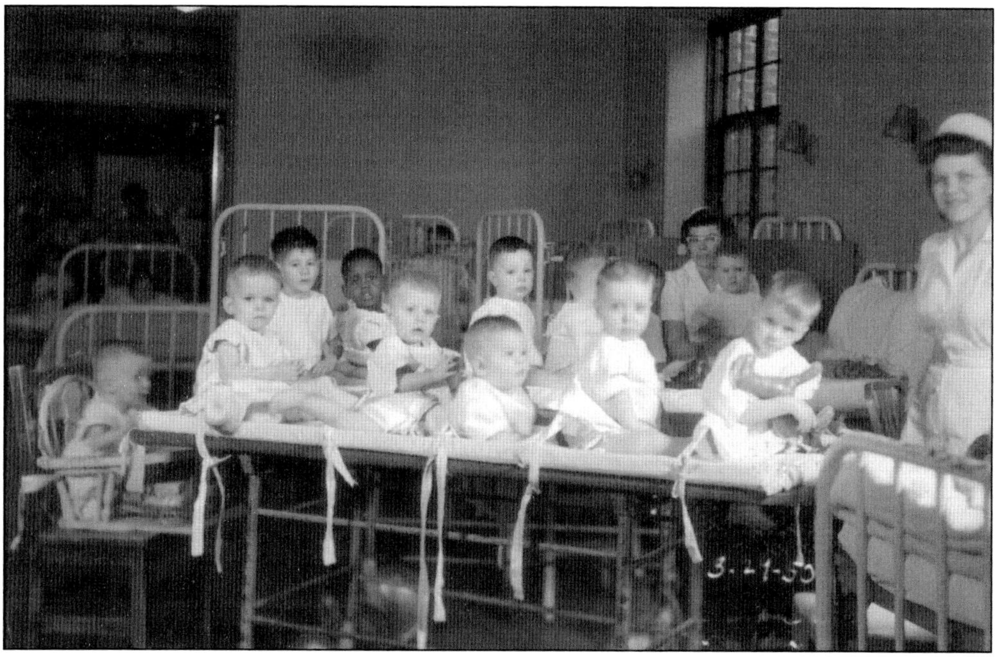

The average length of stay for the children in the hospital was 15 to 19 months. In some cases, a child stayed for years. As late as the 1960s, the average hospital stay for a patient was still a year, and the hospital had more than 3,000 visits annually by outpatients.

Patient rehabilitation included on-campus apartment housing for children and adults transitioning to living at home. The original policy of ending treatment for children when they reached 21 was amended to provide continuation of treatment of current or former patients as adults.

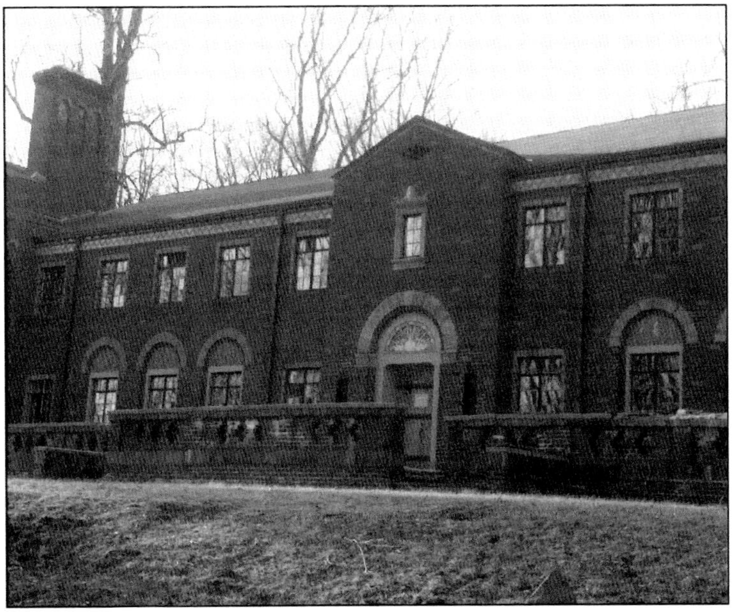

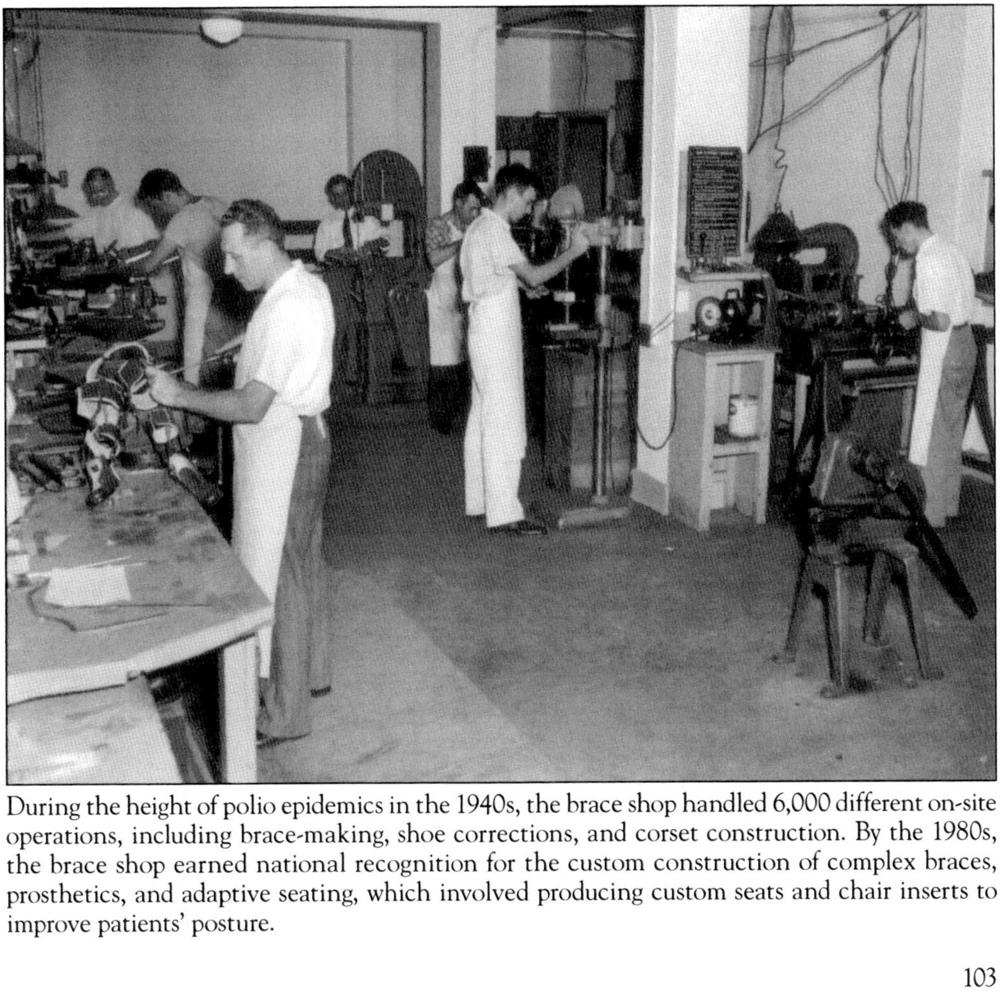

During the height of polio epidemics in the 1940s, the brace shop handled 6,000 different on-site operations, including brace-making, shoe corrections, and corset construction. By the 1980s, the brace shop earned national recognition for the custom construction of complex braces, prosthetics, and adaptive seating, which involved producing custom seats and chair inserts to improve patients' posture.

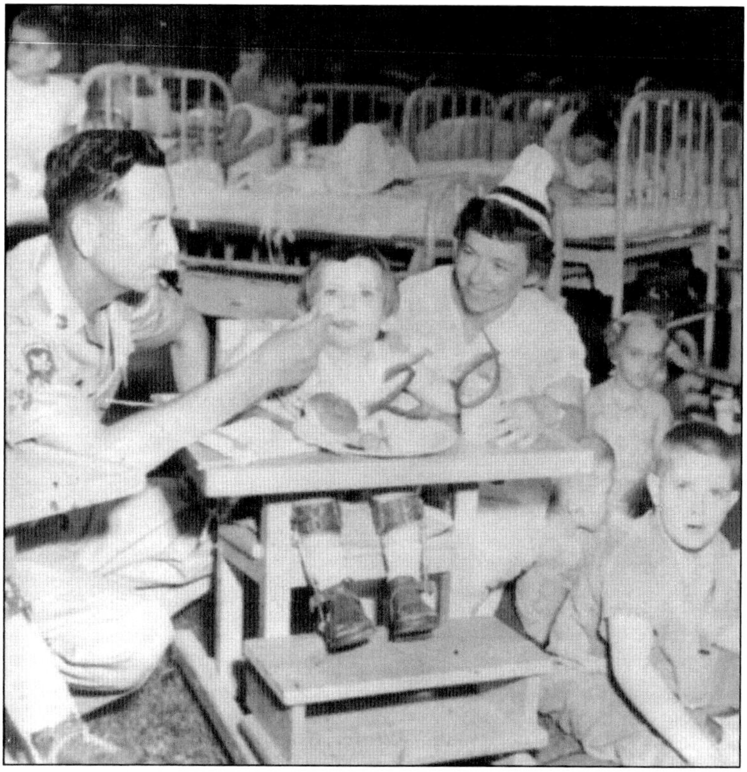

The hospital offered nonrestricted visiting hours for parents and a parents' dormitory. Parents were encouraged to room with their children, and family support groups were created. In 1936, the Division of Crippled Children was added to the Pennsylvania Bureau of Maternal and Child Health.

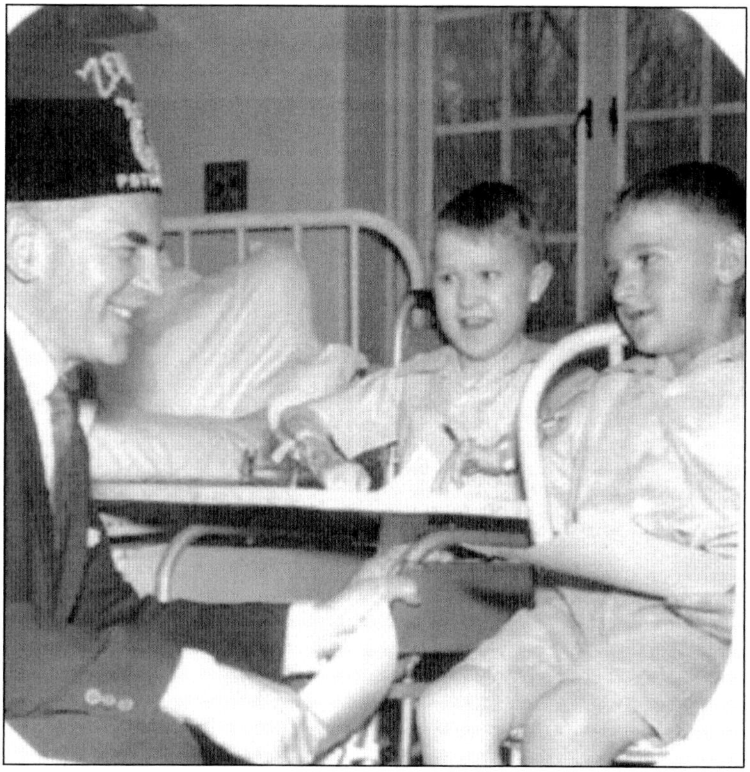

Visitation by local community-service organizations, such as this Shriner talking with patients, was a key part of strengthening the relationship between the Elizabethtown community and the hospital. Local Boy Scouts and Girl Scouts visited with patients. The hospital had both Boy Scout and Girl Scout troops on campus for their patients.

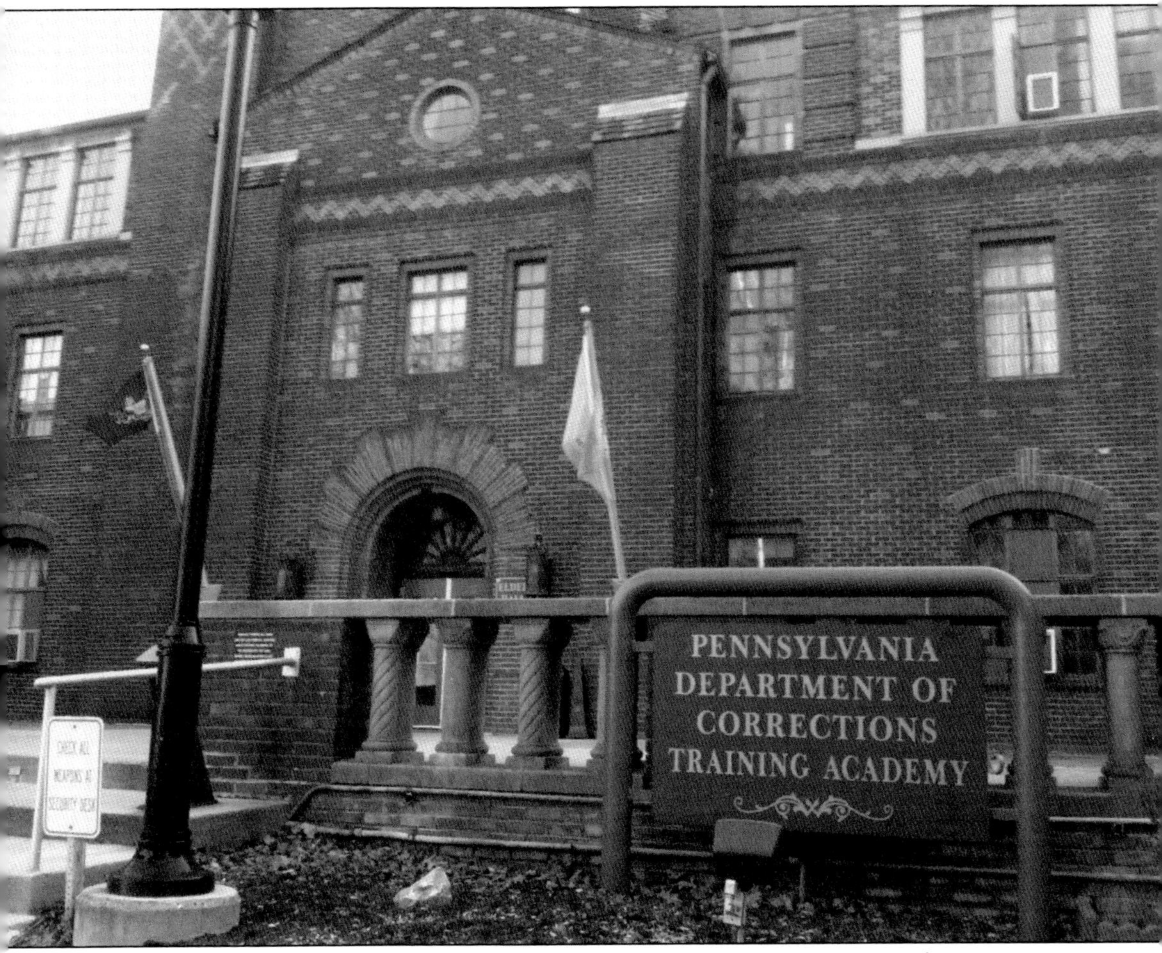

In 1991, the campus became the Training Academy for the Pennsylvania Department of Corrections. The academy trains prison employees working for the state and county. Inmates from the State Correctional Institution at Camp Hill provide daily maintenance and food-service labor, and they participate in vocational training.

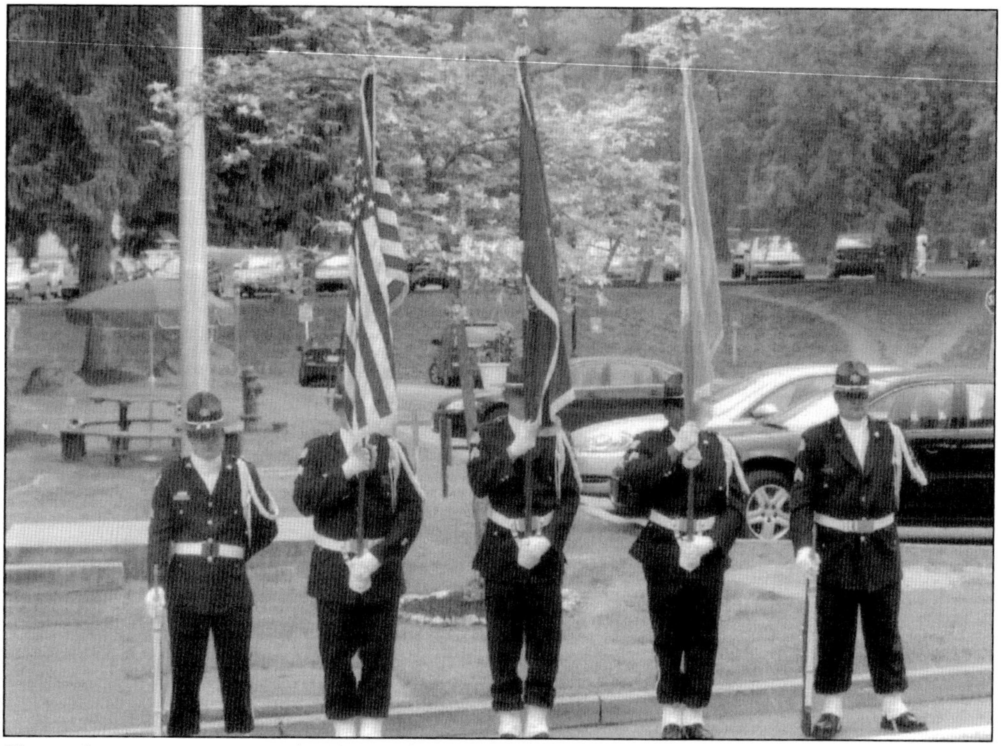

Shown here on campus is the Pennsylvania Department of Corrections Training Academy Honor Guard.

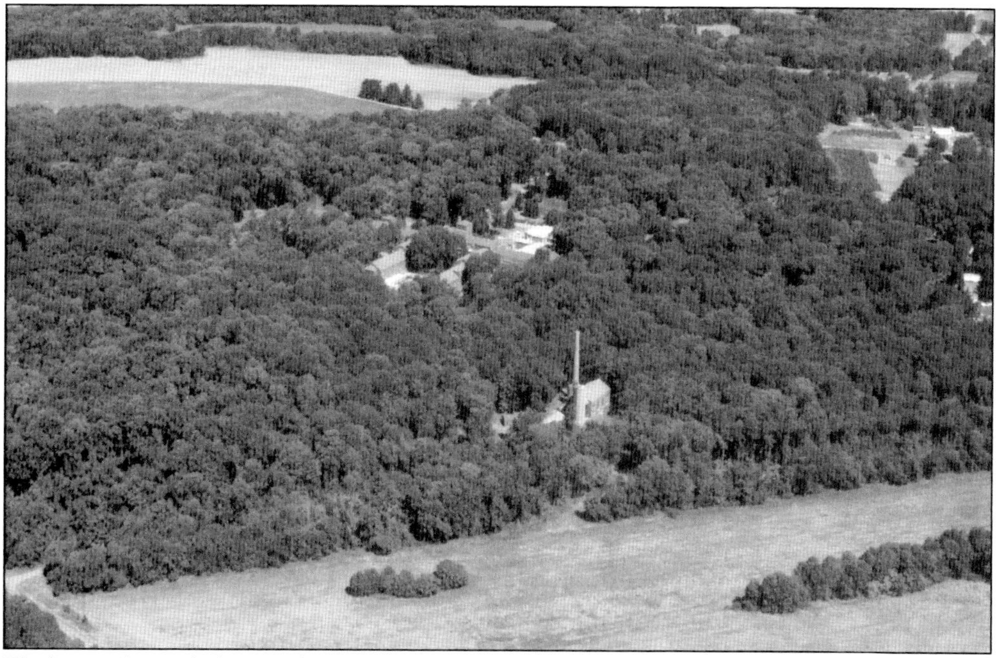

The hospital provided comprehensive care on 265 acres, with its own farm, dairy, and truck garden. Today, some of the acreage is farmed for the training academy by neighboring farmers. Known as "Academy Woods," the property is inhabited by sizeable populations of deer.

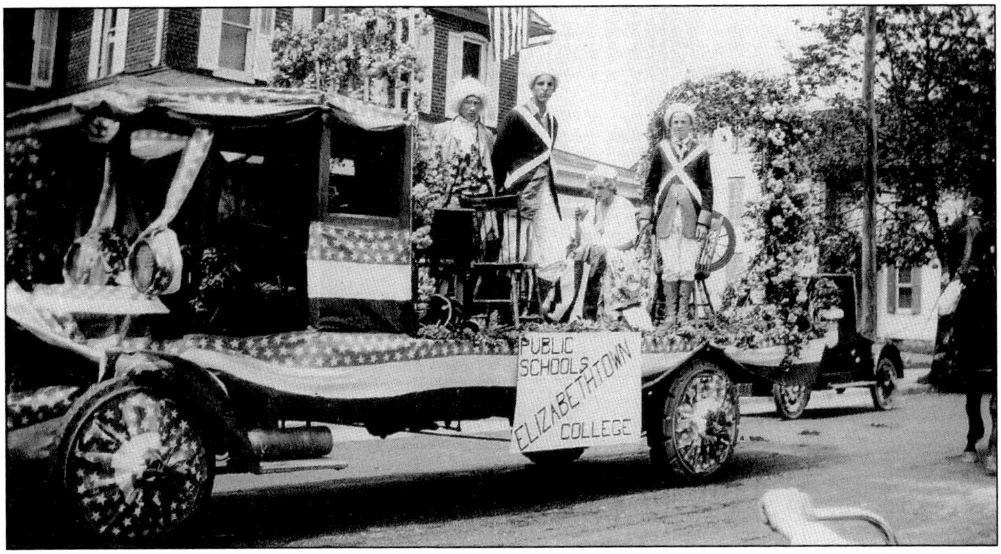

The earliest ecumenical schools were established by St. Peter's. Rev. Bernard Keenan (1823–1877) of St. Peter's advocated establishing public schools. In 1882, a Frenchman, Rev. Jules Foin, with the Sisters of St. Francis, established a parochial school. St. Peter's Elementary School opened in 1957, staffed by the Servants of the Immaculate Heart of Mary and, in 1985, by Daughters of Mercy. When it closed in 2012, students transferred to Seven Sorrows in Middletown.

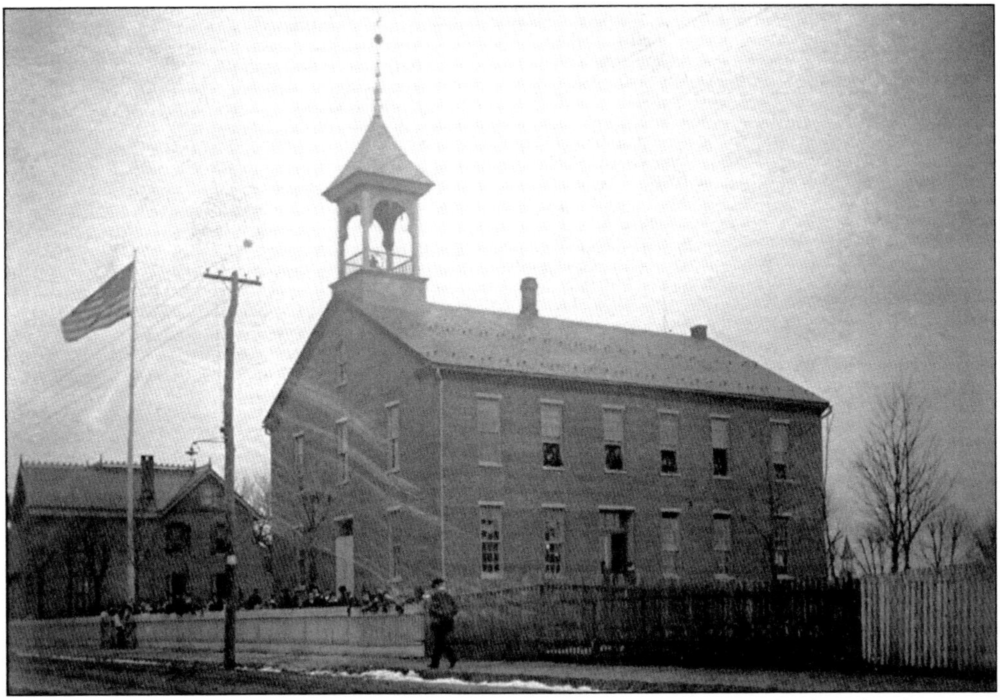

On May 5, 1874, a new consolidated public school (pictured) was dedicated. The school on West High Street was built next to the Peach Alley public schoolhouse on Poplar Street. The first school was constructed in 1818 on Mechanics Street. A second schoolhouse was erected at 45 West High Street. The two institutions merged, and a larger school was built in 1844 on the original Mechanics Street site.

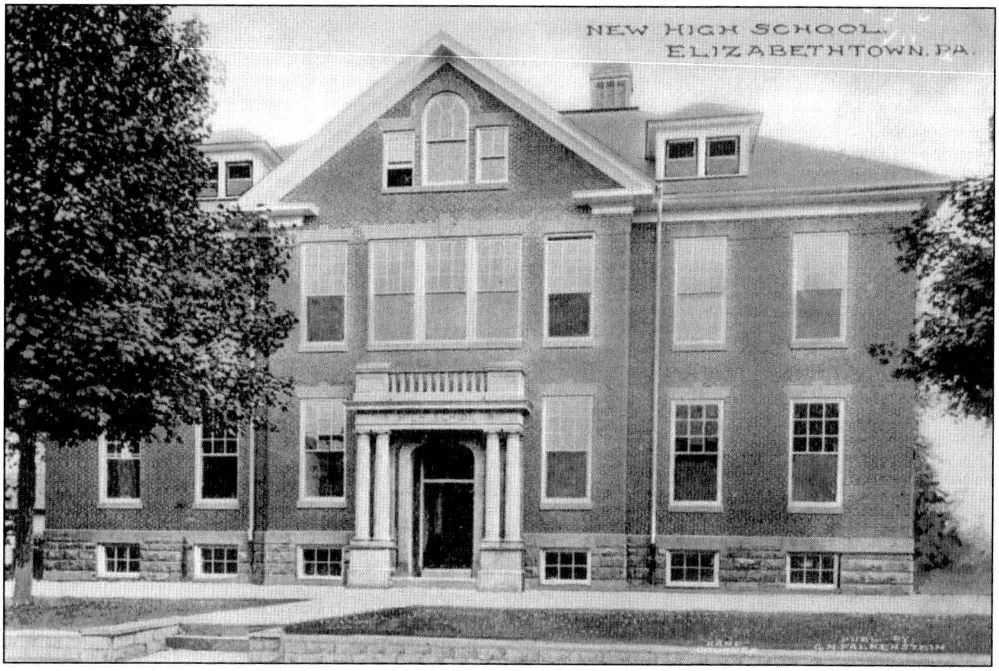

In 1909, the school board erected a larger, three-story building on the same site at Poplar Street near Peach Alley School.

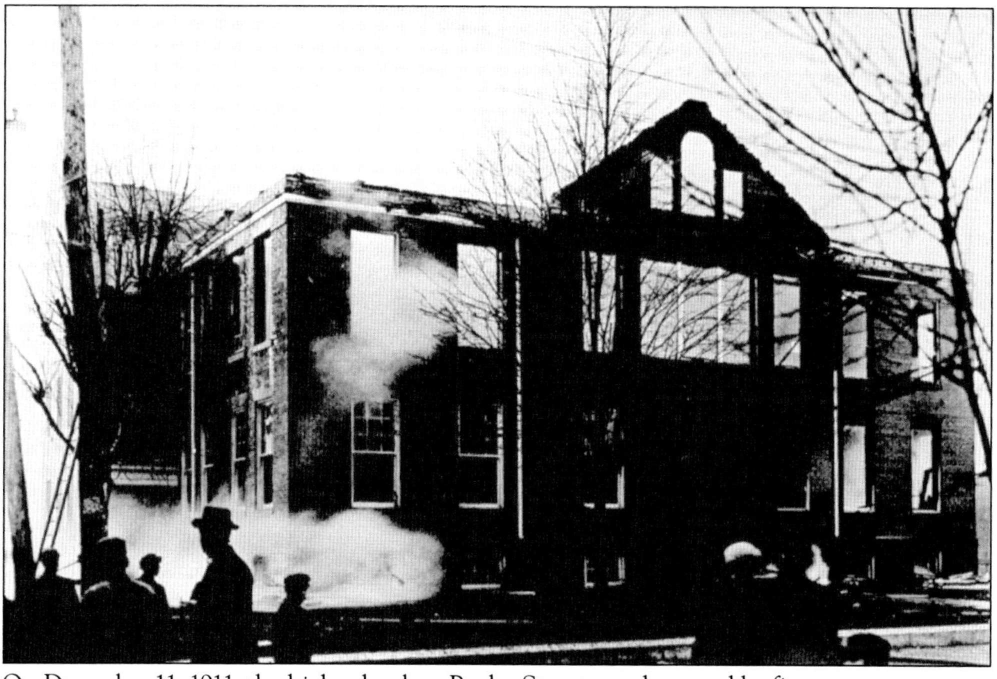

On December 11, 1911, the high school on Poplar Street was destroyed by fire.

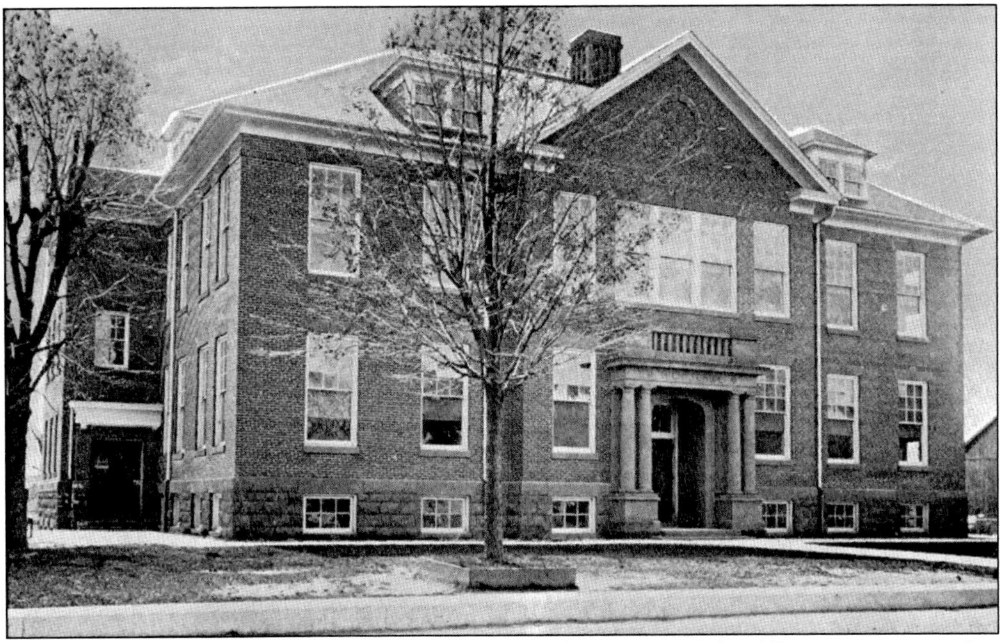

This new public school was built in 1912. The Elizabethtown Area School District was created in May 1954. The following year, three new elementary schools were built with identical architecture: Mill Road, Fairview, and Rheems. Dedication ceremonies for the junior-senior high school were held on April 10, 1958. Bainbridge and East High Elementary Schools were built later on, followed by Bear Creek Intermediate School in 2011.

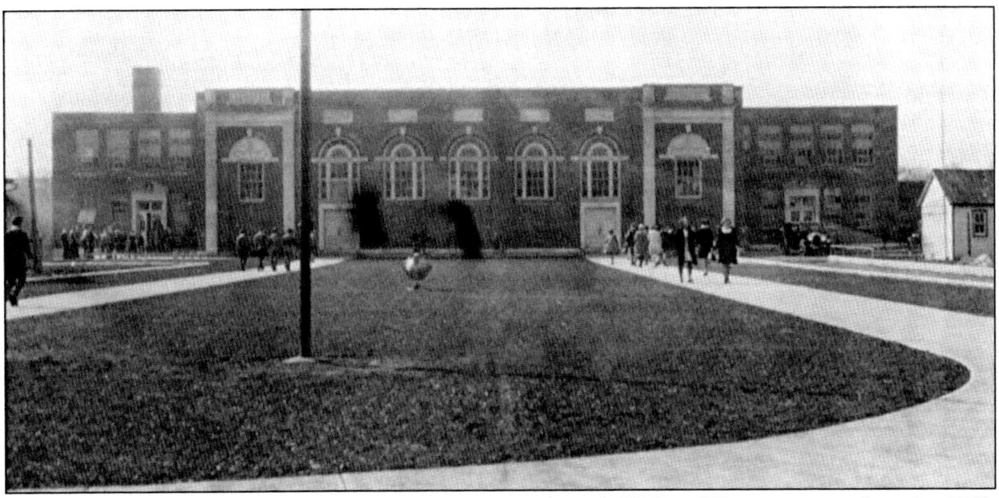

In 1967, the Elizabethtown Senior Citizens organized, with Wilbur Weaver as president. In 1975, Elizabethtown joined the Lancaster County Community Action Program, offering programming for senior citizens. The Elizabethtown Area Recreation Commission was created that same year, and, in 1977, a community center board was established. By 1985, the Elizabethtown Community Center opened in the restored public high school (pictured), built in 1928 on South Poplar Street.

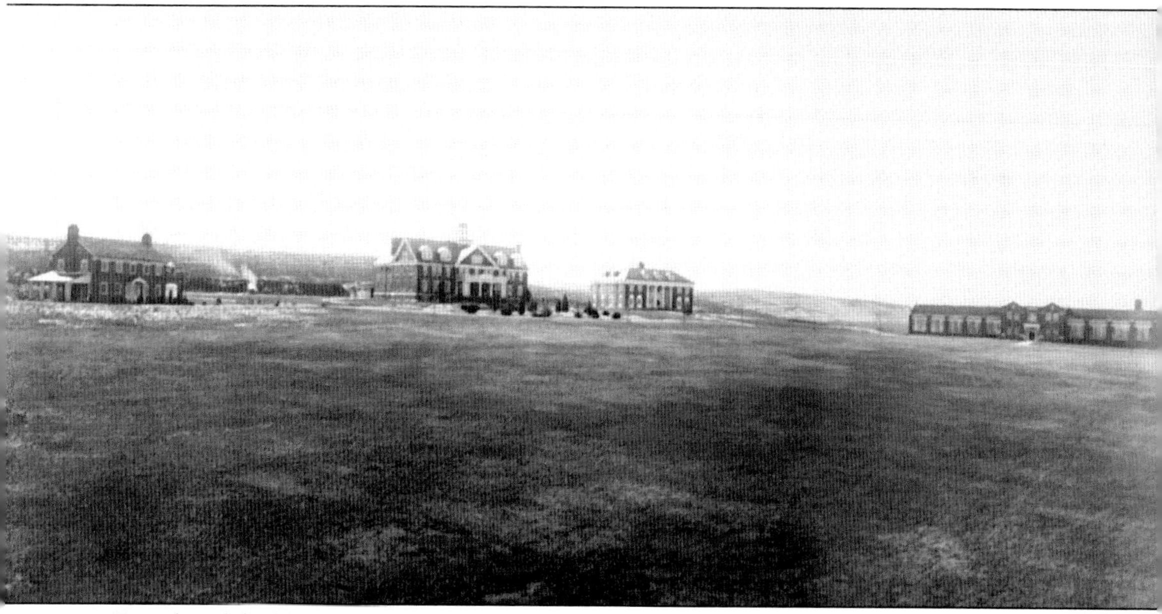

Founder of the Union Trust Company in Philadelphia, Thomas R. Patton, willed his estate for "the establishment of an institution for male orphan children of Master Masons." In 1925, in Elizabethtown, a boarding high school was established. Thomas Ranken Patton Masonic Institution for Boys had an academic and vocational curriculum. The school closed in 1976. Today, the building houses the Patton Conference Center at Masonic Village. (Courtesy Masonic Village).

Four

COMMUNITY

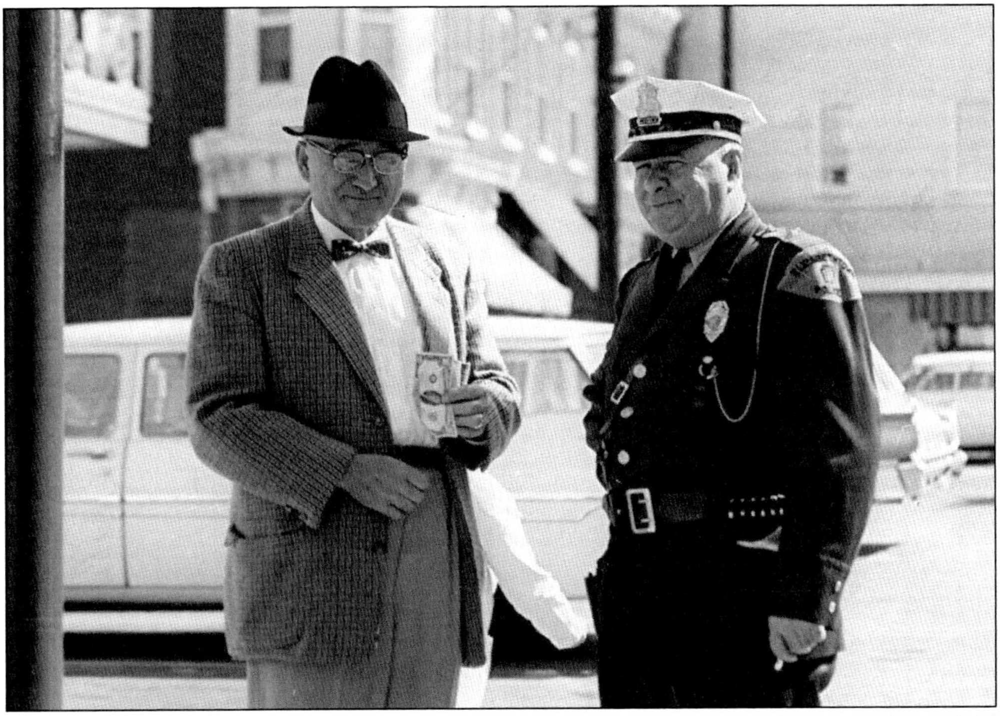

Dr. Troy M. Thompson (left) poses with Police Chief Mumma. In 1949, Thompson donated 25 acres on East High Street to build the public junior-senior high school. In 1968, he donated land adjacent to Elizabethtown College, increasing athletic facilities and playing fields. Philanthropy and civic engagement has driven progress in Elizabethtown. The Greater Elizabethtown Area Recreation and Community Services, public library, community park, and service clubs continue to strengthen the borough.

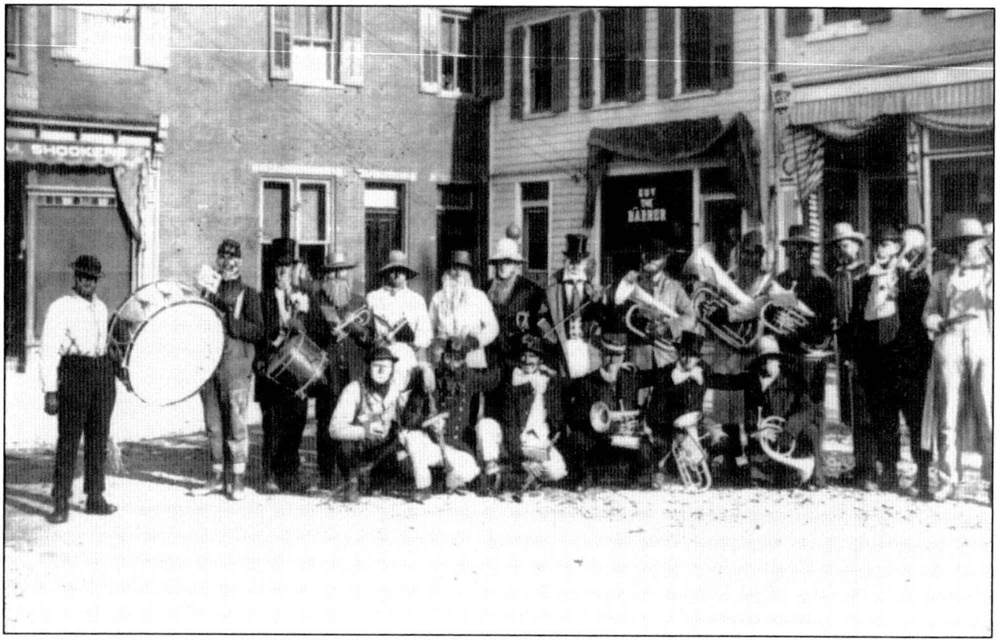

The Elizabethtown Brass Band, under the direction of Dr. Sebastian Keller and J.D. Young, was organized for Whig Party rallies and lasted until 1856. The Elizabethtown Cornet Band (above) was organized on July 19, 1867, with Keller as president. The band practiced every Tuesday and Friday at the Phoenix Hotel, 28 South Market Street. In the 1920s, the Rotary Club sponsored the Elizabethtown Boys Band (below), featuring child musicians.

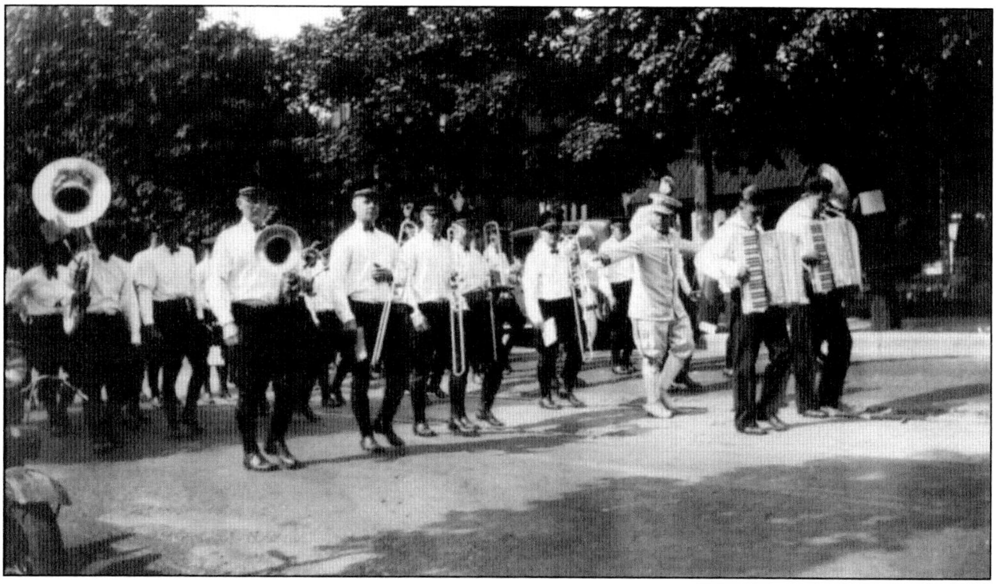

Shown here is a homecoming parade in 1946. The Veterans of Foreign Wars Post No. 5667 was established in April 1946 and was located at the former Wagner's Park. Prior to that, the park had been known as Keener Park. It had also served as the Beulah Heights Bible conference grounds. The park was purchased by Elwood Grimm from Claude Disney.

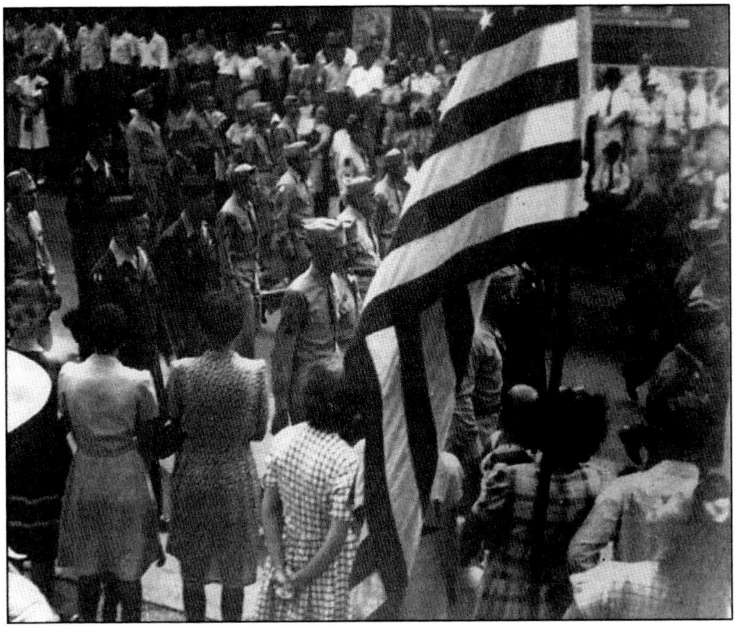

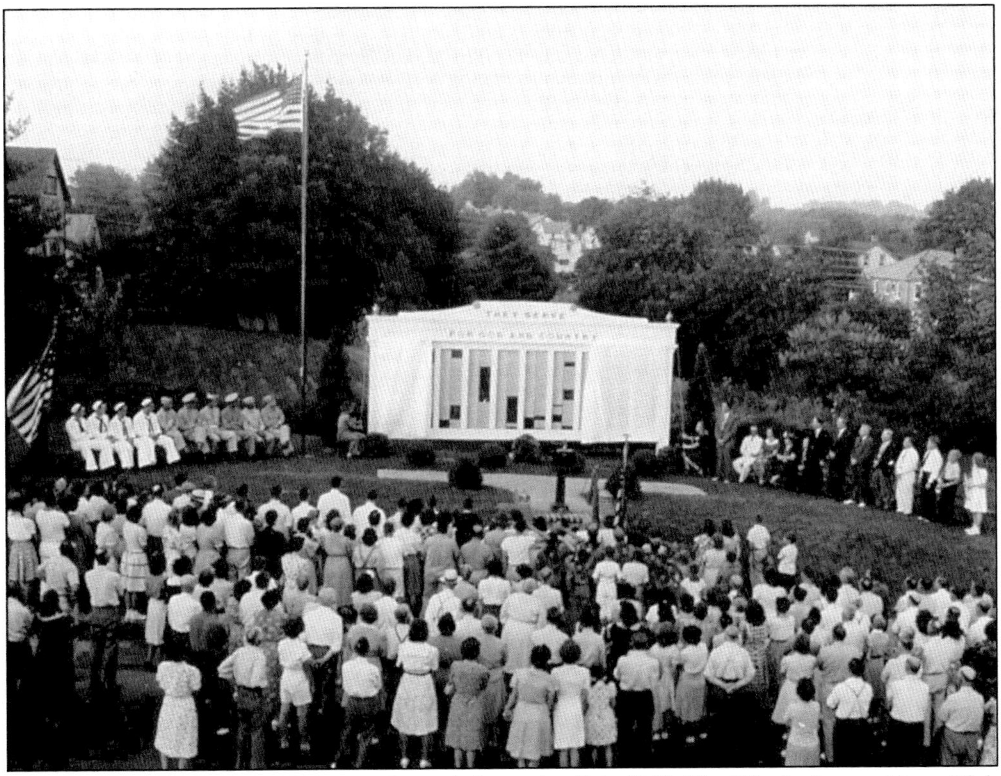

The World War II Veterans Memorial was dedicated in July 1945. The Elizabethtown Lions Club dedicated a service roll honoring 816 local men and women who served in the war. This memorial stood on the corner of South Market Street near Christ Reformed Church. It was replaced in 1959 by other memorials erected at Mount Tunnel Cemetery (formerly Red Hill) and, in 1988, at the Elizabethtown Veterans Memorial in the community park.

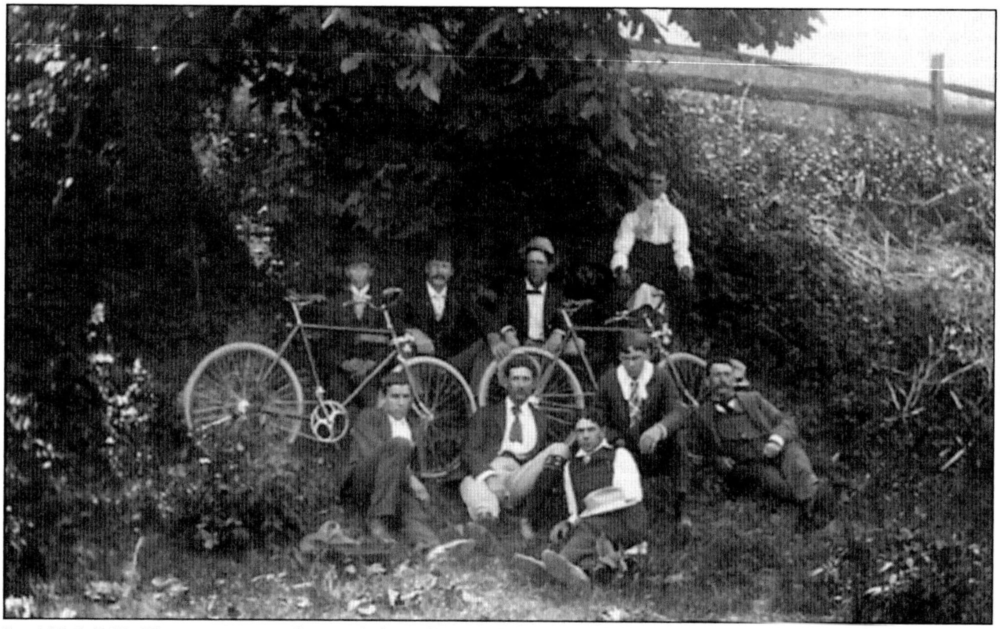

In 1896, J.K. Herr was president of the Elizabethtown Wheelman, a men's bicycle club. Today, Elizabethtown residents walk, run, ride horseback, bicycle, snowboard, and cross-country ski on the 5.5-mile Conewago Recreation Trail. The trail runs along Conewago Creek on the path of the former Cornwall-Lebanon Railroad (1883). Elizabethtown's Rails to Trails Bicycle Shop at 1010 Hershey Road is located adjacent to the former Hershey Transit trolley car substation.

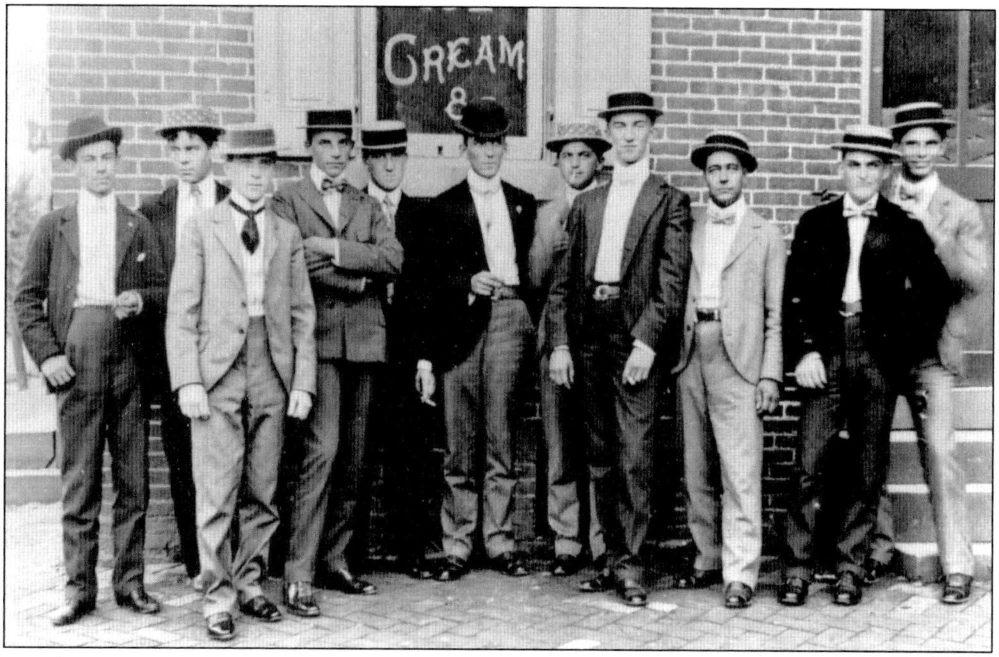

Members of the Crescent Club pose for a photograph. In the 1850s and 1860s, an ordinance was passed to "prevent young men or boys assembling or congregating on the corners of Center Square." On the third floor of 15 Diamond Square was Horst Hall, where the men of the Crescent Club played pinochle and harmonized with piano accompaniment.

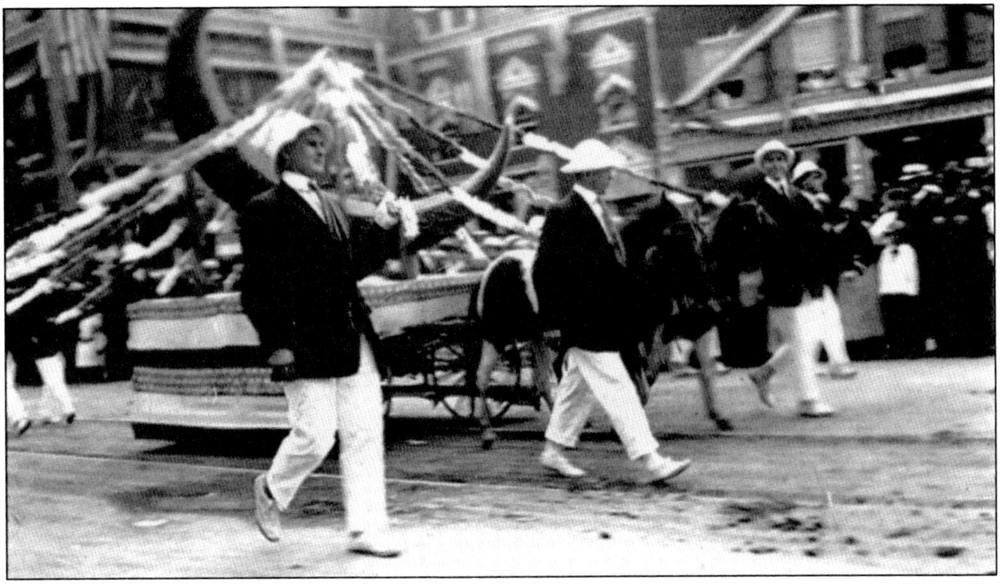

Shriners march through Diamond Square. Elizabethtown native sons Daniel Balmer and Andrew Wade were elected, in 1842 and 1849, respectively, as Whigs to the Pennsylvania General Assembly. The strong support of the Whig Party in Elizabethtown contradicted the fact that Lancaster County was a stronghold for the Anti-Masonic Party. Local Anabaptist Historic Peace Churches opposed secret societies, dismissing Masonic lodges as a closed brotherhood with a concentration of wealth and political power.

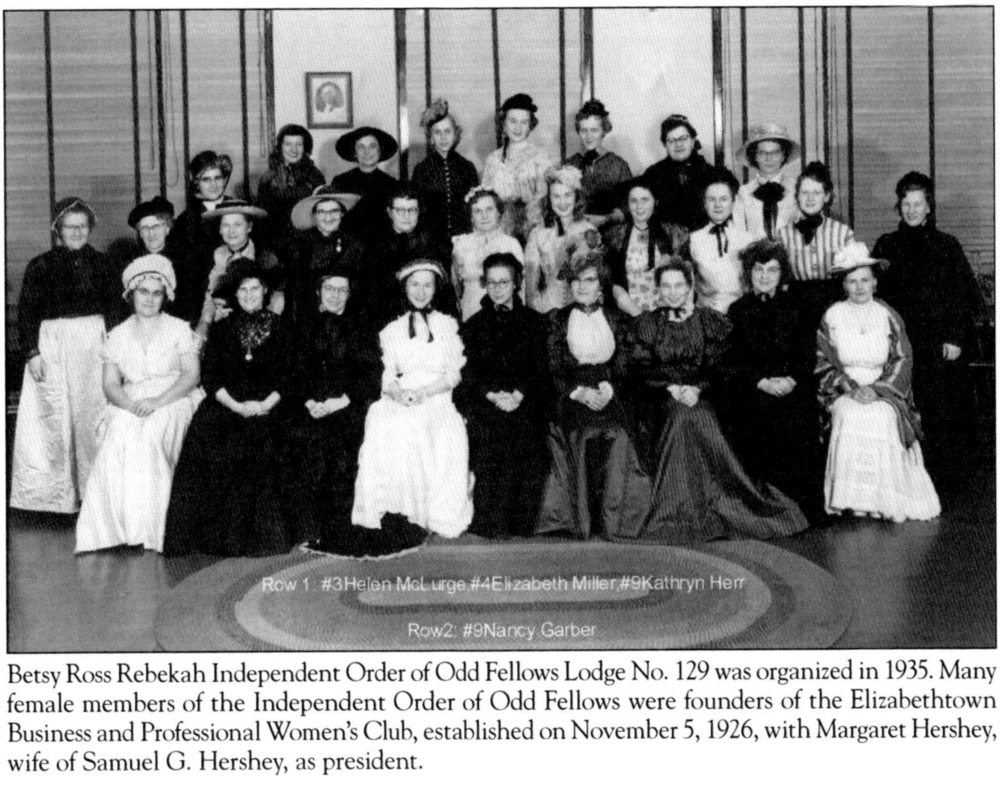

Betsy Ross Rebekah Independent Order of Odd Fellows Lodge No. 129 was organized in 1935. Many female members of the Independent Order of Odd Fellows were founders of the Elizabethtown Business and Professional Women's Club, established on November 5, 1926, with Margaret Hershey, wife of Samuel G. Hershey, as president.

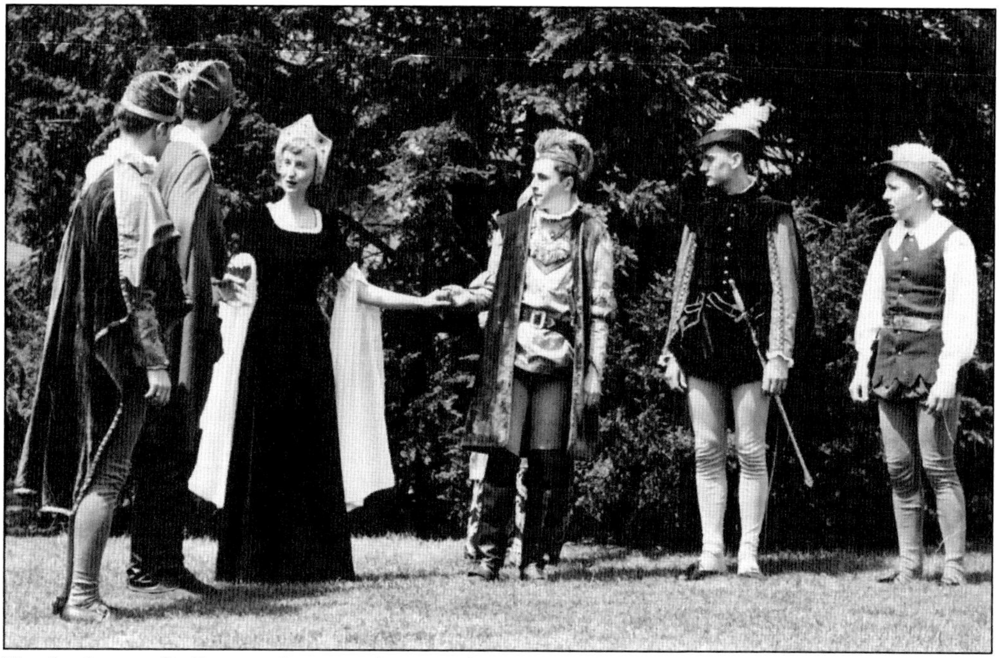

Elizabethtown College students perform in the 1940s. The Elizabethtown Thespian Society, a male theatrical club established in 1842, put on performances, often joined by visiting professional actors, in a large hall with 300 seats. The Elizabethtown Drama Club put on plays in 1933–1934 under the direction of Charlotte Kob. The Little Theater was created by attorney Jack Hornafius in 1954 for community theatrical productions.

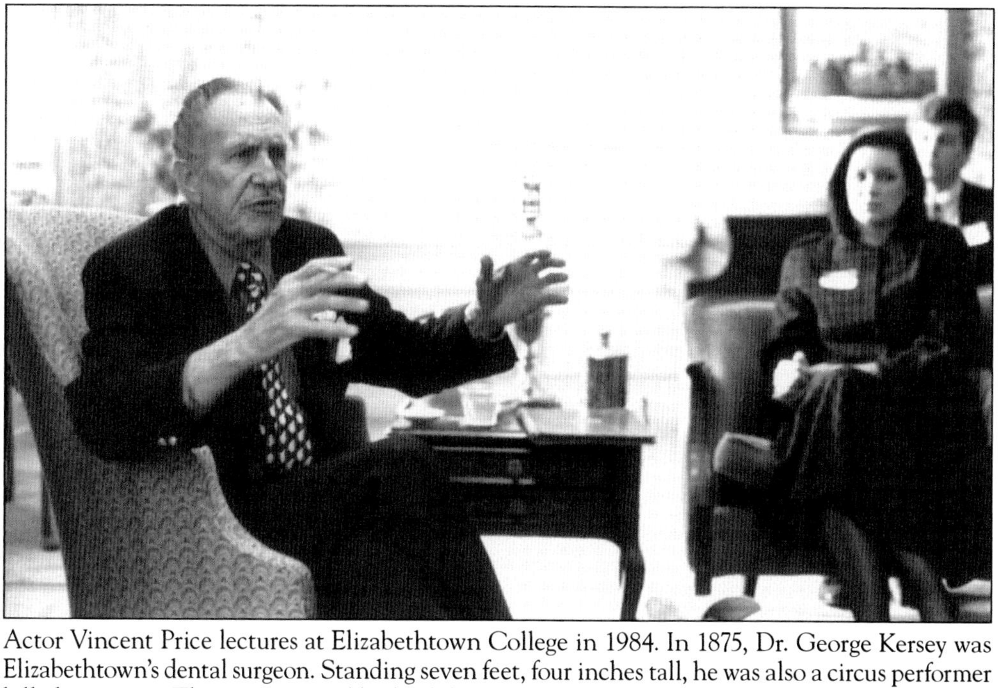

Actor Vincent Price lectures at Elizabethtown College in 1984. In 1875, Dr. George Kersey was Elizabethtown's dental surgeon. Standing seven feet, four inches tall, he was also a circus performer billed as a giant. The town council had a sliding scale of license fees for "menageries and circuses, flying horses, jugglers, puppet and all other shows exhibited in a field or under a canvas."

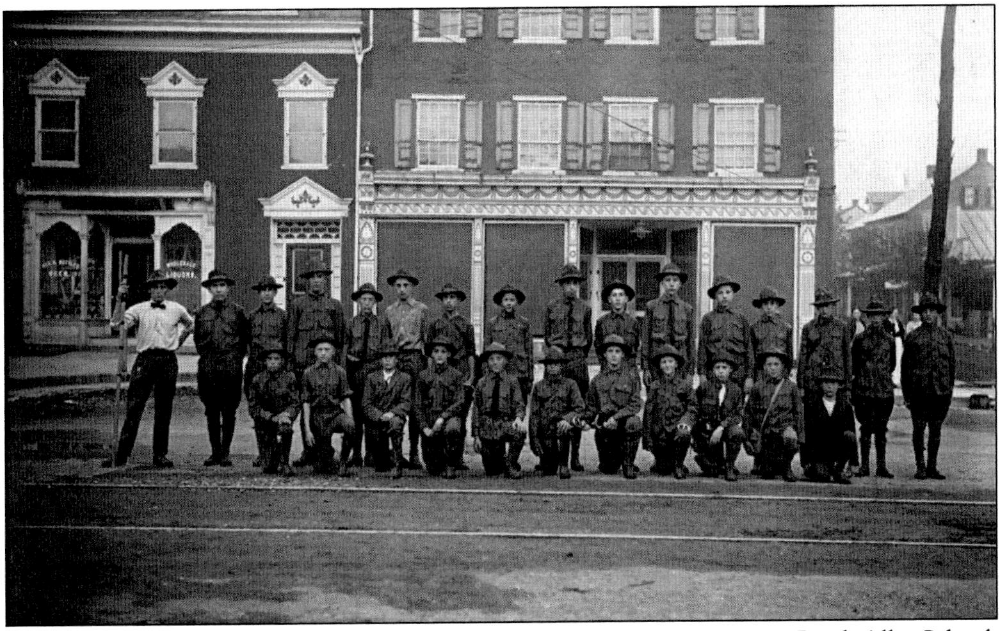

Elizabethtown Boy Scout Troop No. 1 was chartered on July 30, 1914. It met in Peach Alley School, owned by Jacob Olweiler, who was instrumental in starting the troop with Roy Ream and Paul Burkholder. The Episcopalian Heistand brothers were members of St. Elizabeth's Church. Charles Heistand served as assistant chief Scout executive for the United States, and Robert retired after 40 years as Scout executive of the Baltimore Area Council in 1966.

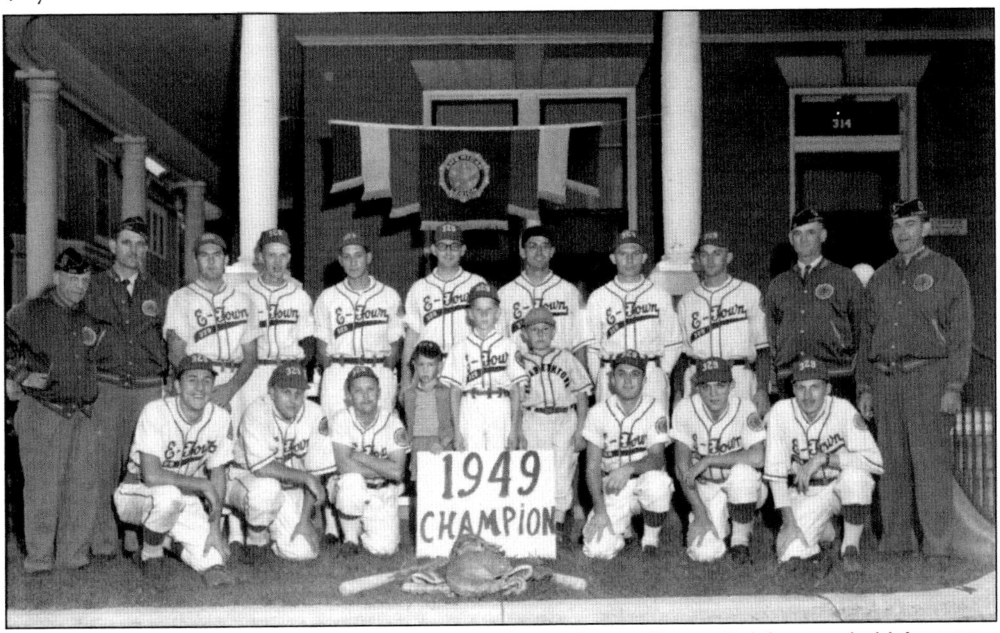

At the end of World War I, the committee for the Welcome Home Celebration held festivities on September 8–9, 1919. In 1920, thirty-nine charter members established Conewago Post No. 329 of the American Legion. In 1934, it purchased a property on South Market Street before building a new location on North Hanover Street in 1954. George Achorn started Elizabethtown Little League baseball in 1952.

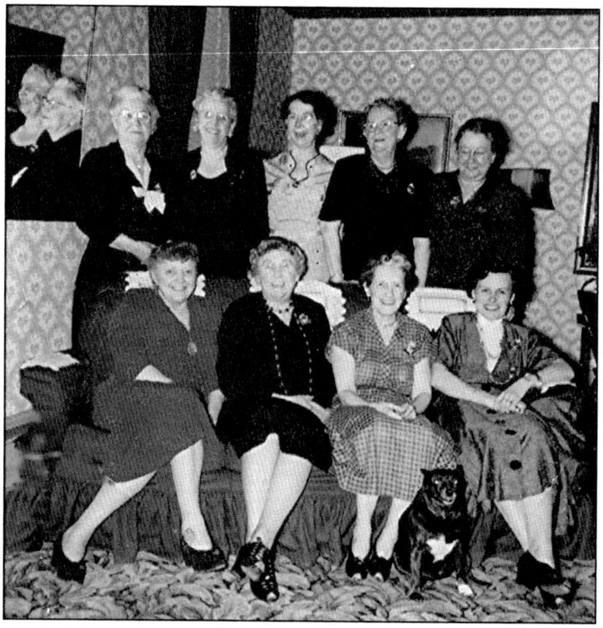

In 1928, the Delphian Society chartered the Elizabeth Hughes Society, named for Mrs. Barnabus Hughes, proprietress of the Bear Tavern and namesake of the borough. In 1874, the Elizabethtown Literary Society commenced. Elizabethtown supported a Lyceum series and an annual Chautauqua. A Chautauqua reading group called the Delphian Course led in 1920 to the formation of the Delphian Society, which opened the public library in 1925 in the Odd Fellows Building. Pictured are members of the Delphian Society.

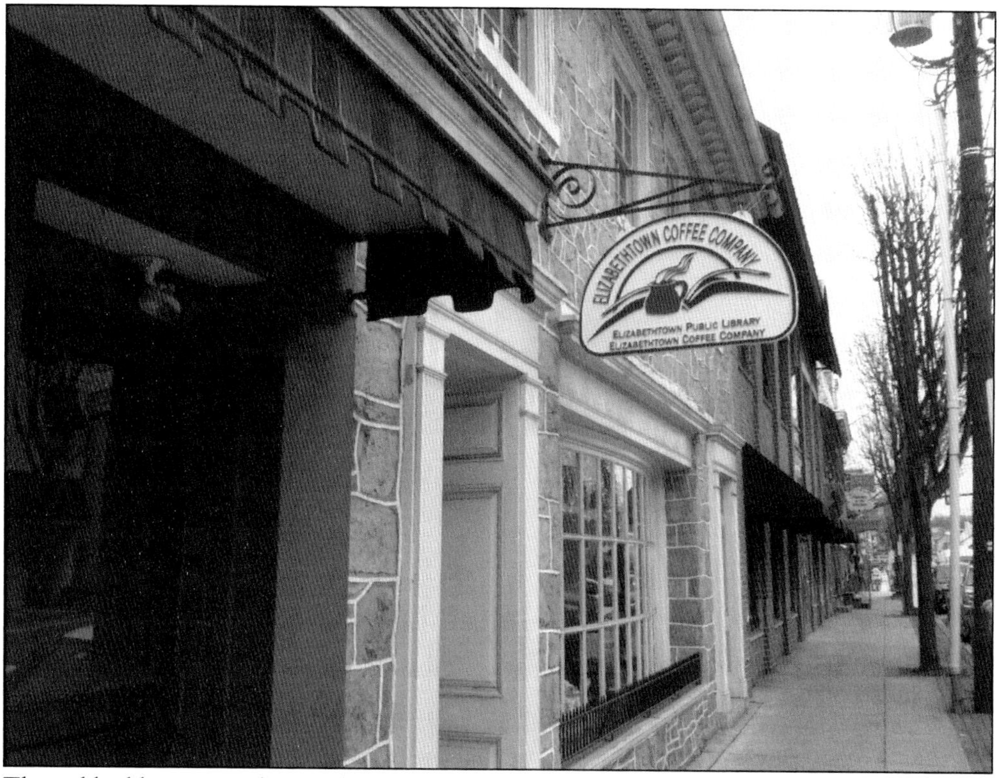

The public library was chartered in April 1959 through leadership by the community service committee of Rotary. It moved from the Odd Fellows Building on Market Street to the former Mount Calvary Church on North Hanover and Oak Streets. Today, the library is at 10 South Market Street, incorporating a structure built in 1787. The new library, constructed in 2001, is at the former site of the Elizabethtown Exchange Bank.

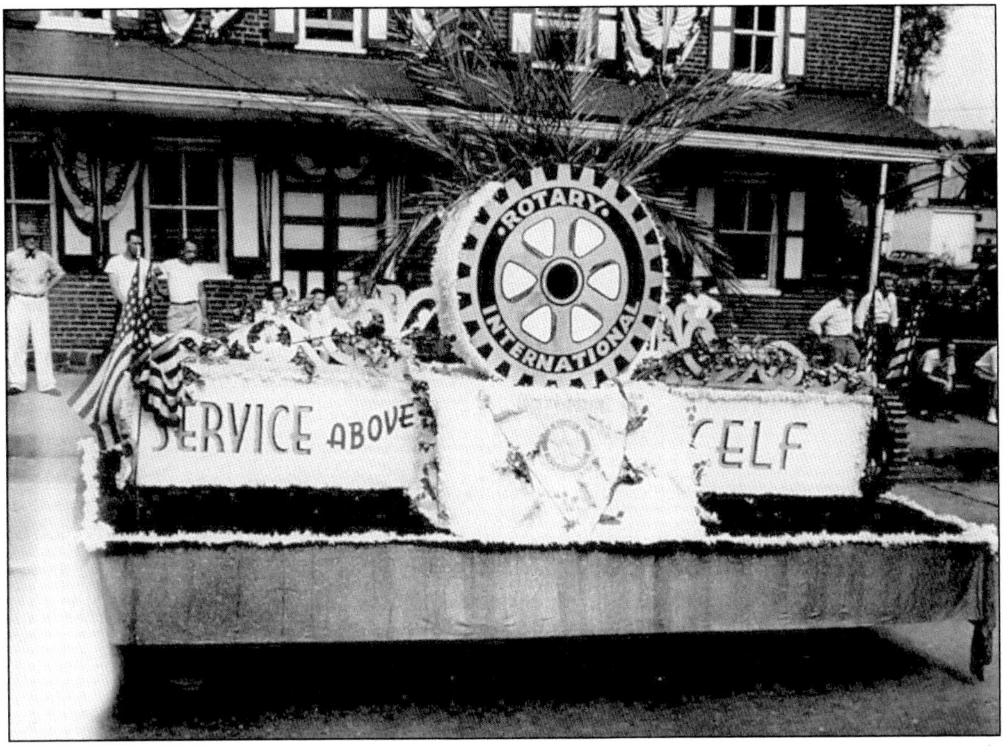

In November 1925, the local Rotary Club was established. In the background of this photograph is 45 North Market Street. The original structure was built as a tavern in 1747, and a brewery was established here in 1831 by Henry Boll. He sold it to Abraham Springer in 1834. In turn, the building was purchased by cattleman Joseph Strouse in 1837. A Messianic Jew, Strouse was a member of St. Peter's Church. He deeded land for the church's expansion in 1859.

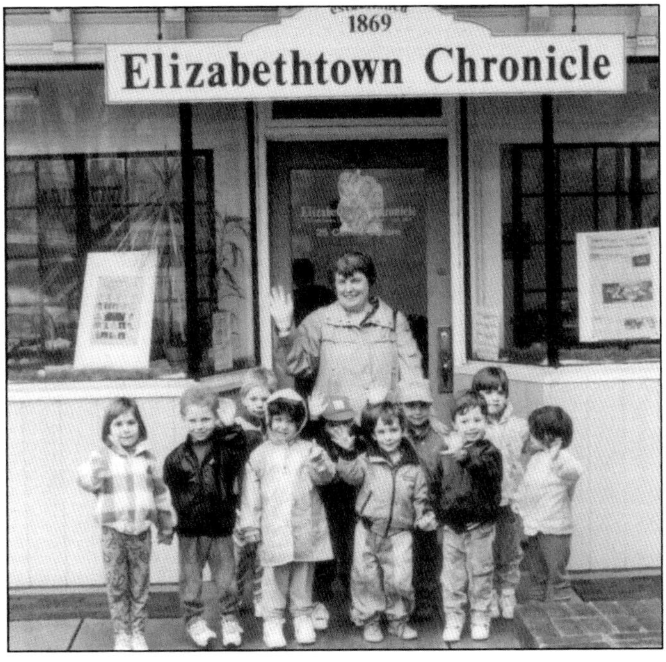

In 1864, Benjamin H. Lehman started publishing a weekly newspaper, the *Elizabethtown Trumpet*, before changing the name in 1866 to the *Elizabethtown Gazette*. In 1869, Stuart McCord, a printer from Lebanon, and John G. Westafer, apprentice on the *Middletown Journal*, came to Elizabethtown and established the *Elizabethtown Chronicle*. The newspaper offices were located on South Market Street. In 1909, Westafer published the *Elizabethtown Chronicle* from printing offices at 3 North Market Street. The paper was in print from 1869 to 2009.

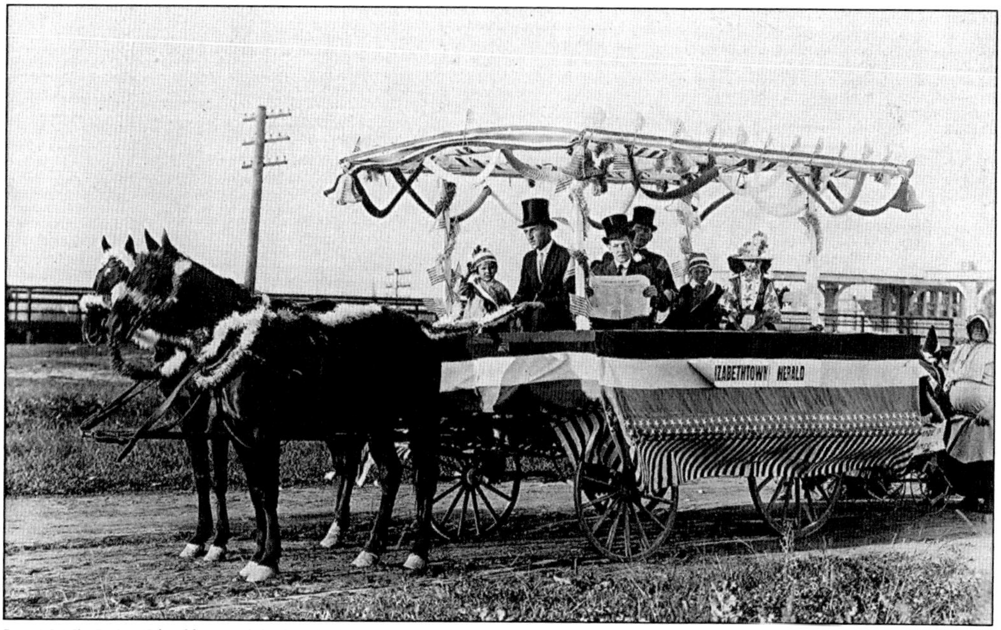

In 1915, I.A. Shiffer published the *Elizabethtown Herald* on West High Street, two doors from Diamond Square. That same year, he moved the newspaper offices to 39 South Market Street and purchased the book and stationery store from the founder of Elizabethtown College, George N. Falkenstein. In 1926, Shiffer sold the store to James Doyle. Today, the newspaper is the *Elizabethtown Advocate*, with offices on 9 South Market Street.

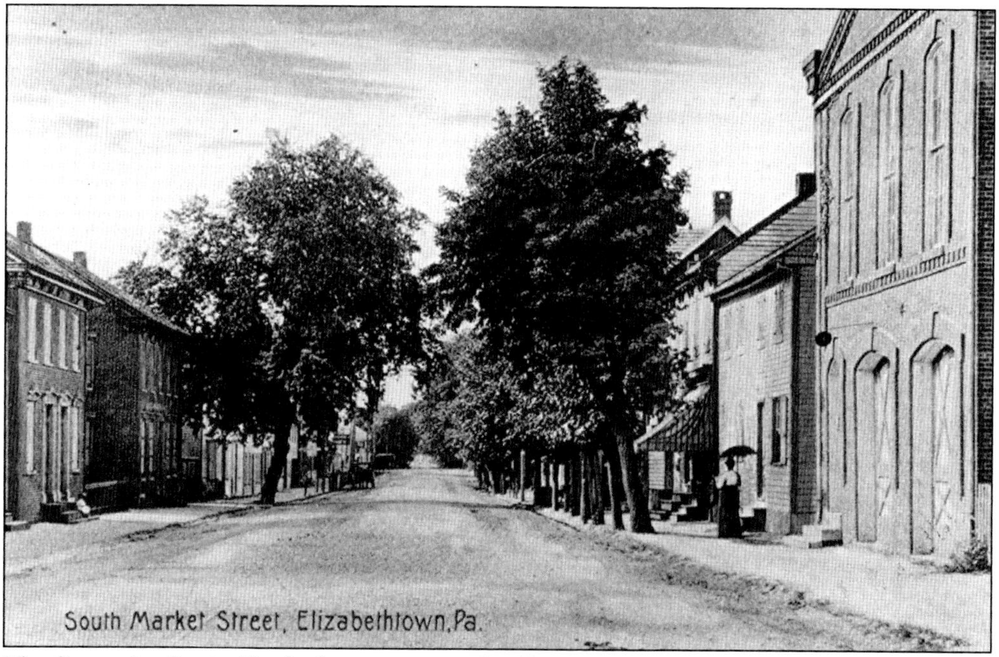

The first major fire in Elizabethtown occurred in January 1836, when Irish railway workers set fire to Maj. Jacob Redsecker's barn behind his Black Horse Inn. Maj. John Maglauchlin chaired a meeting at Col. Abraham Greenawalt's Tavern, and, on January 16, 1836, the Union Fire Company of Elizabethtown was organized.

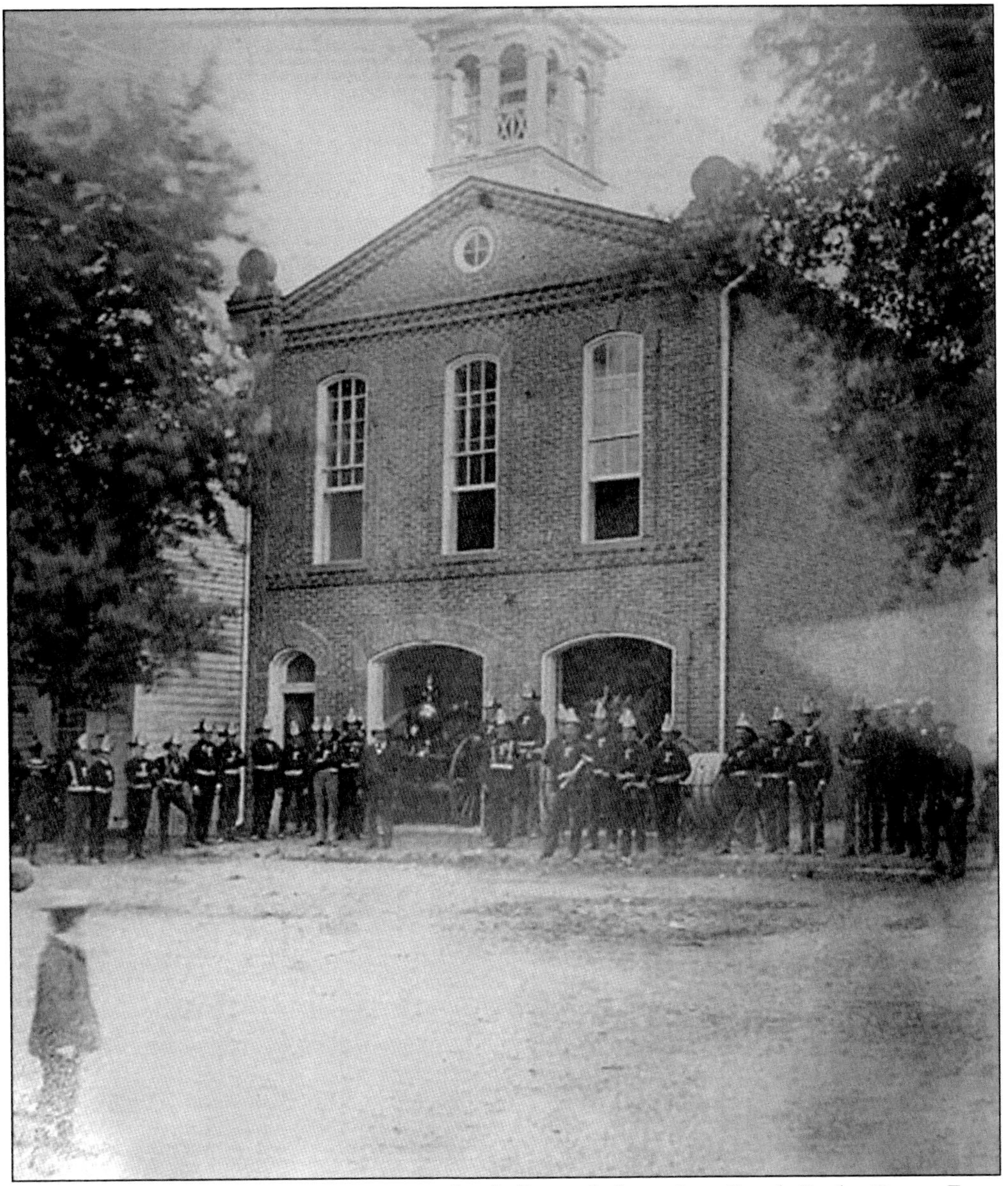

On November 22, 1860, a new, two-story fire hall was dedicated on South Poplar Street. From 1885 to 1976, the fire hall was located at 117 South Market Street, on land purchased from Mennonite Mary Breneman and in a two-story building erected by Church of the Brethren member Benjamin G. Groff. On April 6, 1976, a new firehouse was dedicated at its present location on North Mount Joy Street.

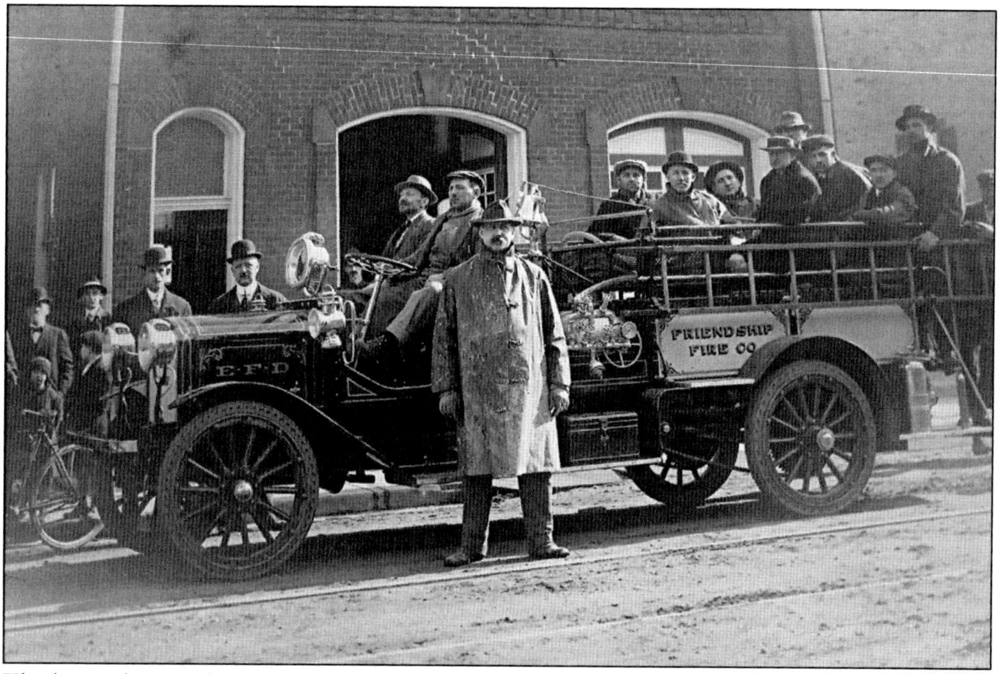

The borough owned a fire engine built in England in 1749. In 1879, a Rogers steam fire engine from Clapp & Jones of Hudson, New York, was purchased. The Union Fire Company was reorganized in 1858 and purchased a new Friendship Fire Engine from Baltimore. On April 23, 1859, a constitution was adopted establishing the Friendship Fire Company.

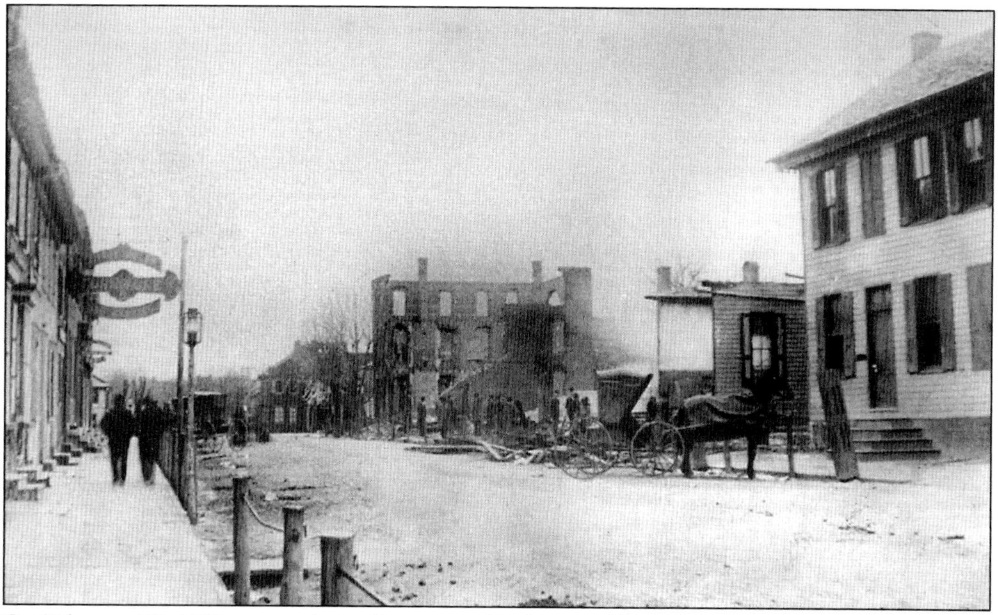

On February 12, 1892, an overheated stove in the dentist office of C.G. Gabel on South Market Street started a fire, destroying much of downtown. The Rogers steam fire engine blew a cylinder, and a bucket brigade brought water from Conoy Creek. In 1895–1896, a reservoir and water-pumping house were built on West High Street at Conoy Creek and fire hydrants were installed throughout the borough.

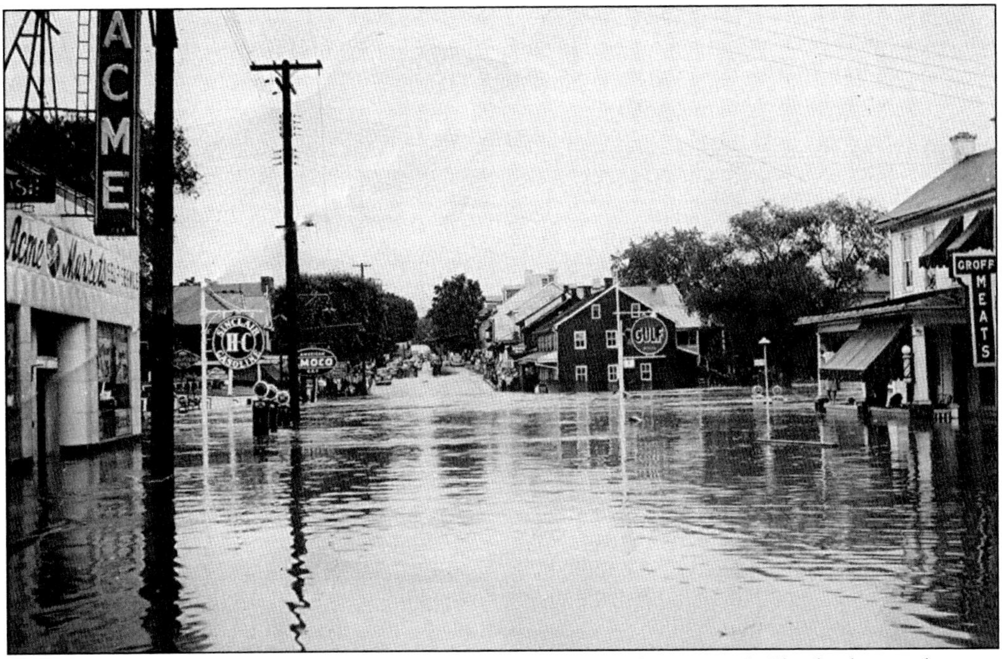

Torrential rains caused the Conoy Creek to overflow on July 22, 1945. Elizabethtown burgess Jacob N. Olweiler estimated damage to public and private property at $100,000.

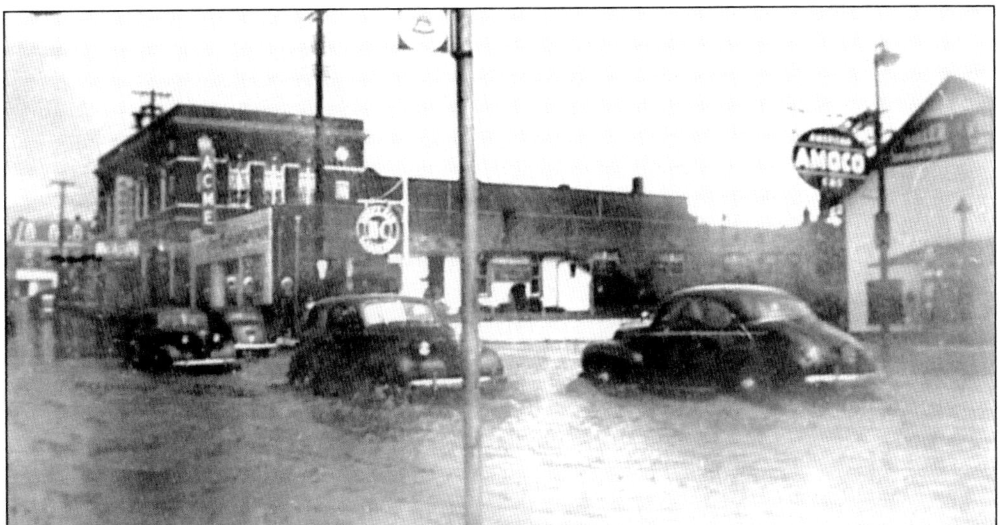

Floodwaters damaged buildings where North Market Street crossed Conoy Creek and in the hollow at College Avenue (formerly Union) and South Market Street.

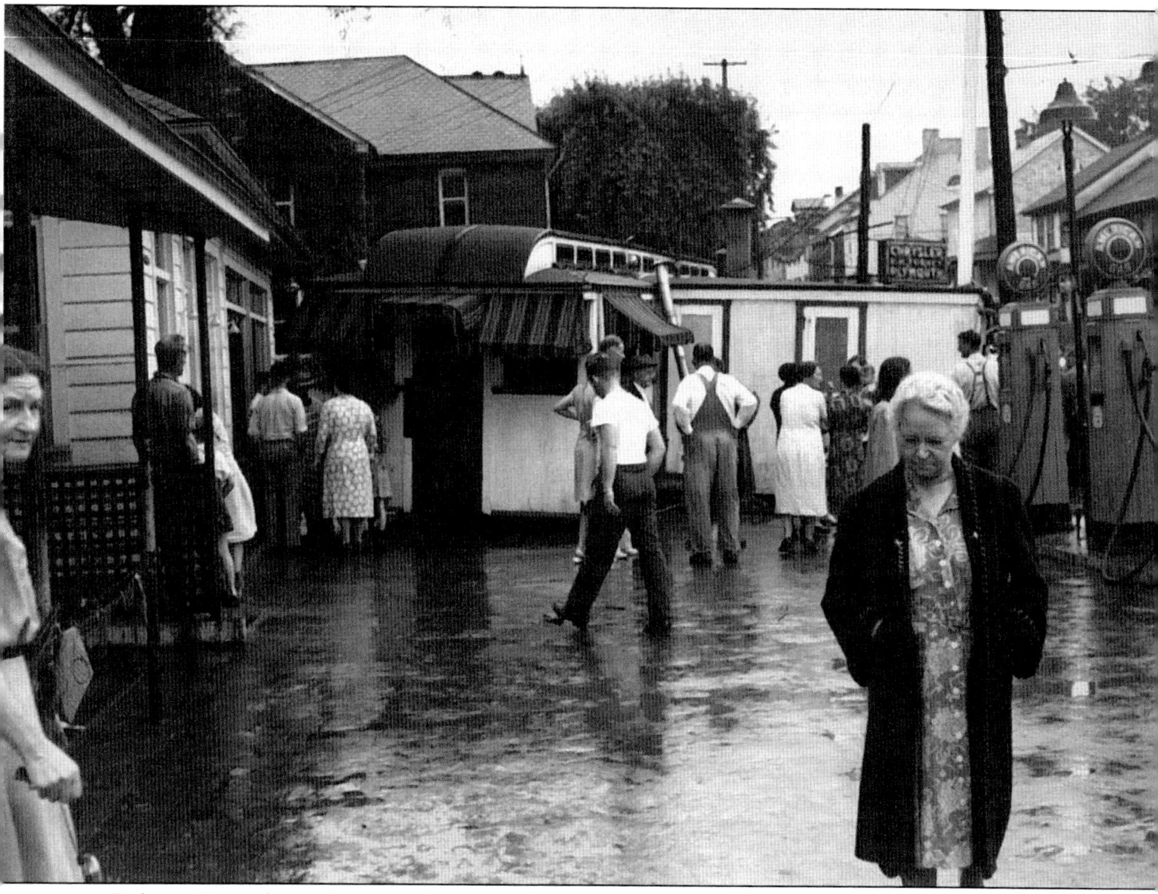

Baker's Diner, located across the street from the tavern and brewery built in 1747 at 45 North Market Street, was torn from its foundation and floated across the road, eventually lodging against R.H. Forney's automobile showroom.

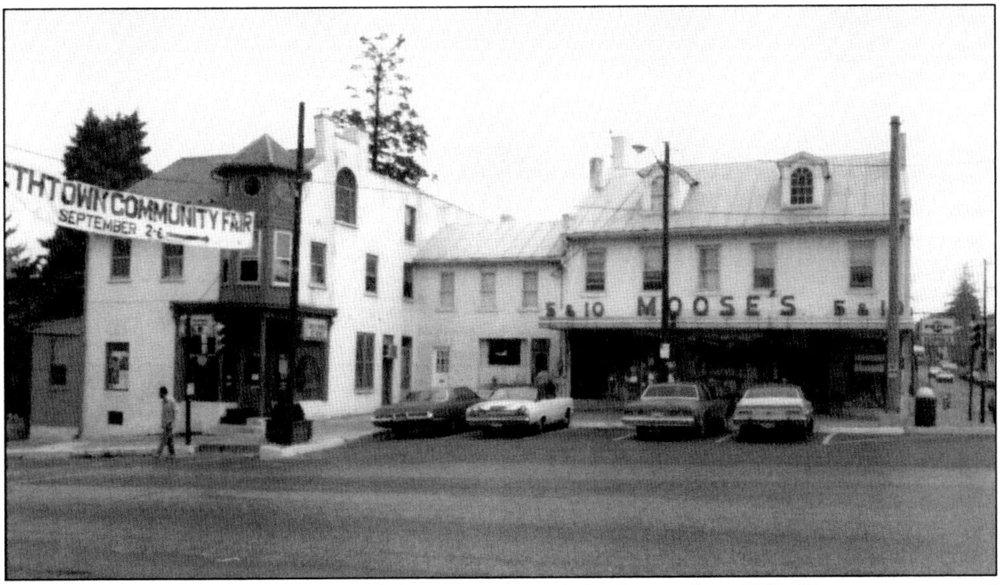

On March 17, 1947, the Kiwanis Club was organized. In September 1950, Kiwanis sponsored the first annual Elizabethtown Community Farm Fair. By 1955, the fairgrounds had moved from Poplar Street to College Avenue opposite Lake Placida. In 1976, for the nation's bicentennial, the Elizabethtown Jaycees sponsored Marketplace Fair before renaming it Elizabethtown Fair in 1978. The following year, fairgrounds opened on East High Street. In 1981, the Elizabethtown Fair Association was established.

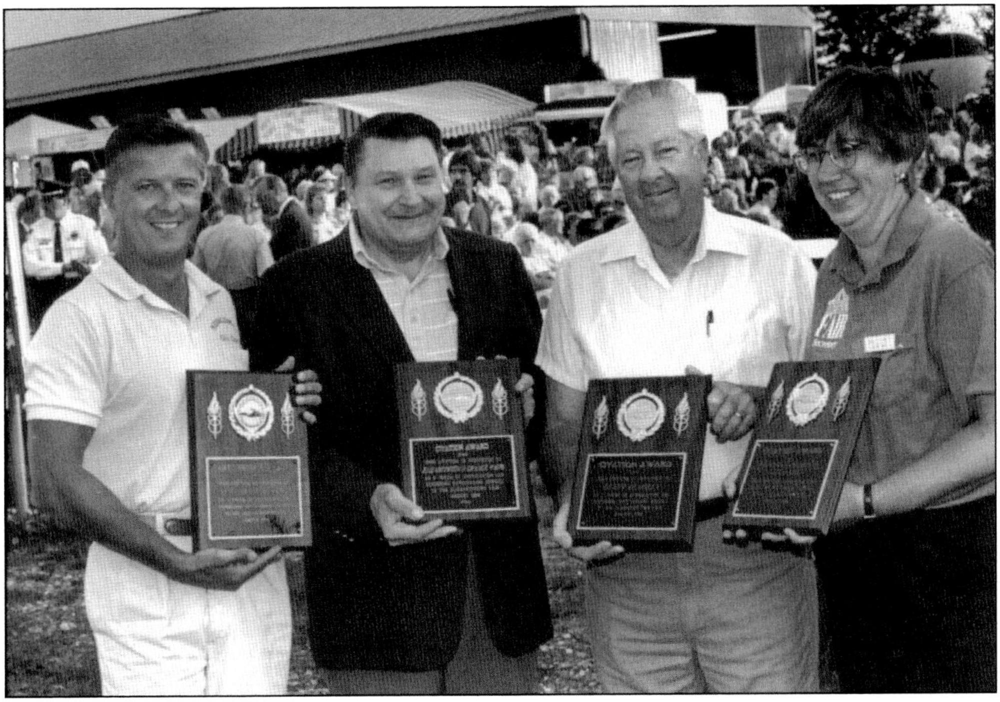

Here, recipients of the 1994 citation award honoring service to the fair community pose for a photograph. They are, from left to right, Len Zvorsky of Newcomer Oil, Ron Shaffer of Elizabethtown Grange, Elvin Yeagley, and Sally Nolt. (Courtesy Elizabethtown Fair Association)

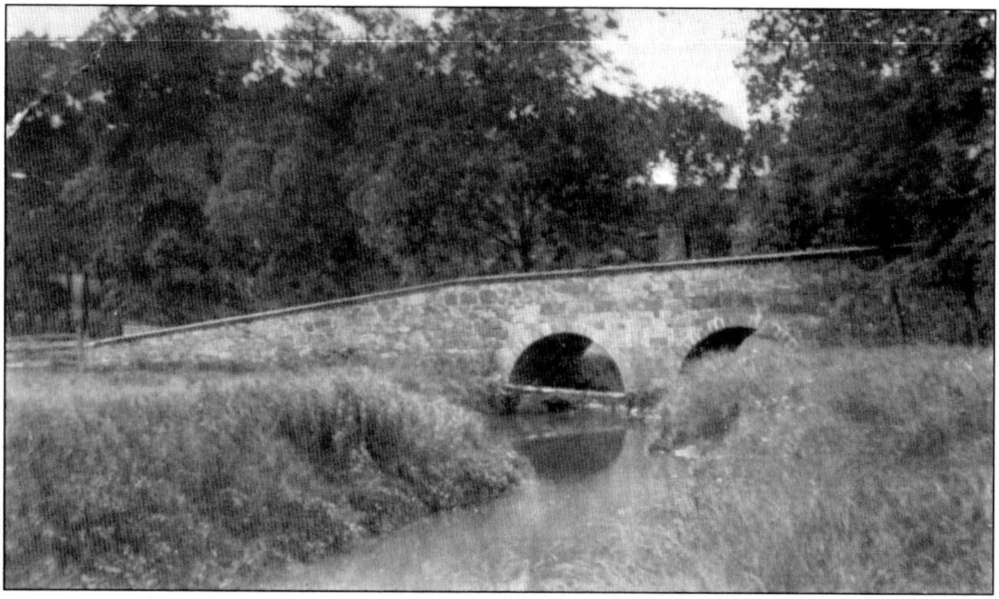

This George N. Falkenstein postcard shows the Conoy Creek—the heart of Elizabethtown.

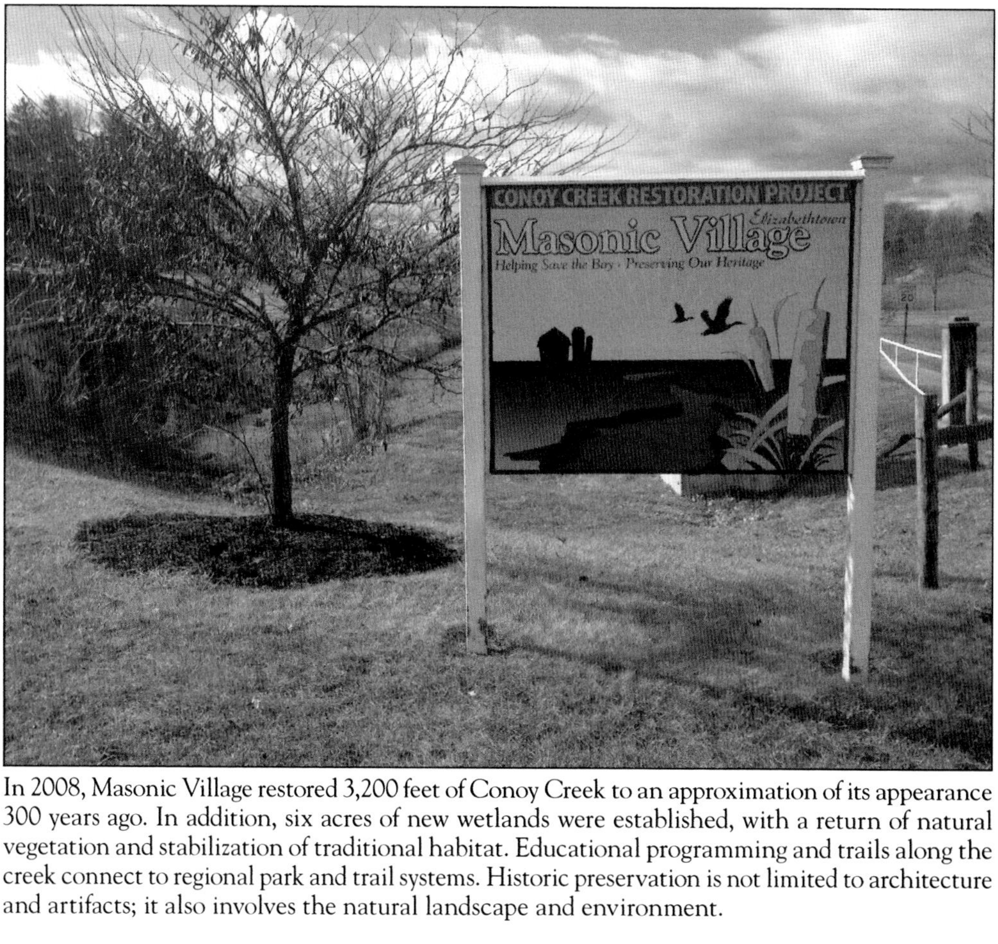

In 2008, Masonic Village restored 3,200 feet of Conoy Creek to an approximation of its appearance 300 years ago. In addition, six acres of new wetlands were established, with a return of natural vegetation and stabilization of traditional habitat. Educational programming and trails along the creek connect to regional park and trail systems. Historic preservation is not limited to architecture and artifacts; it also involves the natural landscape and environment.

Bibliography

de Bien, Lindsay A., ed. *Masonic Village Elizabethtown, PA 1910–2010: 100th Anniversary*. Philadelphia: Masonic Villages of the Grand Lodge of Free and Accepted Masons of Pennsylvania, 2010.

Dunaway, W.F. *A History of Pennsylvania*. New York: Prentice Hall, 1935.

Espenshade, A. Howry. *Pennsylvania Place Names*. State College: The Pennsylvania State College, 1925.

Fink, L.G. *Old Jesuit Trails in Penn's Forest*. New York: Paulist Press, 1935.

Ford, Henry Jones. *The Scotch Irish In America*. Princeton, NJ: Princeton University Press, 1915.

Gibson, William M. *Elizabethtown Hospital for Children and Youth, 1930–1980: Fifty Years New*. Harrisburg: Pennsylvania Department of Health, 1980.

Herrick, C.A. *White Servitude in Pennsylvania, Indentures and Redemption Labor in Colony and Commonwealth*. Philadelphia: John G. McVey, 1926.

Holbrook, Sabra. *The French Founders of North America and their Heritage*. New York: Atheneum Books, 1976.

Klein, Frederic Shriver. *A History of the Jews in Lancaster: Compiled in Commemoration of the Tercentenary of the Arrival of Jews in America in 1654*. Lancaster, PA: Intelligencer Printing Company, 1955.

Lemon, James T. *The Best Poor Man's Country: A Geographical Study of Early Southeastern Pennsylvania*. Baltimore.: Johns Hopkins University Press, 1971.

MacMaster, Richard K. *Elizabethtown: The First Three Centuries*. Elizabethtown, PA: The Elizabethtown Historical Society, 1999.

Martin, David L. *A Clash of Cultures: Native Americans and Colonialism in Lancaster County Pennsylvania*. Morgantown, PA: Masthof Press, 2010.

Mueller, H.R. *The Whig Party in Pennsylvania*. New York: Columbia University Press, 1922.

Williamson, Chet. *Uniting Work and Spirit: A Centennial History of Elizabethtown College*. Elizabethtown, PA: Elizabethtown College Press, 2001.

Wood, Ralph. *The Pennsylvania Germans*. Princeton, NJ: Princeton University Press, 1942.